THE WAR IN VIETNAM

**Other Titles in the Greenwood Press Guides
to Historic Events of the Twentieth Century**
Randall M. Miller, Series Editor

The Persian Gulf Crisis
Steve A. Yetiv

World War I
Neil M. Heyman

The Civil Rights Movement
Peter B. Levy

The Holocaust
Jack R. Fischel

The Breakup of Yugoslavia and the War in Bosnia
Carole Rogel

Islamic Fundamentalism
Lawrence Davidson

Frontiers of Space Exploration
Roger D. Launius

The Collapse of Communism in the Soviet Union
William E. Watson

Origins and Development of the Arab-Israeli Conflict
Ann M. Lesch and Dan Tschirgi

The Rise of Fascism in Europe
George P. Blum

The Cold War
Katherine A.S. Sibley

World War II
Loyd E. Lee

The Unification of Germany, 1989–1990
Richard A. Leiby

THE WAR IN VIETNAM

Anthony O. Edmonds

Greenwood Press Guides to
Historic Events of the Twentieth Century
Randall M. Miller, Series Editor

Greenwood Press
Westport, Connecticut • London

Library of Congress Cataloging-in-Publication Data

Edmonds, Anthony O.
    The war in Vietnam / Anthony O. Edmonds.
        p.   cm.—(Greenwood Press guides to historic events of the
  twentieth century, ISSN 1092–177X)
    Includes bibliographical references (p.   ) and index.
    ISBN 0–313–29847–5 (alk. paper)
      1. Vietnamese Conflict, 1961–1975—United States.   I. Title.
  II. Series.
    DS558.E29   1998
    959.704′3373—dc21   98–15591

British Library Cataloguing in Publication Data is available.

Library of Congress Catalog Card Number: 98–15591
ISBN: 0–313–29847–5
ISSN: 1092–177X

First published in 1998

Greenwood Press, 88 Post Road West, Westport, CT 06881
An imprint of Greenwood Publishing Group, Inc.

Printed in the United States of America

∞™

The paper used in this book complies with the
Permanent Paper Standard issued by the National
Information Standards Organization (Z39.48–1984).

10 9 8 7 6 5 4 3 2 1

Front cover photo: After a firefight in Long Kanh Province, 1966. Photo by Pfc. L. Paul
Epley, U.S. Army, courtesy of National Archives.

Back cover photo: General William Westmoreland congratulates troops. National Archives.

Copyright Acknowledgments

The author and publisher gratefully acknowledge permission to use the following material:

Excerpts from "Interview with Ralph Strang by Rochelle Strang" by Ralph Strang. Unpublished manuscript. Reprinted by permission of Ralph Strang.

"Night Patrol" and "Framer Nguyen" are reprinted from *To Those Who Have Gone Home Tired* by W. D. Ehrhart, New York: Thunder's Mouth Press, 1984, by permission of the author.

Excerpts from *Vietnam: The Heartland Remembers* edited by Stanley W. Beesley (Norman: University of Oklahoma Press, 1987). Reprinted by permission of the University of Oklahoma Press.

From *In the Combat Zone* by Kathryn Marshall. Copyright © 1981 by Kathryn Marshall. By permission of Little, Brown and Company.

From *In the Combat Zone* by Kathryn Marshall. Copyright © 1981 by Kathryn Marshall. Reprinted by permission of Melanie Jackson Agency, L.L.C.

From *Everything We Had* by Al Santoli. Copyright © 1981 by Albert Santoli and Vietnam Veterans of America. Reprinted by permission of Random House, Inc.

Reprinted from *Poems from Captured Documents*, selected and translated from the Vietnamese by Thanh T. Nguyen and Bruce Weigl. (Amherst: The University of Massachusetts Press, 1994), copyright © 1994 by the University of Massachusetts Press.

Excerpts from *Following Ho Chi Minh* by Bui tin (Honolulu: University of Hawaii Press, 1995). Reprinted by permission of the University of Hawaii Press.

From "Why I Can't" by David Connolly in *Lost in America* (Woodbridge, Conn.: Burning Cities Press, 1994). Reprinted by permission of David Connolly.

Excerpts from *Understanding Vietnam: The Vietnamese, the Americans, and Social Change* by Neil L. Jamieson. Copyright © 1993 by The Regents of the University of California. Reprinted by permission of the University of California Press.

Excerpts from *A Time for War* by Robert Schulzinger (New York: Oxford University Press, 1997). Reprinted by permission of Oxford University Press.

Excerpts from biographical sketch of Walter McIntosh (1998). Used by permission of Walter McIntosh.

Contents

A photo essay follows page 92

Series Foreword

As the twenty-first century approaches, it is time to take stock of the political, social, economic, intellectual, and cultural forces and factors that have made the twentieth century the most dramatic period of change in history. To that end, the Greenwood Press Guides to Historic Events of the Twentieth Century presents interpretive histories of the most significant events of the century. Each book in the series combines narrative history and analysis with primary documents and biographical sketches, with an eye to providing both a reference guide to the principal persons, ideas, and experiences defining each historic event, and a reliable, readable overview of that event. Each book further provides analyses and discussions, grounded in both primary and secondary sources, of the causes and consequences, in thought and action, that give meaning to the historic event under review. By assuming a historical perspective, drawing on the latest and best writing on each subject, and offering fresh insights, each book promises to explain how and why a particular event defined the twentieth century. No consensus about the meaning of the twentieth century emerges from the series, but, collectively, the books identify the most salient concerns of the century. In so doing, the series reminds us of the many ways those historic events continue to affect our lives.

Each book follows a similar format designed to encourage readers to consult it both as a reference and a history in its own right. Each volume opens with a chronology of the historic event, followed by a narrative overview, which also serves to introduce and examine briefly the main themes and issues related to that event. The next set of chapters is composed of topical essays, each analyzing closely an issue or problem of interpretation introduced in the opening chapter. A concluding chapter suggesting the long-term implications and meanings of the historic event brings the strands of the preceding chapters together while placing the event in the larger historical context. Each book also includes a section of short biographies of the principal persons related to the event, followed by a section introducing and reprinting key historical documents illustrative of and pertinent to the event. A glossary of selected terms adds to the utility of each book. An annotated bibliography—of significant books, films, and CD-ROMs—and an index conclude each volume.

The editors made no attempt to impose any theoretical model or historical perspective on the individual authors. Rather, in developing the series, an advisory board of noted historians and informed high school history teachers and public and school librarians identified the topics needful of exploration and the scholars eminently qualified to examine those events with intelligence and sensitivity. The common commitment throughout the series is to provide accurate, informative, and readable books, free of jargon and up to date in evidence and analysis.

Each book stands as a complete historical analysis and reference guide to a particular historic event. Each book also has many uses, from understanding contemporary perspectives on critical historical issues, to providing biographical treatments of key figures related to each event, to offering excerpts and complete texts of essential documents about the event, to suggesting and describing books and media materials for further study and presentation of the event, and more. The combination of historical narrative and individual topical chapters addressing significant issues and problems encourages students and teachers to approach each historic event from multiple perspectives and with a critical eye. The arrangement and content of each book thus invite students and teachers, through classroom discussions and position papers, to debate the character and significance of great historic events and to discover for themselves how and why history matters.

The series emphasizes the main currents that have shaped the modern world. Much of that focus necessarily looks at the West, especially Europe and the United States. The political, commercial, and cultural expansion of the West wrought largely, though not wholly, the most fundamental changes of the century. Taken together, however, books in the series reveal the interactions between Western and non-Western peoples and society, and also the tensions between modern and traditional cultures. They also point to the ways in which non-Western peoples have adapted Western ideas and technology and, in turn, influenced Western life and thought. Several books examine such increasingly powerful global forces as the rise of Islamic fundamentalism, the emergence of modern Japan, the Communist revolution in China, and the collapse of communism in eastern Europe and the former Soviet Union. American interests and experiences receive special attention in the series, not only in deference to the primary readership of the books but also in recognition that the United States emerged as the dominant political, economic, social, and cultural force during the twentieth century. By looking at the century through the lens of American events and experiences, it is possible to see why the age has come to be known as "The American Century."

Assessing the history of the twentieth century is a formidable prospect. It has been a period of remarkable transformation. The world broadened and narrowed at the same time. Frontiers shifted from the interiors of Africa and Latin America to the moon and beyond; communication spread from mass circulation newspapers and magazines to radio, television, and now the Internet; skyscrapers reached upward and suburbs stretched outward; energy switched from steam, to electric, to atomic power. Many changes did not lead to a complete abandonment of established patterns and practices so much as a synthesis of old and new, as, for example, the increased use of (even reliance on) the telephone in the age of the computer. The automobile and the truck, the airplane, and telecommunications closed distances, and people in unprecedented numbers migrated from rural to urban, industrial, and ever more ethnically diverse areas. Tractors and chemical fertilizers made it possible for fewer people to grow more, but the environmental and demographic costs of an exploding global population threatened to outstrip natural resources and human innovation. Disparities in wealth increased, with developed nations prospering and underdeveloped nations starving. Amid the crumbling of former European colonial empires, Western technology, goods, and culture increasingly enveloped the globe, seeping into, and undermining, non-Western cultures—a process that contributed to a surge of religious fundamentalism and ethno-nationalism in the Middle East, Asia, and Africa. As people became more alike, they also became more aware of their differences. Ethnic and religious rivalries grew in intensity everywhere as the century closed.

The political changes during the twentieth century have been no less profound than the social, economic, and cultural ones. Many of the books in the series focus on political events, broadly defined, but no books are confined to politics alone. Political ideas and events have social effects, just as they spring from a complex interplay of non-political forces in culture, society, and economy. Thus, for example, the modern civil rights and woman's rights movements were at once social and political events in cause and consequence. Likewise, the Cold War created the geopolitical framework for dealing with competing ideologies and nations abroad and served as the touchstone for political and cultural identities at home. The books treating political events do so within their social, cultural, and economic contexts.

Several books in the series examine particular wars in depth. Wars are defining moments for people and eras. During the twentieth century war became more widespread and terrible than ever before, encouraging new efforts to end war through strategies and organizations of international cooperation and disarmament while also fueling new ideologies and instruments of mass persuasion that fostered distrust and festered old national rivalries. Two world wars during the century redrew the political map, slaughtered or uprooted two generations of people, and introduced and hastened the development of new technologies and weapons of mass destruction. The First World War spelled the end of the old European order and spurred communist revolution in Russia and fascism in Italy, Germany, and elsewhere. The Second World War killed fascism and inspired the final push for freedom from European colonial rule in Asia and Africa. It also led to the Cold War that suffocated much of the world for almost half a century. Large wars begat small ones, and brutal totalitarian regimes cropped up across the globe. After (and in some ways because of) the fall of communism in eastern Europe and the former Soviet Union, wars of competing cultures, national interests, and political systems persisted in the struggle to make a new world order. Continuing, too, has been the belief that military technology can achieve political ends, whether in the superior American firepower that failed to "win" in Vietnam or in the American "smart bombs" and other military wizardry that "won" in the Persian Gulf.

Another theme evident in the series is that throughout the century nationalism has continued to drive events. Whether in the Balkans in 1914 triggering World War I or in the Balkans in the 1990s threatening the post–Cold War peace—or in many other places—nationalist ambitions and forces would not die. The persistence of nationalism is yet another reminder of the many ways that the past becomes prologue.

We thus offer the series as a modern guide to and interpretation of the historic events of the twentieth century and as an invitation to consider how and why those events have defined not only the past and present but also charted the political, social, intellectual, cultural, and economic routes into the next century.

Randall M. Miller
Saint Joseph's University, Philadelphia

Preface

On a cold November night in 1969 I was marching down Riverside Avenue in Muncie, Indiana—part of a peaceful demonstration for peace in Vietnam. I was carrying a sign and singing a very off-key rendition of "Give Peace a Chance," when a local citizen poked his head out of the window of his passing truck and called me a "mother— communist who belonged in Hanoi." Almost thirty years later, in November 1997, I had the temerity to call Ho Chi Minh a nationalist during a discussion on the Internet. A veteran of the war, who was part of the cyberdiscussion, responded by calling me a dupe of communist propaganda who was clearly not a good citizen of the United States. At least he omitted the expletive. The Vietnam War seems to be a conflict that will not end and still divides a nation.

Perhaps in part because of the Vietnam War's continued prominence, American college and high school students display a particularly keen interest in the war. We know that there are hundreds of classes being offered on the conflict, with thousands of other courses devoting at least some attention to the American experience in Vietnam. Moreover, new books and movies about the war continue to appear with great frequency, clearly indicating that the general public is fascinated by the topic. This book is intended to help these students and other interested parties begin to understand America's longest war.

Like other volumes in this series, *The Vietnam War* contains a variety of materials designed to assist the reader: a brief chronology, a general overview, a series of interpretative essays, representative documents, brief biographical sketches, an annotated bibliography, and a glossary of terms. The focus of all the material is on the American experience in the war.

I have tried to be fair in discussing a number of controversial issues, especially in the interpretative essays following the overview. But interpretation requires taking a stand, and I have attempted to do so using the best evidence available. If there is a central theme running through all the elements of this study, it is the desire to understand rather than demonize. Thus, for example, I cast Lyndon Johnson as neither a war monger nor a noble defender of freedom, but rather as a complex leader who was caught in circumstances difficult to control. The same kind of ambiguity can be seen in Ho Chi Minh, the antiwar movement, the media, and American, South Vietnamese, and communist troops. There are few sinners and saints in this story, only a lot of people facing a terrible war and its aftermath. If those who read this book better understand the war and learn not to point fingers of blame but extend handshakes of reconciliation, my effort here will have done some small good. As for me, I'd like to find that man who called me a communist so long ago, buy him a beer, and talk with him, without acrimony, about the war in Vietnam.

ACKNOWLEDGMENTS

I want to thank a number of people who have helped make this book possible. Several of my colleagues read portions of the text and caught both factual and interpretative errors. I especially appreciate the assistance of Walter McIntosh, a former CIA officer whose story appears as one of the documents. As "Internet buddies" we have corresponded extensively about the war. Although we have had passionate disagreements, his insights have helped me greatly. I also thank the hundreds of Ball State University students who have taken my course on America and the Vietnam War. It is primarily for students like them that this book is written. The Department of History at Ball State has provided released time for research and writing, and the university awarded me a special assigned leave to complete my writing. The John Fisher Fellowship Committee kindly awarded me a handsome grant that allowed me time off in the summer to work on this project. My student assistant Rachel Popma actually learned to read my handwriting. My editors at Greenwood, Barbara Rader and Norine Mudrick, showed enormous patience with my lousy proofreading and missed deadlines. And their work made this a better book. But my deepest thanks goes to series editor, Randall Miller. He gave me the opportunity to work on this project in the first place, and his thoughtful comments and careful criticism helped me enormously to sharpen my focus and understand my audience. Finally, I dedicate *The War in Vietnam* to my three sons, Anthony, Daniel, and Samuel, and to my wife, Joanne. May they never have to know the horrors of a war like the American War in Vietnam.

Chronology of Events

Late 3rd century B.C.	Chao T'o (Trieu Da) conquers what is now northern Vietnam; establishes kingdom of Nam Viet ("Land of the Southern Viets").
111 B.C.	Han Dynasty China conquers Nam Viet.
A.D. 39–40	Trung Sisters' rebellion against Chinese rule.
938–39	Led by Ngo Quyen, Vietnamese defeat Chinese; Ngo becomes emperor of independent Vietnam.
1428	China recognizes Vietnamese independence under Emperor Ly Loi.
1627	French missionary Alexander de Rhodes adapts the pictographic Vietnamese language to the Roman alphabet.
1771–1802	Nguyen Anh puts down a rebellion and becomes Emperor Gia Long, ending thirty years of internal turmoil.
1852	Napoleon III becomes Emperor of France and supports French military expeditions to Vietnam to protect missionaries and secure trade concessions.
1858	French fleet captures Saigon.
1862–1893	France extends control over Vietnam, Cambodia, and Laos, creating French Indochina.
1890	Nguyen Sinh Cung born. Later identifies himself as Ho Chi Minh.

1930	Ho Chi Minh and other nationalists create Indochinese Communist party.
1940	Japan occupies French Indochina.
1941	Ho Chi Minh establishes "Viet Nam Doc Lap Dong Minh" (League for Vietnamese Independence, shortened to "Vietminh").
1945 (August)	Japan surrenders, ending occupation of Vietnam.
1945 (September)	Ho Chi Minh declares Vietnamese independence from France, creating the Democratic Republic of Vietnam (DRV).
1946 (March)	French-Vietminh agreement recognizes Vietnam as a "free state" within the French Union and authorizes French troops to return to Vietnam.
1946 (November–December)	French warships bombard Haiphong after dispute with Vietminh over customs collections; Vietminh forces withdraw from Hanoi; French war begins in Vietnam.
1949	French install Bao Dai as nominal head of government of Vietnam.
1950 (January–February)	Most communist nations extend diplomatic recognition to DRV; United States recognizes French-controlled State of Vietnam.
1950 (July)	The United States begins military and economic aid in support of French in Vietnam.
1950 (September)	U.S. Military Assistance Advisory Group—Indochina (MAAG) created.
1954 (March–May)	Battle of Dienbienphu; Eisenhower refuses to intervene militarily in Vietnam.
1954 (June)	Geneva Accords signed ending French War and temporarily dividing Vietnam at 17th parallel pending a national reunification election.
1954 (September)	Southeast Asia Treaty Organization (SEATO) created.
1955–1956	The United States begins to send economic and military aid to southern Vietnam; Premier Ngo Dinh Diem becomes new head of state, proclaims Republic of Vietnam (RVN) in the south, and consolidates power; with U.S. approval, Diem refuses to participate in reunification elections; Ho Chi Minh sponsors disastrous land reform policy in northern Vietnam.

1957–1958	Anti-Diem communist guerrilla activity intensifies in RVN.
1959	Communist Party Central Committee in Hanoi recognizes need for armed struggle in South Vietnam; Major Dale Buis and Sergeant Chester Ovnand killed at Ben Hoa, the first "official" American casualties of the "Vietnam War Era."
1960 (December)	Under Hanoi's direction, South Vietnamese communists create the National Liberation Front (NLF), political wing of the southern revolutionary forces, and the Peoples Liberation Armed Forces (PLAF, called "Vietcong" by South Vietnamese and Americans); about 900 American advisors in South Vietnam.
1961 (January)	President John F. Kennedy's inaugural address confirms American commitment to defend freedom worldwide.
1961 (October)	Kennedy increases military assistance to Diem, including more American advisors.
1961 (December)	3,205 American advisors in-country.
1962	Strategic Hamlet Program initiated.
1962 (February)	U.S. Military Assistance Command, Vietnam (MACV) established under General Paul Harkins.
1962 (December)	11,300 American advisors in-country.
1963 (January)	The Battle of Ap Bac fought.
1963 (November)	Ngo Dinh Diem ousted in American-approved coup; Diem and his brother/advisor Ngo Dinh Nhu are murdered; John F. Kennedy assassinated; Lyndon Johnson becomes president.
1963 (December)	16,300 American advisors in-country.
1963–64	Johnson affirms commitment to Kennedy policy of aiding South Vietnam against communists.
1964 (June)	General William Westmoreland replaces General Harkins as commander of U.S. military forces in Vietnam.
1964 (July)	Covert South Vietnamese operations against the North intensify.
1964 (August)	Gulf of Tonkin incidents; first U.S. air strikes against North Vietnam in retaliation; Congress passes Gulf of Tonkin Resolution, giving Johnson the equivalent of war-making power in Vietnam.
1964 (November)	Johnson defeats Republican Barry Goldwater in 1964 presidential election.

1964 (December)   23,300 American advisors in-country.

1964 (December)– Vietcong launch attacks against American installations.
1965 (February)

1965 (February)   Johnson orders sustained bombing attack against North
                   Vietnam, code-named "Rolling Thunder."

1965 (March)   First official U.S. combat troops arrive in Vietnam—two
                   Marine battalions tasked to guard American airbase at Danang.

1965   Antiwar teach-ins at several American universities.
(March–May)

1965 (April)   Johnson's peace proposals in Johns Hopkins University speech
                   offer economic development for North Vietnam; North
                   Vietnam rejects them.

1965 (July)   Johnson agrees to increase number of American troops by
                   forty-four battalions.

1965 (October)   Battle of the Ia Drang Valley, the first major combat
                   confrontation between American and North Vietnamese troops.

1965 (December)   American troop strength at 184,300.

1966 (February)   Honolulu Conference in which pacification is stressed as a
                   strategy in the war; Senator William Fulbright (D-Ark.) chairs
                   Senate Foreign Relations Committee hearing on purposes and
                   conduct of the war.

1966 (June)   Rolling Thunder targets expanded to include oil depots near
                   Hanoi and Haiphong.

1966 (December)   American troop strength at 385,300.

1967 (January–   Operations Cedar Falls and Junction City, major American and
February)   South Vietnamese clear-and-destroy/pacification campaigns
                   carried out.

1967 (September)   Nguyen Van Thieu and Nguyen Cao Ky elected President and
                   Vice President of South Vietnam.

1967 (October)   Antiwar March on the Pentagon attracts 50,000 demonstrators.

1967 (December)   American troop strength at 485,600.

1968 (January–   Communist Tet Offensive; Battle of Hue.
February)

1968 (January–   North Vietnamese seige of Marine military base at Khe Sanh.
April)

1968 (February)   Westmoreland requests additional 206,000 American troops; new Secretary of Defense Clark Clifford begins study of the war, advises rejection of troop buildup.

1968 (March)   Westmoreland replaced as MACV commander by General Creighton Abrams; Senators Eugene McCarthy (D-Minn.) and Robert Kennedy (D-NY) emerge as viable antiwar contenders for the Democratic nomination for president; Johnson suspends Rolling Thunder air attacks, offers peace talks, and chooses not to run for a second term.

1968 (May)   Peace talks between Americans and North Vietnamese begin in Paris.

1968 (June)   Robert Kennedy assassinated in Los Angeles.

1968 (August)   Antiwar demonstrations at Chicago Democratic National Convention lead to violence and mass arrests; Hubert Humphrey is the Democratic nominee for president.

1968 (November)   Republican Richard Nixon elected president; promises "secret plan" to end the war.

1968 (December)   American troop strength at 536,100.

1969 (March)   Secret bombing of Cambodia begins. Defense Secretary Melvin Laird unveils strategy of Vietnamization.

1969 (June)   Nixon announces first withdrawal of American troops (25,000) and reaffirms strategy of Vietnamization.

1969 (September)   Ho Chi Minh dies in Hanoi.

1969 (October– November)   Vietnam Moratorium antiwar marches nationwide on October and November 15.

1969 (November)   My Lai massacre uncovered.

1969 (December)   American troop strength at 475,200.

1970 (February)   U.S. National Security Advisor Henry Kissinger begins secret negotiations with North Vietnam's Le Duc Tho.

1970 (April)   American and South Vietnamese troops launch attacks on suspected enemy sanctuaries in Cambodia; major antiwar protests occur on many American college campuses; Ohio National Guard troops kill four students at Kent State University.

1970 (December)   Congress repeals Gulf of Tonkin Resolution.

1970 (December)   American troop strength at 334,600.

1971 (February–April)   Operation Lan Son 719, in which ARVN troops, supported by U.S. air power, launch attacks against Ho Chi Minh Trail in Laos.

1971 (March)   Army Lieutenant William Calley convicted of premeditated murder for role in My Lai massacre.

1971 (April)   Major antiwar protest in Washington, D.C., featuring Vietnam Veterans Against the War.

1971 (June)   Right to publish Pentagon Papers upheld by Supreme Court.

1971 (December)   American troop strength at 156,800.

1972 (April–June)   Communist Easter Offensive directed against northern provinces of South Vietnam.

1972 (April–May)   Nixon authorizes bombing near Hanoi and Haiphong and mining of Haiphong harbor in North Vietnam.

1972 (November)   Nixon reelected president.

1972 (December)   Peace talks break down after Thieu balks at tentative agreement and North Vietnamese boycott talks; Nixon orders massive bombing of North Vietnam; American troop strength at 24,500.

1973 (January)   North Vietnamese return to talks; Paris Accords signed, ending official American involvement in the war.

1973 (November)   War Powers Act limiting presidential war-making power passed by Congress over Nixon's veto.

1974   Communist and ARVN forces jockey for position; North Vietnam plans offensive for 1974–1975 dry season.

1975 (January–April)   Communists launch offensive against South Vietnam.

1975 (April)   Cambodia falls to communist Khmer Rouge troops; Saigon falls to communists on April 30, 1975, as last Americans are evacuated.

1975 (May)   *Mayaguez* incident occurs.

1975 (August)   Communist Pathet Lao assume control of Laos.

1977   Newly elected President Jimmy Carter pardons most Vietnam era draft evaders.

1978 (October)   United States postpones potential normalization of relations with Vietnam over issue of alleged remaining American POWs and unaccounted for MIAs.

1978 (December)   Exodus of Vietnamese boat people; Vietnam invades Cambodia, establishes pro-Vietnamese puppet government.

1979   Vietnam-Peoples Republic of China war between January and March.

1982   Vietnam Veterans Memorial dedicated in Washington, D.C.

1984   Out-of-court settlement in Agent Orange case.

1986   Vietnam begins free-market economic reforms known as *doi moi*.

1990   With Vietnamese troops withdrawn, Cambodian factions agree to coalition government.

1994   President Bill Clinton lifts American economic embargo of Vietnam.

1995   The United States officially grants diplomatic recognition to Vietnam.

THE WAR IN VIETNAM
EXPLAINED

I

The United States and Vietnam: An Overview

When does a war begin? For most conflicts involving the United States, the answer is relatively simple. The Civil War started with the bombardment of Fort Sumter; declarations of war in 1917 and 1941, respectively, marked America's "official" entrance into World Wars I and II. Even the undeclared Korean War had a relatively clear beginning with the North Korean invasion of the South and the subsequent United Nations (U.N.) resolution supporting a U.N. military response. But for the Vietnam War, the answer to this question (and to so many others) is more complicated. Not only was war never officially declared, but America seemed to slide gradually, almost imperceptibly into armed conflict. Perhaps the war began with the first American death by hostile fire, when Colonel Peter Dewey was killed by anti-French Vietminh in September 1945. Or was it in July 1950 when the United States began to supply military and economic aid to the French in Indochina? Perhaps the real war began in October 1954 when President Dwight D. Eisenhower assured South Vietnamese leader Ngo Dinh Diem of American support of his anticommunist government. The Gulf of Tonkin incident in 1964? Rolling Thunder in early March 1965? Or was it, finally, the introduction of American combat units on March 8, 1965, that marked the beginning of the Vietnam War?

There probably is no definitive answer to this question, but the history of Vietnam suggests that the roots of the conflict lay deep in the past. Any brief introduction to American involvement in Vietnam must begin with a central fact of Vietnamese history: The people of Vietnam are deeply conscious of their past. For them, the "American War" was a small though highly destructive incident in a long tradition of conflict. As historian Robert Schulzinger notes, "For the Vietnamese the fight [against the Americans] represented the latest phase of a century-long, even millennial effort to define themselves and cast out invaders."[1] Crucially, for most of its history, Vietnam suffered foreign occupation, and most Vietnamese developed a deep desire to resist such occupation. In 208 B.C. what is now the northern part of Vietnam was occupied by a renegade Chinese general Chao T'o, who turned it into his personal fiefdom, calling it Nam Viet. Almost a century later, in 111 B.C., an expansive Han dynasty absorbed Nam Viet, which then remained a part of China until a successful rebellion in A.D. 938. (The Chinese reoccupied the country in 1407 but were defeated in 1426.)

During the century of Chinese rule, the Vietnamese adopted some Chinese customs and habits but also consistently tried to remove the yoke of foreign domination. The Trung Sisters in A.D. 39, Trieu Au in A.D. 248, Ly Bon in A.D. 543, Ngo Quyen in A.D. 938, among others, rebelled against Chinese rule. After Ngo's successful fight for independence, Chinese and Mongols attempted to reconquer their lost province on several occasions during the next nine centuries, always meeting fierce resistance. These confrontations became a legacy of Vietnamese resentment of outsiders. This "persistent opposition to Chinese domination," finally, led the Vietnamese to create what historian William Turley describes as "a myth of national indomitability." Worshiping their military heroes, according to Turley, "the Vietnamese forged a strong collective identity early in their history, certainly long before Europeans appeared off their shores."[2]

The appearance of Europeans forms another major part of the history of the war. Understanding the French role in southeast Asia is necessary if we are to fathom American policy there. France's first contact with Vietnam occurred in the early seventeenth century when a French Jesuit missionary, Alexandre de Rhodes, traveled there. Rhodes combined religion and politics as he converted scores of Vietnamese to Catholicism and cooperated with French merchants in establishing a commercial foothold in Vietnam.

During the next two centuries French interest in Vietnam waxed and waned, as did Vietnamese hostility toward the European interlopers. By the mid-nineteenth century, however, France became deeply committed to establishing a colonial empire in southeast Asia. For a complex series of reasons, including missionary zeal, economic self-interest, and perhaps most important, imperial jealousy of the colonial expansion of other European nations, France launched a successful military assault on Saigon in 1859. Over the next two decades, the French took advantage of internal weaknesses and divisions among competing Vietnamese factions and extended their control over all of Vietnam, as well as neighboring Laos and Cambodia.[3] (See Map 1.)

France claimed that its rule in Indochina was benevolently intended and carried out in a Christian fashion. Writing in 1900, Charles Depincé, a member of the Union Coloniale Française (a pro-empire pressure group), claimed that the French presence in Indochina had "only one justification: the improvement, as a result of the conquering nation's efforts, of the material and moral standards of the conquered race."[4]

Though a few Catholic missionaries may have felt such altruism, this French version of the "white man's burden" was largely a smoke screen to cover an especially vicious brand of imperialism. France exploited Vietnam ruthlessly. Although French technology helped make the Mekong River delta into one of the leading rice-producing areas of the world, for example, the exportation of rice outstripped the increases in land under cultivation and population, ultimately contributing to profound economic hardship for most Vietnamese peasants, the majority of whom became landless under French rule. Symbolic of this economic exploitation was the infamous water buffalo tax of 1935. An epidemic that year killed large numbers of these draft animals vital to the tenuous economic survival of Vietnamese farmers. The French were predictably callous; as historian Edward Doyle notes, they not only "refused to lower taxes . . . they continued to demand payment of the livestock tax for the now-dead water buffalo." After all, the animals had been alive "during a portion of the tax year"![5]

French rule profoundly affected Vietnamese culture as well. A government opium monopoly sanctioned the production of a drug that had been outlawed prior to French rule, helping to create a major addiction problem. The French also established an alcohol monopoly, making village rituals, which had traditionally used small amounts of intoxicants, more expensive. In an attempt to diminish the influence of Confucianism, France also abolished Vietnamese schools, setting up French ones that were available to only a few of the best students. By 1940 only about 20 percent of school-age children in Vietnam attended school, and the illiteracy rate skyrocketed. As the French eliminated education in classical Chinese, one French observer suggested the larger symbolic meaning: "Traditional Annamite society, so well organized to satisfy the needs of the people, had been destroyed by us."[6]

Some Vietnamese collaborated with their European overlords. Often native converts to Catholicism who learned French, these "culture brokers" served as actual and symbolic interpreters for the colonial class. They were, in the words of one Frenchman, the "dependable Vietnamese" who them-

Map I

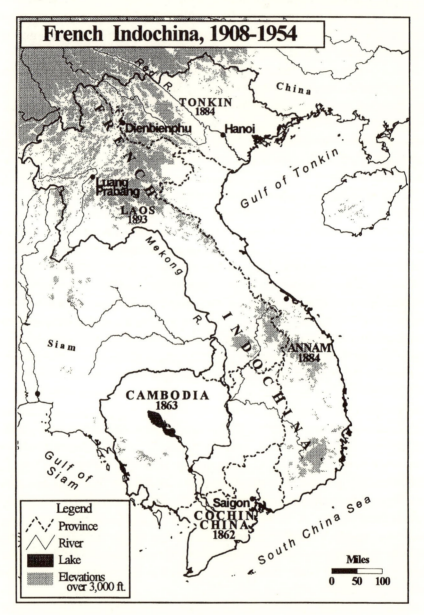

French Indochina, 1908–1954

China

TONKIN
1884

Dienbienphu   Hanoi

Gulf of Tonkin

Luang
Prabang

LAOS
1893

Mekong R.

Siam

ANNAM
1884

INDOCHINA

CAMBODIA
1863

Gulf of
Siam

Saigon
COCHIN
CHINA
1862

South China Sea

Legend
Province
River
Lake
Elevations
over 3,000 ft.

Miles
0   50   100

Generated by Connie McOmber, Department of Geography, Ball State University.

selves became dependent on French rule.[7] Most Vietnamese, however, chafed under French domination—some silently, others as part of that long tradition of open rebellion against foreign control. None became more prominent than Ho Chi Minh. His leadership and profound commitment to both anti-French patriotism and a communist social revolution ultimately helped end French rule in all of Indochina.

Born Nguyen Sinh Cung in 1890 in Nghe An province in central Vietnam, Ho developed a powerful sense of anti-French nationalism as a youth. He traveled to France and in 1919 tried to press demands for Vietnamese independence on American President Woodrow Wilson, who would not meet with the young Vietnamese. Ho then became a founding member of the French Communist party in 1920, as he was deeply impressed with the dedication and ideological sophistication of Marxism as interpreted by Lenin. Believing that national and social revolution could be combined, Ho (using the pseudonym Nguyen Ai Quoc) studied in Moscow in the 1920s and became a member of the Communist International. In 1930 he helped create the Indochinese Communist party and by 1940 had returned to Vietnam where he established the Vietnam Independence League (Vietminh), a multifactional but communist-controlled organization committed to Vietnamese independence. When Japanese troops occupied Vietnam in 1940–1941, Ho plotted a war of independence against both France and Japan. For the next four years, the Vietminh fought against both oppressors.

The Vietnam that the United States confronted in the twentieth century, then, had a long tradition of both foreign domination and resistance to that domination. Because of Ho Chi Minh's communist affiliation, America's relation to Vietnam almost from the outset was premised on fears of communist expansion. Indeed, the major themes surrounding American involvement in Vietnam concern the omnipresence of Cold War politics and diplomacy. According to diplomatic historian Thomas J. McCormick, "anticommunism . . . provided a unifying sense of purpose and mission" for American foreign policymakers during the period between 1945 and 1975.[8] In addition, and with considerable irony, as it turns out, the United States was never profoundly concerned with Vietnam per se. Indeed, that small Southeast Asian country was largely viewed as a symbol and a pawn, first as a counter to help the United States defeat Japan in World War II, then as a chip in the complex game to keep postwar France happy and noncommunist, and finally as a domino, whose collapse to communism might well cause "more important" nations like Japan or even Australia to fall victim to the Red Menace during the Cold War era. A final theme involves America's strategic and tactical approach to "stopping" communism in Vietnam. Following the classic bureaucratic form known as the Goldilocks Syndrome, American policymakers generally followed the "middle" option when making major decisions about the war. As options tended to shift toward deeper military involvement over time, the middle term shifted as well.

Vietnam was no more than a blip on the American consciousness prior to the closing days of World War II, and because of this lack of interest the government never developed a coherent policy toward Indochina. To be sure, President Franklin D. Roosevelt was no fan of colonialism, and he seemed to have a particular animus against the French variety of it in Indochina. In 1944 an irritated Roosevelt noted to Secretary of State Cordell Hull that "France has had the country [Indochina] for nearly one hundred years, and the people are worse off than they were at the beginning. . . . The people of Indochina are entitled to something better than that."[9] At one point, the American president suggested that Indochina be placed under an international trusteeship. But later, partly because of British opposition, he speculated that France could reclaim Vietnam if it pledged to grant eventual independence. Roosevelt's inconsistencies were part and parcel of the fact that he was simply concerned with matters that he saw as more crucial than Indochina.

One group of Americans, however, was deeply interested in and concerned about Vietnam during World War II. The Office of Strategic Services (OSS), a World War II precursor of the Central Intelligence Agency (CIA), positioned agents in Vietnam to assist Vietnamese under Ho Chi Minh fight against Japanese forces who had occupied Vietnam at the beginning of the war. One of these agents, medic Paul Hoagland, probably saved Ho's life in early 1945 when he treated him for various tropical diseases. Several of these agents, including Major Archimedes Patti, were taken by what they saw as Ho's sincere nationalism and quietly lobbied for the cause of a free Vietnam. In fact, Ho asked Patti's advice in drafting the 1945 Vietnamese Declaration of Independence. Indeed, the opening lines of the Vietnamese Declaration of Independence were lifted directly from the American Declaration of 1776: "All men are created equal." And several OSS agents stood with Ho on the reviewing stand when he announced independence in September 1945. Significantly, a Vietnamese band played "The Star Spangled Banner." Of course, Ho might well have been trying to manipulate his OSS friends with these moves in hopes of gaining a favorable hearing in Washington for his independence movement. As journalist-historian Stanley Karnow points out, Ho could be quite cynical about America's role in the world: "They [Americans] are only interested in replacing the French," Ho observed in late 1945. "They are capitalists to the core."[10]

This positive view of Ho, however, basically fell on deaf ears in Washington. For at precisely the time Ho was hoping for American support, Soviet communist intransigence in Europe and growing American fears of communist expansion combined to create a kind of "anticommunist paranoia" in official Washington. Initially, Ho's communism was not the problem; rather, those who manned the State Department's European desk feared that American support for Vietnamese independence would alienate France. And France was to be a crucial component in a stable, anticommunist Western Europe, which in turn would become a barrier to Soviet expansion. Given the sad state of the postwar French economy and the growing strength of the French Communist party, many French politicians worried that even the most innocent discussions of colonial independence would injure France and make it a less willing and able participant in the Western anticommunist phalanx. The French were also probably suffering feelings of inferiority, which the loss of its "jewel," Indochina, would only exacerbate. "Gloire" has always been an important part of French imperial motivation.

Whatever the French motives, President Harry S Truman listened to his pro-French advisors, and in the summer of 1945 he indicated to French president Charles DeGaulle that the United States would not undermine the French in Indochina. Meanwhile, in Vietnam that fall, Ho Chi Minh was desperately trying to hold on to the fragile independence he had declared on September 2. In the South, British troops, supposedly in Saigon to disarm the Japanese, were rearming former French prisoners of the Japanese (and in some cases giving weapons back to the Japanese) in order to attack pro-independence nationalist Vietminh. France spent the next several months in complicated negotiations with Ho, ultimately reaching an agreement with him in March 1946. This pact seemed to offer at least a modicum of independence to the northern part of Vietnam as a "free state" within the French Union and promised "free elections" in Cochin China. In return, France was allowed to station troops in northern Vietnam. France almost immediately reneged, and after a French naval bombardment of Haiphong in late 1946, full-scale war broke out between the Vietminh and France.

The late 1940s also witnessed the intensification of the Cold War and the development of a basic American strategy for combating the threat of communist expansion. After World War II, the Soviet Union installed communist-dominated governments in eastern Europe, in spite of American protests. In 1946 American diplomat George Kennan in his famous "long telegram" argued that Soviet communism was an implacable, expansionistic foe. When President Truman determined that communism threatened Greece and Turkey in early 1947, he promulgated the Truman Doctrine, calling for American economic and military assistance to those two nations. Truman feared that the fall of Greece or Turkey to communism would imperil other European and Middle Eastern nations—an early articulation of what later became the domino theory.

The Truman Doctrine formed the basic precedent for what came to be called the "containment policy." As enunciated by Kennan in 1947, the United States would attempt to contain communist expansion in Europe through a combination of economic and military assistance. Over the next two years, America developed a series of responses to the communist threat. The Marshall Plan (1947) provided for extensive economic assistance to European nations threatened by communism; the National Security Act (1947) created the Central Intelligence Agency (CIA) to promote covert anticommunist activity. In 1948 an American airlift helped break a Soviet-sponsored blockade of the noncommunist zones in Berlin; in 1949 the North Atlantic Treaty Organization (NATO) committed America to the military defense of western Europe. When the Soviets backed down in Berlin and communist expansionistic ambitions were thwarted in the rest of Europe, containment seemed to have succeeded.

When the containment policy was exported to Asia, however, the results were more ambiguous. In spite of massive American aid, in China the anticommunist Nationalist government fell to Mao Zedong's (Mao Tse-tung's) communist forces in 1949. This was a severe blow to American prestige and was viewed as a telling example of a worldwide communist effort to expand power and influence. Many Americans, especially conservative Republicans, blamed the Truman Administration for the "loss of China." Thus, when communist North Koreans invaded South Korea in June 1950, Truman acted quickly. Working through the United Nations, he sent American troops to Korea to join South Korean and other United Nations forces to stem the invasion. Thus, by 1950, Asia, not Europe, formed the crucible for the Cold War.

It was within this context that the United States sought to assist France in its struggle against the Vietminh. America's commitment to a French-controlled Indochina became more than just an attempt to keep the French happy. In the American mind, Ho Chi Minh's communist identity superseded his nationalist one. As a communist, Ho now became a threat to southeast Asian stability, as Americans increasingly seemed to share the monolithic view of communism expressed by Secretary of State Dean Acheson, when he noted in 1949 that whether "Ho Chi Minh is as much a nationalist as a Commie is irrelevant. . . . All Stalinists in colonial areas are nationalists."[11]

And the "loss" of any of these areas to a communist movement like Ho's would, in the minds of American leaders, result in the "fall" of neighboring countries to communism. Thus, if Ho triumphed in Vietnam, then Malaysia, the Philippines, and Indonesia might well be at risk. Even Japan, in the words of a 1952 National Security memorandum, might then be subject "to such economic and political pressures as to make it extremely difficult to prevent Japan's eventual accommodation to the Soviet bloc."[12] This "domino theory"—itself an elaboration of earlier American policy justifications in Europe—and its variants became the operating metaphor supporting American policy in Vietnam from the 1950s on.

Thus, support of France in Indochina became a vital American interest, although U.S.-French relations involving Vietnam were quite complicated. America pressured France to offer a noncommunist Vietnam at least a semblance of self-rule with an eye toward eventual independence. In part as a response to American concerns, France installed Bao Dai, a former Vietnamese emperor, as head of the Vietnamese state in 1949 but continued to control most of the country's government apparatus. In spite of considerable skepticism about French sincerity, the Truman administration ultimately recognized the Bao Dai government, largely because Truman believed that the alternatives were unacceptable. Indeed, in the spring of 1950, the Truman administration began to provide direct political, economic, and military support to French anticommunist forces in Vietnam. By 1954 the United States had supplied more than $2 billion in aid to France's effort—a stunning 75 percent of the total cost of the conflict.

Yet interestingly, America's commitment to a noncommunist Vietnam had its limits. Though the United States would not desert all of Vietnam, neither would it intervene with combat forces. In spite of massive infusions of American military aid, by 1954 French forces in Vietnam were clearly losing as the result of a combination of fierce determination on the part of the Vietminh, strategic and tactical errors by the French, and war weariness within France. In a last attempt to win a stunning victory, French General Henri Navarre hoped to lure Vietminh General Vo Nguyen Giap's troops into a set-piece battle at a village called Dienbienphu near the border between Vietnam and Laos. Vietminh troops managed to trap several thousand French there in the spring of 1954. President Dwight Eisenhower, Truman's successor, was deeply worried about a communist victory in Vietnam. Some of his advisors urged deeper American military involvement in the war. For example, Air Force Chief of Staff Nathan Twining went so far as to suggest that the United States "drop three small atomic bombs on the Vietminh around Dienbienphu 'and clean those commies out of there and the band could play "The Marseillaise" and the French would come marching out in fine shape.' "[13] Ultimately, Eisenhower was unwilling to commit American troops or even sanction an air strike to help the French at Dienbienphu. The risk was simply greater than any potential gain.

Dienbienphu fell on May 2, 1954, shortly after a conference in Geneva convened to deal with problems in southeast Asia. Ultimately, the war-sated French and Vietminh agreed to a cease-fire and a temporary division of the country at the 17th parallel, with the northern half under the control of Ho Chi Minh and the southern half nominally ruled by Bao Dai. An internationally supervised nationwide election would be held within two years to unify the country. Miffed at communist Chinese participation in the conference, the United States did not sign the Geneva Accords. In fact, American Secretary of State John Foster Dulles left the conference, refusing to shake hands with Chinese leader Chou En-lai. The United States did issue a unilateral statement through American observer Walter Bedell Smith in which it "recognized" the agreement and indicated that it would "refrain from the threat or the use of force to disturb" it. Smith also noted that the United States would "view any renewal of aggression . . . [in Vietnam] with grave concern."[14] (See Map 2.)

Such a "recognition" did not mean that the United States approved of the results of the Accords. In fact, the Eisenhower administration was determined to maintain a noncommunist South Vietnam. Shortly after the Geneva conference, for example, America joined several nations in an anticommunist alliance called the Southeast Asia Treaty Organization (SEATO), one major purpose of which was to protect the southern part of Vietnam from a communist takeover. Eisenhower also threw his support to Ngo Dinh Diem, a fiercely anticommunist, anti-French Catholic. Diem managed to silence several opposition groups within the South, and in 1955, with U.S. help, he won a clearly corrupt national referendum: "In an election that saw 605,000 of Saigon's 405,000 registered voters cast ballots," as historians James Olson and Randy Roberts point out, Diem won 98.2 percent of the vote against sitting emperor Bao Dai.[15] Shortly after the election, Diem formally proclaimed the Republic of Vietnam, known to Americans as "South Vietnam."

Once in power, Diem consolidated control and received the enthusiastic support of the Eisenhower administration when he refused to participate in the nationwide reunification elections called for in the Geneva Accords. (American CIA head Allen Dulles had predicted "an overwhelming victory . . . by Ho Chi Minh," an unappealing outcome to both Diem and the Americans.[16]) Diem placed numerous family members in high positions, gave large plots of land to fellow Catholics who had migrated from the north,

Map 2

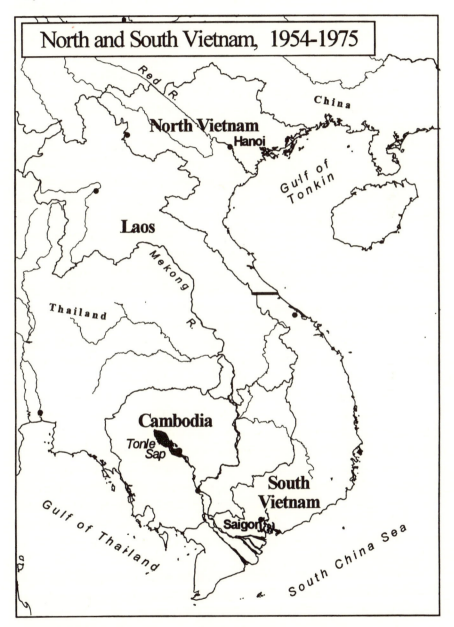

North and South Vietnam, 1954-1975

Red R.

China

North Vietnam

Hanoi

Gulf of Tonkin

Laos

Mekong R.

Thailand

Cambodia

Tonle Sap

South Vietnam

Saigon

Gulf of Thailand

South China Sea

Generated by Connie McOmber, Department of Geography, Ball State University.

and abolished local village elections in order to place supporters in positions of local power. In spite of some reservations about Diem's authoritarian methods, over the next five years, the United States provided considerable economic and military aid—including some American military advisors—to the Diem government as a bulwark against communist expansion in Asia.

Meanwhile, in northern Vietnam, Ho Chi Minh was also consolidating power, much more harshly and brutally than Diem. A disastrous land reform program, in which thousands of peasants were killed because they were allegedly landowning capitalists, marred Ho's rule. (He later apologized for the program's rigidity.) The communist government there was also deeply disappointed by the failure to hold the elections promised by the Geneva Accords but was initially unwilling to use force to attempt the reunification of the country. By 1959, however, communist remnants of the Vietminh who had remained in the South after the Geneva Accords convinced their northern comrades to sanction a combination of political and armed revolutionary struggle to liberate "South" Vietnam. In that year, forces loyal to Ho carried out a number of assassinations and kidnappings of Diemist village officials. In December 1960, southerners sympathetic to Ho formed the National Liberation Front (NLF), which became the umbrella political organization under which guerrilla warfare against the Diem government was waged. The NLF designated its military arm the Peoples Liberation Armed Forces (PLAF), dismissively referred to as Vietcong (Vietnamese communists) by the Diem government.

When President John F. Kennedy took office in 1961, Vietnam was still not a primary concern of American foreign policy. (In fact, Kennedy recalled that President Eisenhower "never mentioned it [Vietnam]" in transition meetings.[17]) Nonetheless, Kennedy was from the outset committed to using American power to thwart communist expansion. In the words of his famed inaugural address: "We shall pay any price, bear any burden, meet any hardship, support any friend, oppose any foe to assure the survival and success of liberty."[18] With South Vietnam clearly a "friend" and communist North Vietnam obviously an enemy, Kennedy planted himself firmly within the aggressive anticommunist nexus.

Throughout most of the Kennedy administration, however, Vietnam remained a tangential concern. In fact, the first Gallup public opinion poll involving Vietnam was not conducted until 1964, underscoring the relatively small role played by Vietnam in the national consciousness. Soviet threats to Berlin and American-Cuban relations monopolized national attention. Even in southeast Asia, a civil war raging in Laos was much more a front-burner issue than was Vietnam. In fact, Kennedy worried that Laos might fall to communist insurgents. Yet, given the country's small population, limited strategic value, and unfriendly terrain for military operations, he chose to avoid military confrontation. Ultimately, the Laotion struggle ended in 1962 with an agreement by which the country would remain neutral in the Cold War.

This does not mean that Kennedy ignored the problem of Vietnam. Much like Eisenhower, he was committed to a noncommunist South Vietnam, but like Eisenhower, Kennedy was reluctant to expand American involvement to include ground combat troops. Thus, in 1961 when several advisors, including Maxwell Taylor, Kennedy's military advisor, and Walt Rostow, his Deputy Special Assistant for National Security Affairs, urged him to commit some thirteen thousand combat troops, Kennedy rejected the counsel, musing that "the troops will march in, the bands will play; the crowds will cheer; and in four days everyone will have forgotten. Then we will have to send in more troops."[19] When his Undersecretary of State, George Ball, advised the president to cut his losses and withdraw from Vietnam, however, Kennedy balked at such a policy that would in essence surrender another nation to communism, with a negative impact on both American security and the Kennedy presidency.

Over the next two-and-a-half years, then, the Kennedy administration chose the classic middle path, as it increased the number of American military advisors to more than sixteen thousand, while pouring in additional money and equipment. Although Congress passed no declaration of war or resolution of support, in essence, America was an integral part of a hot war against communism in Vietnam. In spite of new tactical approaches such as counterinsurgency through the Green Berets and a Strategic Hamlet Program designed to move South Vietnamese to safe new hamlets, the war was not going well. By the summer of 1963, the public became increasingly aware of the problem of Vietnam. When protests against the government of President Diem escalated with the self-immolation of a Buddhist monk, many Americans were horrified. Most American policymakers saw the Diem government as unpopular and ineffective. In the fall of 1963, the Kennedy administration secretly indicated to anti-Diem forces that the United States would not attempt to stop a military coup against the unpopular leader. The Kennedy administration clearly hoped that new leadership in the South would help in the struggle against the communists.

Kennedy's assassination in November 1963 brought to office a man with little foreign policy experience, Vice President Lyndon Johnson. The new president retained Kennedy's chief foreign policy advisors, from Secretary of State Dean Rusk to Secretary of Defense Robert McNamara to State Department and intelligence bureau heads, and he remained firmly committed to Kennedy's primary goal in Vietnam: to keep South Vietnam noncommunist. In his public rhetoric, however, Johnson tended to couch American objectives in Vietnam in the highest moral terms. He talked about the "need to give the people on the periphery of Asian communism . . . the help they needed to . . . live in peace and stability."[20] America wanted nothing for itself, only freedom for South Vietnam.

Such high-flown moral rhetoric tended to obscure the deeper reason for Johnson's firmness. Lyndon Johnson was very much a product of the Cold War mentality; the expansion of communism was a threat to American security, and Vietnam was an area of the world in which communism was trying to expand. Johnson also accepted the domino theory wholeheartedly, although his version tended to emphasize the importance of American credibility: If the United States allowed South Vietnam to fall to communism, then America's more important allies—Japan and West Germany in particular—would lose faith in America's promises to protect them. In fact, in a 1965 memorandum to Secretary of Defense Robert McNamara, Assistant Secretary John T. NcNaughton boldly stated that "70%" of "U.S. Aims" in the war was an attempt "to avoid a humiliating U.S. defeat (to our reputation as a guarantor)," while only "10% involved permitting the people of SVN [South Vietnam] to enjoy a freer, better way of life."[21] In other words, Vietnam remained a pawn, albeit a crucial one, in the "great game" between the United States and the forces of communism.

If the Johnson administration was sure of its central objective—a noncommunist Vietnam—it was less certain of the proper combination of methods to achieve the goal. While continuing the Kennedy policy of providing money, matériel, and advisors, Johnson also embarked on a "secret" war against the North, which included the use of naval vessels with electronic intelligence capacity. In early August 1964, one such ship was attacked by communist patrol boats in the Gulf of Tonkin off the coast of North Vietnam. An alleged second attack led the president to order a limited retaliatory air strike against North Vietnamese bases. He also introduced, and Congress overwhelmingly passed, a resolution in essence giving the president a free hand to combat communist aggression in Vietnam by all means necessary.

In the midst of a presidential election campaign against Republican Barry Goldwater, Johnson was able to use the Gulf of Tonkin incident to show both his boldness and restraint. He responded to a communist attack yet did not unleash a full-scale war. Goldwater, generally perceived as more militantly anticommunist than Johnson, could only applaud the president's actions. And Johnson's Vietnam policy probably helped assure him a landslide victory.

After his election triumph, Johnson had to face a deteriorating situation in Vietnam. Particularly galling was continued political instability in South Vietnam. After the 1963 coup against Diem, the South Vietnamese government underwent a bewildering series of changes in leadership. Taking advantage of this instability, the Vietcong, assisted by some units of the North Vietnamese Army (NVA), stepped up guerrilla warfare in the South, so that by late 1964, the communists were winning the war. Enemy attacks on American installations at Pleiku and Qui Nhon in early 1965 led Johnson to approve Operation Rolling Thunder, a sustained air attack on North Vietnam. Responding to the request of General William Westmoreland, the American military commander in Vietnam, Johnson ordered two Marine battalions into Vietnam in March 1965, ostensibly to guard the now very active American air base at Danang.

Over the next five months, Johnson and his advisors debated the future course of the war. While only Undersecretary of State George Ball spoke firmly against further American involvement, Johnson's other advisors urged various kinds of escalation. Once again choosing a middle option—this time between withdrawal and massive escalation—the president agreed to increase the number of combat troops markedly and confirm their change in mission from defensive protection of bases to offensive activity. Even though the additional troops (some 184,300 combat troops were in Vietnam by the end of 1965) probably prevented a victory by revolutionary forces, they certainly did not convince these forces to desist in their attempts to unify the country under Ho's rule.

For the rest of the Johnson administration, the United States continued its gradual escalation of the war by committing ever more troops, supplies, and dollars, so that by December of 1968, 536,100 American combat troops were in the country.[22] The air assault against North Vietnam also intensified; in July 1966 Rolling Thunder expanded to include ammunition dumps and oil storage facilities, and in the spring of 1967 it was further enhanced to include power plants, factories, and airfields in the Hanoi-Haiphong area.

The strategy and tactics accompanying this escalation moved along two different, often mutually contradictory tracks. On the one hand, General Westmoreland fought a war of attrition, in which, ideally, American ground units on "search and destroy" missions would engage the enemy, then call in massive firepower through artillery and air strikes, thereby killing and maiming so many of the enemy that North Vietnam would sue for peace. Relying heavily on America's technological superiority would also reduce American casualties and avoid a long war. Thus, enemy body count, not territory gained, became the chief barometer of military success. At the same time, South Vietnamese military units would engage in pacification (in addition to some combat missions), convincing villagers to support the South Vietnamese government—winning "the hearts and minds" of the people.

Johnson also made several overtures to the North Vietnamese, suggesting negotiations to end the war between 1965 and 1968. He called for bombing halts of the North as a token of American good faith. However, neither side was willing to concede on the central negotiating point: the existence of a noncommunist South Vietnam.

American strategy was only partly successful in the 1965–1968 period. Revolutionary forces learned rather quickly to avoid major set-piece battles, relying more on hit-and-run tactics. They also used villages as fortified places so that during battles, civilians were killed and maimed, and property was destroyed when Americans responded with heavy firepower. Such attacks often alienated villagers, who tended to blame the Americans for the damage. Moreover, the enemy was able to replenish its forces by increased infiltration of North Vietnamese Army units; in spite of American bombing, the revolutionary forces also moved sufficient supplies either down the Ho Chi Minh Trail through Laos or by sea through Cambodia.

Some senior military officials, including General Westmoreland and members of the Joint Chiefs of Staff, wanted the president to order "a brief, intensive [air] campaign to isolate North Vietnam from external sources of supply."[23] They also urged him to approve expanded military action in Cambodia and Laos, where the enemy had built base camps and supply trails in technically neutral areas. Johnson rejected this advice, choosing only a limited air war via Rolling Thunder and ground activity only in South Vietnam. He feared that large-scale bombing of the North and escalation in Laos and Cambodia might provoke a military response from the Soviet Union or communist China, thus leading to a wider war.

By early 1968, then, the war had reached what historian Vincent H. Demma terms "a strategic stalemate: neither side faced imminent defeat or victory."[24] The war, it seemed, would drag on and on.

This stalemate had devastating effects on the Johnson administration. His overwhelming victory in the 1964 election and subsequent legislative triumphs for his Great Society program in 1965 and 1966 boded well for continuing success. He even sought to apply his New Deal-Great Society paradigm to the war itself, as he promised Vietnam a veritable Tennessee Valley Authority (TVA) on the Mekong River if Ho Chi Minh would cease aiding the insurgency in the South. But the war gradually sapped Johnson's energy and destroyed his popularity. A Gallup public opinion poll taken in later 1965 showed 56 percent of Americans approving of Johnson's handling of the situation in Vietnam, with only 26 percent disapproving. By February 1968, the numbers had virtually flip-flopped, with only 35 percent approving and 50 percent disapproving of the president's handling of the war. By mid-March 1968, only 36 percent of Americans approved of Johnson's overall performance as president, a precipitous drop from just three years earlier when 67 percent approved.[25]

The military stalemate in Vietnam also probably encouraged the growing antiwar movement in the United States. From fitful beginnings in 1965, by early 1968, hundreds of thousands of Americans actively opposed the war. These so-called doves on the war were a diverse lot, difficult to generalize about, although most saw the war as contrary to American interests and urged withdrawal. The Johnson administration, however, seemed little moved by the antiwar movement. A major attack by revolutionary forces during the Tet holiday in early February 1968, however, would shake the president and his advisors. Although this massive assault, in which the enemy struck thirty-six of forty-four provincial capitals, as well as scores of other towns and cities, including Saigon, was ultimately crushed by American and ARVN forces, the psychological impact on America was devastating. Johnson's political base was narrowing, as he was challenged in his own party for the presidential nomination by Senators Eugene McCarthy and Robert Kennedy. Within three months after Tet, Johnson had decided not to seek another term as president, to end Rolling Thunder air attacks north of the 20th parallel, and to open peace talks in Paris. In essence, Johnson sought to end the war in a negotiated settlement.

But the peace talks accomplished little, given the intransigence of the two sides over major issues like the legitimacy of the South Vietnamese government and the role that revolutionary forces would play in a new regime. Thus, when Richard Nixon, the newly elected president, took office in January 1969, the war essentially remained a strategic stalemate. In many ways, Nixon shared Johnson's basic worldview about the war: A communist victory in Vietnam would weaken American credibility. As he explicitly stated in a November 1969 speech, "A nation cannot remain great if it betrays its allies and lets down its friends. Our defeat and humiliation in South Vietnam . . . would promote recklessness in the councils of those great powers who have not yet abandoned their goals of world conquest."[26]

However, because Nixon had promised a "secret plan" to end the war during the election campaign, he needed to come up with something that appeared new and promising. Moreover, he was vitally interested in reaching some kind of modus vivendi with both the Soviets and the communist Chinese; the Vietnam War was a major impediment to this goal. Finally, he needed to deal with growing antiwar sentiment, much of it based upon the anguish accompanying American casualties in the war. Because he wanted neither to capitulate nor to escalate the war, he refurbished and renamed a strategy of "Vietnamization," which actually was first discussed during the last days of the Johnson administration. In essence, Nixon would gradually withdraw American combat troops while turning the fighting over to the South Vietnamese. To make up for the diminution of American troops, the president enhanced the role of American air power.

Nixon succeeded in withdrawing American combat personnel. Shortly after he took office, there were 543,400 American troops in-country. By June 1971 the number had been more than halved to 239,200, and by December 1972 the number stood at 24,200.[27] But the viability of turning the bulk of the fighting over to South Vietnamese forces was questionable. Although a joint U.S.-ARVN incursion into Cambodia in April–May 1970 probably killed some enemy and temporarily disrupted supply lines, this was mainly an American-controlled operation. An ARVN thrust against the Ho Chi Minh Trail in Laos in 1971, although supported by American air and artillery attacks, was beaten back by the North Vietnamese and generally considered a defeat for the South. A year later, an "Easter Offensive" by revolutionary forces almost succeeded in permanently capturing much of the northern part of South Vietnam; it failed only after massive American air attacks. Thus, American force again saved the South Vietnamese, confirming that the ARVN alone could not stop determined enemy attacks.

The mixed performance of South Vietnamese forces did not deter Nixon in his attempts to end the war. The president's National Security Advisor, Henry Kissinger, and North Vietnam's Le Duc Tho embarked on a series of secret negotiations in 1969. By 1972 both sides saw the need to compromise. North Vietnam had suffered severely during the abortive Easter Offensive and, according to historian George Herring, "wanted peace if it could be attained without abandoning long-term goals."[28] Nixon faced growing public discontent, a Congress threatening to cut off financial support for the war, and an election in the fall. The two sides had reached virtual agreement in the fall of 1972, but South Vietnamese president Nguyen Van Thieu refused to accept the treaty. When North Vietnamese negotiators then left the table, President Nixon ordered a massive air assault on the Hanoi area, probably as much to reassure Thieu of American support as to intimidate the North. For whatever reason, North Vietnamese negotiators returned to the negotiations, and President Nixon bluntly told Thieu to accept an agreement or face the loss of American assistance (while secretly promising him American retaliation if North Vietnam violated the peace).

The warring parties ultimately agreed to a series of "accords" signed in January 1973. In essence, the United States agreed to remove its forces from Vietnam, and North Vietnam agreed to return American prisoners of war and to allow the Thieu government to remain in power in the South. Revolutionary forces in the South held on to positions they controlled, while the two Vietnams were supposed to negotiate a reconciliation under international supervision. Over the next two years, both Vietnams violated the agreement, the North more blatantly and successfully than the South. American public and congressional opinion had turned so overwhelmingly against the war that President Gerald Ford, Nixon's successor, was unable to generate any support for additional American aid to South Vietnam. In 1975 in a conventional attack, revolutionary forces overwhelmed the South Vietnamese army and unified Vietnam under communist rule. The American war in Vietnam ended on April 30, 1975, as the last evacuation helicopter departed from the roof of the American Embassy in Saigon.

The United States clearly failed to achieve its central goal in Vietnam: saving South Vietnam from communist control. More than fifty-eight thousand Americans died in Vietnam, as did countless Vietnamese and soldiers from other nations. More than three hundred thousand Americans were wounded, as were probably millions of others. Millions in neighboring Cambodia and Laos were also killed and wounded. The war helped convince Lyndon Johnson not to run for another term as president and led the Nixon Administration to approve illegal activities against its opponents. For example, men hired by Nixon advisors broke into the office of antiwar activist Daniel Ellsberg's psychiatrist, an action that helped lay the groundwork for President Nixon's resignation.

And the war remains very much a part of Vietnamese and American life. Vietnam has suffered through devastating economic and political problems since the war. In America, the legacy of the war has included cynicism about government and a loss of faith in political officials, deep reluctance to become involved militarily in distant areas of the world, and a sense of bitterness on the part of many veterans who have felt ignored by the nation that sent them off to war. Although the diplomatic recognition of the socialist Republic of Vietnam by President Bill Clinton in 1995 brought a kind of formal conclusion to the war, its legacy will no doubt live on.

In the essays that follow, we look in more detail at selected aspects of this conflict that will not die as we delve further into the central issues of America's longest war.

NOTES

1. Robert D. Schulzinger, *A Time for War: The United States and Vietnam, 1941–1975* (New York: Oxford University Press, 1997), p. 3. In using the term "Vietnamese" here, Schulzinger, like some other American historians of the war, oversimplifies a very complex arrangement of loyalties among the inhabitants of Vietnam. Clearly, large numbers of southern Vietnamese did not see the Americans as invaders but rather as protectors against the perceived horrors of communist domination from the North.

2. William Turley, *Second Indochina War: A Short Political and Military History* (New York: New American Library, 1986), p. 2.

3. Administratively, France established three territories in Vietnam in 1883: The northern third was called Tonkin; the middle third Annam; and the southern third Cochin China. Laos and Cambodia were added to comprise "French Indochina." Although only Cochin China was directly ruled by the French, France did effectively control the entire area.

4. Charles Depincé, "Protection of Indigenous Peoples," in *Vietnam: Anthology and Guide to a Television History*, ed. Steven Cohen (New York: McGraw-Hill, 1983), p. 9.

5. Edward Doyle, et al., eds., *Setting the Stage*, in *The Vietnam Experience*, ed. Edward Doyle, et al. (Boston: Boston Publishing Co., 1981), p. 129.

6. Ibid., p. 123.

7. Ibid., p. 107.

8. Thomas J. McCormick, "Troubled Triumphalism: Cold War Veterans Confront a Post-Cold War World," *Diplomatic History* 21 (Summer 1997): 482.

9. George Donelson Moss, *Vietnam: An American Ordeal*, 2nd ed. (Englewood Cliffs, N.J.: Prentice-Hall, 1994), p. 23.

10. Stanley Karnow, *Vietnam: A History* (New York: Viking Press, 1983), p. 138.

11. James S. Olson and Randy Roberts, *Where the Domino Fell: The United States and Vietnam, 1945–1995*, 2nd ed. (New York: St. Martin's Press, 1996), p. 32.

12. Ibid., p. 33.

13. Stephen Ambrose, *Rise to Globalism: American Foreign Policy since 1938*, 6th rev. ed. (New York: Penguin Books, 1991), p. 143.

14. "Statement by Walter Bedell Smith at the Geneva Conference July 21, 1954," in *Vietnam*, ed. Steven Cohen, pp. 49–50.

15. Olson and Roberts, *Domino*, p. 62.

16. Ibid., p. 64.

17. Ibid., p. 73.

18. John F. Kennedy [really Ted Sorensen], "Inaugural Address," in *Vietnam,* ed. Steven Cohen, p. 75.

19. Olson and Roberts, *Domino,* p. 86.

20. George Herring, *America's Longest War: The United States and Vietnam, 1945–1975,* 3rd. ed. (New York: McGraw-Hill, 1996), p. 129.

21. John T. McNaughton, "Memo to McNamara," March 24, 1965, in *A Vietnam Reader: Sources and Essays,* ed. George Donelson Moss (Englewood Cliffs, N.J.: Prentice-Hall, 1991), pp. 80, 81.

22. Daniel T. Bailey, "Order of Battle: U.S. Military," in *Encyclopedia of the Vietnam War,* ed. Stanley I. Kutler (New York: Charles Scribner's Sons, 1996), p. 413. Defense analyst Thomas Thayer estimates that the total cost of the war was $150 billion (Thomas C. Thayer, *War without Fronts: The American Experience in Vietnam* [Boulder, Colo.: Westview Press, 1985], p. 23).

23. John F. Guilmartin, "Rolling Thunder," in Kutler, *Encyclopedia,* p. 477.

24. Vincent H. Demma, "Strategy and Tactics," in Kutler, *Encyclopedia,* p. 520.

25. George H. Gallup, ed., *The Gallup Poll: Public Opinion, 1935–1971,* Vol. 3 (New York: Random House, 1972), pp. 1982, 2105, 2113, 1936.

26. Richard Nixon, "Speech," November 3, 1969, in Moss, *Vietnam Reader,* p. 140. The phrase "great powers who have not yet abandoned their goals of world conquest" is a none-too-subtle euphemism for the communist Soviet Union and the communist Peoples Republic of China.

27. Bailey, "Order of Battle: U.S. Military," p. 413.

28. George C. Herring, "Diplomacy," in Kutler, *Encyclopedia,* p. 172.

2

Ho Chi Minh and the Vietnamese Tradition of Rebellion

In 1978 Nguyen Co Thach, one of North Vietnam's negotiators at the Paris Peace Conference in the early 1970s, observed that "Vietnam is nobody's dog."[1] Even to Westerners, the meaning of this sentiment should have been clear: Vietnam did not whine or wheedle to gain its objectives; nor was it loyal to "masters."[2] Vietnam's long history of rebellion and resistance to foreign invaders who have tried to control and dominate her has attested to the fierce and proud desire for independence. In fending off modern enemies—be they French or, in the eyes of many, Americans—Vietnamese brandished their history of rebellion as a cultural and political weapon to rally opposition to foreign rule. Even, and especially, communist leader Ho Chi Minh draped his Vietminh and anti-American cause in the memory of Vietnamese rebellion and the call for national unity.

As noted in the introduction, a renegade Chinese warlord occupied the northern part of Vietnam in 208 B.C., and the Han dynasty absorbed it in 111 B.C. Almost from the beginning of Chinese rule, there were Vietnamese who rose up against the "foreigners." Between A.D. 39 and 40, for example, Trung Trac, a Vietnamese noblewoman, sought revenge for the murder of her husband by a Chinese military commander. She and her sister, Trung Nhi, then launched the first major rebellion against Chinese rule, leading a band of dissident nobles and their vassals. One of their comrades, a woman named Phung Thi Chin, allegedly fought against the Chinese while she was pregnant. According to Vietnamese accounts: "Surrounded by Chinese attackers, she delivered her baby. She then strapped the newborn to her back, grabbed a sword in each hand, and opened a bloody escape route through the ranks of the enemy."[3] Although ultimately put down by the Chinese, the Trung Sisters' rebellion has become part of Vietnamese folklore—both in the North and the South: "The Communists acclaim them as pioneer nationalists," and Ngo Dinh Diem's sister-in-law, Madame Nhu, had a statue of them erected in Saigon in 1962 "to commemorate their patriotism—and also promote herself as their reincarnation."[4]

This tradition of rebellious women was reprised two hundred years later when Trieu Au raised an army of a thousand men to contest the rule of the "cruel and cantankerous" Chinese. When her brother tried to dissuade her, "she defiantly replied, 'I want to rail against the wind and tide, kill the whales in the ocean, sweep the whole country to save the people from slavery, and I have no desire to take abuse.' " This no-nonsense young woman, known as the Vietnamese Joan of Arc, took after the Chinese in golden armor as she perched atop a war elephant. Defeated by a larger force, she "committed suicide rather than submit to the shame of surrender."[5]

Vietnamese men also peopled the pantheon of rebel heroes. In 938, Ngo Quyen, a provincial aristocrat, defeated a Chinese flotilla with a crafty ruse. As the enemy approached the Bach Dang River, his men implanted iron-tipped spikes just under the water (arguably, the first use of punji stakes). At high tide, Ngo lured the Chinese forward as his ships gradually retreated. When the Chinese vessels were impaled, Ngo's forces destroyed them.

A few years after this important battle, the Chinese granted Vietnam virtual independence as a tributary state. However, Vietnamese relations with China remained turbulent. For example, Kubla Khan, the legendary Mongol emperor, invaded Vietnam three times during the thirteenth century. Vietnamese military leader Tran Hung Dao managed to repulse all of the encroachments by using an early version of guerilla warfare, relying "on mobile methods . . . abandoning cities, avoiding frontal attacks, and harassing his enemies until . . . they were ripe for final attack." When his outnumbered forces defeated three hundred thousand Mongol troops in 1287, one of his generals composed a victory poem that affirmed that "this ancient land shall live forever." Vietminh commander Vo Nguyen Giap invoked Tran's memory in a battle against the French seven centuries later—a not surprising example of uses modern Vietnamese made of history and poetry.[6]

We should be careful, however, not to overly romanticize Vietnamese dedication to freedom. Having temporarily shed Chinese rule, Vietnam showed considerable unconcern for the independence of its neighboring state, Champa. After Tran's victory, the Vietnamese launched what would become a two-century assault against the Champans. So weakened was

Vietnam by the struggle that in 1406 the Chinese again successfully invaded the country. And once again the Vietnamese rose in rebellion. Led by another almost mythical hero, Le Loi, the Vietnamese finally expelled their Chinese overlords in 1426.[7] (Chinese forces tried to defeat the insurrection by "[clinging] to towns, venturing out only by day [with] their big battalions sticking to roads." They also built a series of "fortified towers along main routes"—all abortive tactics used by the French five centuries later!)[8]

Le Loi's great victory inspired one Nguyen Trai, a Vietnamese poet, to write a hymn of hope:

> Henceforth our country is safe.
> Our Mountains and rivers begin life afresh.
> Peace follows war as day follows night.
> We have purged our shame for a thousand centuries.
> We have regained tranquility for ten thousand
> generations.[9]

Trai's optimism was somewhat premature, as his blessed "tranquility" lasted, at best, a mere four hundred years. From 1859 to 1887 France gradually spread its control over Vietnam, Laos, and Cambodia, creating the Indochinese Union in 1887. (See map 1 in chapter 1.) As might have been predicted, based on national history, rebellions against French rule shadowed its expansion. As early as 1859, the year Saigon fell to French forces, "Vietnamese partisans appeared . . . and insurgent movements spread through Cochinchina soon afterward." As the commander of French forces in Indochina noted in 1862: "We have enormous difficulty in enforcing our authority. . . . Rebel bands disturb the country everywhere. They appear from nowhere in large numbers, destroy everything and then disappear into nowhere."[10]

One of the chief "everywheres" where rebellion was rife was a region just to the north of old Annam called Nghe Tinh, consisting of the provinces Nghe An and Ha Tinh. As French journalist Jean Lacouture points out, it was from this region that "had come for many centuries all but a few of the country's revolutionaries."[11] Among these revolutionaries was one Nguyen Sinh Huy, a peasant-turned-intellectual who in 1885 reputedly had participated in an abortive uprising known as "The Scholars' Revolt." Huy also supposedly urged his friends and family to study the famous anti-French writings of Vietnamese nationalist Phan Boi Chau. Huy's son, who would become Vietnam's greatest modern revolutionary, Ho Chi Minh, was born into this atmosphere of rebellion in 1890 as Nguyen Sinh Cung.

Unfortunately, we know little of Ho's early life. His mother died when he was ten, and at fifteen he attended a secondary school where he learned French. He probably participated in "the insurrectional movements of 1908" at his school. In 1911 he moved to Phan Tiet, a small seaport, where he taught Quoc Nhu (romanized Vietnamese). One day in September 1911, calling himself "Ba," he signed on as a mess boy on a ship that plied the waters between Haiphong and Marseilles.[12] For the next four decades, as a student and an intellectual, Ho would travel in North America, Europe, and the Far East, gaining knowledge and skill as he worked to free his country from French control.

Although the details of Ho's childhood and adolescence are sketchy, one fact is clear: He absorbed his father's hatred of French domination and fierce sense of Vietnamese nationalism. He also, no doubt, learned to despise the Mandarin system and the social and ecomomic inequality it engendered. After all, according to Lacouture, Ho's father was fond of saying that "being a mandarin . . . is the ultimate form of slavery."[13] Ho saw communism as a way to eliminate the inequalities inherent in the Mandarin system. Thus, his early upbringing sowed the seeds of both nationalism and socialism in the young Ho.

Over the next six years, Ho traveled extensively and was probably deeply influenced by visits to other colonial sites in Africa. In 1917, while World War I raged, he was in Paris, where, he says, "I made my living . . . now as a retoucher at a photographer's, now as a painter of 'Chinese antiquities' (made in France!)."[14] He also was attracted to the French left, especially the critique of imperialism offered by some of its luminaries. He adopted a new name, Nguyen Ai Quoc ("Nguyen the Patriot"), joined the Young Socialists, and wrote articles for three left-wing newspapers. At the end of World War I, he and two Vietnamese émigré friends, Phan Van Truang and Phan Chu Trinh, wrote a detailed plan for Vietnam's ultimate emancipation and forwarded it to the secretariat of the Versailles Peace Conference. From today's perspective, the plan seems quite moderate. Influenced by the Fourteen Points enunciated by American president Woodrow Wilson, it sought, among other concessions, "permanent representation in the French parliament; . . . freedom to hold meetings and form associations; . . . and equality of legal rights between French and Annamese [Vietnamese]."[15] Ho tried to obtain an audience with President Wilson to plead the case for his country, but Wilson refused to see him. The American leader, no doubt, felt he had bigger fish to fry, with more-crucial self-determination problems involving Europe and the Mideast—Trieste, Arabs, Kurds, Armenians, and others. Vietnam was barely a speck on the American horizon in 1919.

If Wilson chose to ignore Ho Chi Minh's plea, fellow Vietnamese in Paris found it absolutely exhilarating. According to student Bui Lam, "It was like a flash of lightning, the first thunderclap of spring. . . . Here was a Vietnamese insisting that his people be accorded their rights. We took our hats off to him."[16] Wilson's lack of interest in Ho's case meant the loss of a potential friend of Vietnamese independence. Thus, it may have encouraged Ho to look to communism as an ally, although he was probably headed in that direction anyway.

Ho Chi Minh's crucial decision to join the French Communist party in 1920 grew out of his nationalism first and foremost. In Paris, he discovered the works of the great communist revolutionary V. I. Lenin, and, in his own words, "admired Lenin because he was a great patriot who liberated his compatriots."[17] In other words, Lenin's communist ideology was less important than his national patriotism in inspiring the young Vietnamese. As a member of the Young Socialists, Ho began criticizing those colleagues who failed to emphasize anticolonialism. As he passionately argued in one meeting, "If you do not condemn colonialism, if you do not side with the colonial people, what kind of revolution are you waging?" Ho himself admitted that "at first patriotism, not yet Communism, led me to have confidence in Lenin, in the Third [Communist] International." In other words, Marxist-Leninist ideology was a means to a nationalist end. But, as he continued his study of the doctrine, he concluded that "only Socialism and Communism can liberate the oppressed nations and the working people throughout the world from slavery."[18] Thus, he came to that unique combination of Vietnamese nationalism, communism, and world revolution that informed the rest of his life.

For the next three years, Ho organized and wrote in Paris, focusing on the connections between Leninism and anticolonialism. He saved his bitterest barbs for French colonial officials. As Lacouture puts it, for Ho Chi Minh, "no colonial official could be anything but a sadistic blackguard, no French professional soldier anything but a loathsome butcher."[19] In one article, for example, he commented on the departure of a French military official from Rabat: "The disreputable old fogey is leaving Morocco so that he can nurse his 'syph[ilis]' in France."[20]

Ho's organizing skills (and perhaps his vitriolic prose) came to the attention of the communist leadership in the Soviet Union, and in 1923 Ho traveled to Moscow to work for the Communist International (Comintern). After a year of training, he was sent to China where he created the Vietnamese Revolutionary Youth League, a precursor of the Indochinese Communist Party (ICP), which Ho helped establish in 1930. During the next eleven years, he was arrested by the British, hounded by French police agents, even suspected by Soviet leader Joseph Stalin of being excessively "independent minded," and finally served with communist Chinese forces in 1940.[21]

The Japanese occupation of Vietnam in that year provided Ho Chi Minh with another problem. Some Vietnamese saw Japan as a kind of liberator, fellow Asians showing the white French a version of "yellow power." But for Ho and most Vietnamese nationalists, Japan was just another conquerer, an authoritarian state bent on dominating the weaker Vietnamese. Thus, Ho began a complicated two-pronged assault on both French and Japanese rule. Clearly seeing that he needed support from Vietnamese other than peasants, workers, and fellow communists, in 1941 he formed the Viet Nam Doc Lap Dong Minh (League for Vietnamese Independence, or Vietminh) in an attempt to appeal to his middle-class and professional countrymen. According to historian William Duiker, Ho pragmatically "downplayed ideological issues and emphasized anti-imperialism . . . in order to win the support of moderate elements of all social classes against the twin enemies of French colonialism and Japanese fascism." Ho also cleverly disguised the fact that the ICP played "a leading role" in the Vietminh.[22] During the war, Ho also adopted the name "Ho Chi Minh" ("He who enlightens"), which became the way he wanted to present himself to the world.

During World War II, Ho set up a headquarters north of the Red River near the Chinese border. Gradually, he built up an effective guerrilla force. On a trip to China in 1942, he was arrested by the Chinese Nationalists (who were supporting a rival group in Vietnam). He languished in jail for more than a year.

During his imprisonment, Ho wrote some of his most moving poetry. Part of a profound love of poetic expression that has characterized Vietnamese culture, Ho's prison poetry probably helped keep him alive. As he wrote, "It is your body which is in prison/not your mind." He saw his verse as a political tool, noting, "I versify until such time as I see freedom." At that point, the poet becomes the warrior: "The poems of our day must be clad in steel./Poets too must know how to fight."[23] He was released in 1943, apparently because his captors now believed him to be an effective opponent of Japan. In order to fight the Japanese (and ultimately the French), Ho realized that he needed American help. Although we will never be certain of his motives, he apparently believed that a nation founded on anticolonialism like the United States would be well-disposed toward a Vietnam also struggling to throw off the shackles of imperialism. He was also quite aware that the Americans would welcome help in their struggle against the Japanese. Thus, in 1945 Ho and the American Office of Strategic Services (OSS) reached an agreement whereby Ho would provide intelligence about Japanese movements and help rescue downed American pilots in return for American weapons. The OSS airdropped a team into Vietnam, which actually helped train Vietminh forces. Indeed, many OSS agents became so impressed with Ho that they tended to support the idea of Vietnamese independence after the war.

In his relations with the OSS team, Ho once again showed a powerful streak of pragmatism. According to historian Robert Schulzinger, "The Vietminh considered OSS officials as a ticket for ending their isolation and as a counter to the French."[24] American Major Allison Thomas, who led one of the OSS missions into Vietnam in 1945, became an enthusiastic friend and supporter of Ho. Convinced of the sincere patriotism of the Vietminh, in July 1945, he naively cabled his superiors in Washington: "[T]he Vietminh is not Communist. Stands for freedom and reforms from French harsh-ness."[25] Aware of the favorable opinion of OSS people, Ho fervently wanted the American government to "assist Indochina in achieving independence." On August 12, 1945, Vo Nguyen Giap, Ho's trusted comrade and military commander of the Vietminh, convened a congress, which sent a message asking that the United States "prohibit, or at least not help, the French from returning to Indochina." The note also included the rather remarkable request that Vietnam be "placed on the same status as the Philippines for an un-determined period."[26]

At this time, the rapid collapse of Japan after Hiroshima provided the Vietminh with an unprecedented chance to act. Moving into a power vacuum as the only viable nationalist organization in the country, between August 12 and August 25, 1945, Ho's forces captured Hanoi and Hue. On August 24, Emperor Bao Dai abdicated his throne in favor of the Vietminh, proclaim-ing, as historian Joseph Buttinger notes, that he "would rather be a simple citizen in a free country . . . than the ruler of one that is enslaved."[27] Thus, within ten days of the Japanese surrender, "the Vietminh," in the words of French historian Phillippe Devillers, "controlled the entire territory of Vietnam."[28]

Ho hoped to cement his relationship with the United States via its OSS agents during the next few days as he prepared to proclaim independence. American flags dotted Hanoi; Ho asked Archimedes Patti, one of his OSS friends, to help him write the Vietnamese Declaration of Independence. On September 2, as he read the speech declaring independence for the Demo-cratic Republic of Vietnam, Ho quoted from the American declaration: "We hold these truths that all men are created equal." And at the end of the day of celebration, "with United States officials [as] invited guests[,] a Vietminh band played 'The Star-Spangled Banner.' "[29]

Of course, Ho Chi Minh did more than butter up the Americans on Vietnam's Independence Day. In the grand tradition of centuries of rebellion, he
hammered the outside oppressor. The French, he railed, "have built more
prisons than schools. . . . They have drowned our revolution in blood." He
went on to praise the brave Vietnamese who had fought against the imperialists, who had "smashed the yoke which has pressed so hard upon us for
nearly one hundred years and finally made our Viet Nam an independent
country."[30] Vietnam, it seemed, was at last free, independent, and unified.

That condition did not last long. France was determined to regain control
of its colony. In March 1946, realizing that French forces could easily invade
the North and beset with internal dissent from noncommunist nationalists,
Ho tried to buy time by signing an agreement with France that supposedly
would lead to ultimate Vietnamese independence. As part of the agreement,
France was allowed to station troops in Vietnam. For the next several
months, Ho engaged in a campaign of absorption and elimination of competing nationalist groups, thus consolidating his power. When the French violated the agreement by attacking Haiphong in November 1946, war between
the Vietminh and France ensued.

During the war against the French, Ho left military strategy largely to his
friend and military commander, Vo Nguyen Giap. He would, however, often
appear throughout areas controlled by the Vietminh, boosting morale and
serving as a symbol of resistance. He actively participated in the diplomacy
of the war, as the Vietminh sought assistance from communist China and the
Soviet Union.

After the Geneva Accords ending the French War in 1954, Ho spent the
next two years trying to rebuild North Vietnam and instituting a socialist
economic system and a totalitarian political state. His approval of a repres-
sive land reform program, which resulted in the deaths of thousands of allegedly "bourgeois" landowners, was an example of his rigid adherence to
Marxist doctrine. Indeed, so negative were the effects of this policy that Ho
actually apologized for it.

By 1959 it became clear to Ho that armed struggle would be necessary to
reunify North and South Vietnam under communist control. And in that
same year his position as president of the Democratic Republic of Vietnam
(North Vietnam) was reaffirmed in a new constitution. Ho's health began to
decline, however, and according to historian William Duiker, "after the
mid-1960s, his role in decision making was reportedly primarily ceremo-
nial."[31] Ho Chi Minh died on September 2, 1969. Appropriately, the 1975
communist military action that ultimately won the war for the North was
called the "Ho Chi Minh Campaign."

How, finally, are we to judge this most important of all the modern inheritors of the Vietnamese tradition of rebellion? Was Ho Chi Minh simply a sincere, dedicated patriot determined to free a unified Vietnam from foreign domination? Was he a faithful and doctrinaire communist bent on overthrowing the remnants of the Mandarin system and turning his country into a Marxist-Leninist "paradise"? Or was he a cruel, brutal, self-serving "pragmatic" authoritarian who cynically used any means necessary to achieve his goals?

Most historians would probably agree that, ironically, he was all of these things. In 1946 he did cause the elimination of leading members of opposing noncommunist groups. He also can be held responsible for the rigid land reforms of 1954–1956 that caused the deaths of thousands of innocent people. And not surprisingly, most Americans who served in Vietnam would see him as a vicious and cruel leader. He was also most emphatically a communist, with a powerful faith in the world and historical efficacy of Marxism-Leninism. The Democratic Republic of Vietnam was a communist state, and Ho wanted to export that communism to the South. However, at root, Ho's most important characteristic was probably his fierce patriotism. Although historians can hardly mind-meld with people from the past, it seems clear from his own words and actions that a unified Vietnam free of foreign domination was always Ho's ultimate goal. Indeed, the one constant through all his evolution as a communist and adaptations as a pragmatist was his Vietnamese patriotism. Like other communist leaders who fought "wars of national liberation"—such as Marshal Tito in Yugoslavia and Fidel Castro in Cuba—nationalism would inform the character of the kind of communism each would adapt to local circumstances. Authoritarian methods and communist doctrine were, at least in large measure, means to that ultimate end. And although events were to prove him terribly wrong, Ho Chi Minh was no doubt convinced that the communist system would be the best system for the country he so deeply and passionately loved.

Whatever our final judgment of Ho Chi Minh, after 1945 the French and then the Americans would face a leader and an organization that seemed dedicated to their defeat and who carefully and effectively used the images of rebellion that resonated deep in the Vietnamese past.

NOTES

1. James S. Olson and Randy Roberts, *Where the Domino Fell: The United States and Vietnam, 1945–1995*, 2nd ed. (New York: St. Martin's Press, 1996), p. 5.

2. This aphorism takes on additional meaning when we recall that in some sections of Vietnam, dog meat is considered a delicacy—or at least suitable for a

meal. Anecdotal evidence suggests that American troops in Vietnam had difficulty understanding this particular culinary custom. For an interesting take on dogs and Americans during the war, see Kenn Miller, *Tiger the Lurp Dog* (Boston: Little, Brown, 1983).

3. Edward Doyle, et al., eds., *Setting the Stage*, in *The Vietnam Experience*, ed. Edward Doyle, et al. (Boston: Boston Publishing Co., 1981), p. 54.

4. Stanley Karnow, *Vietnam: A History* (New York: Viking Press, 1983), p. 100. Many of the details surrounding the Trung Sisters—as well as other early rebel leaders—are probably in the realm of myth. However, the fact that so many Vietnamese seem to believe them and worship these opponents of Chinese rule as national heroes and heroines attests to the power of the tradition of hatred of foreign intervention.

5. Doyle, et al., *Setting the Stage*, p. 55.

6. Karnow, *Vietnam*, p. 101.

7. According to the Vietnamese legend, Le Loi was a poor fisherman "who one day cast his net into a lake, only to bring up a magic sword that made him superhuman" (Karnow, *Vietnam*, p. 103). In fact, he was "an aristocratic landowner" (Joseph Buttinger, *Vietnam: A Political History* [New York: Praeger, 1968], p. 45).

8. Karnow, *Vietnam*, p. 104.

9. Ibid., p. 104.

10. Ibid., p. 107.

11. Jean Lacouture, *Ho Chi Minh: A Political Biography*, trans. Peter Wiles (New York: Vintage Books, 1968), p. 7.

12. This information comes from Lacouture, *Ho Chi Minh*, pp. 15–16.

13. Ibid., p. 14.

14. Ibid., p. 30.

15. Ibid., p. 24.

16. Ibid., p. 25.

17. Ibid., p. 30.

18. Ibid., p. 31.

19. Ibid., p. 39.

20. Ibid., p. 40.

21. Ibid. Ho was certainly aware of rival noncommunist nationalist groups in Vietnam during the 1920s and 1930s. When the need arose, he fought to diminish their influence. For example, in June 1925 he betrayed legendary nationalist Phan Boi Chau to the French in 1925 for 100,000 piastres (Cecil B. Currey, *Victory at Any Cost: The Genius of Viet Nam's Gen. Vo Nguyen Giap* [Washington, D.C.: Brassey's Inc., 1997], p. 15).

22. William J. Duiker, "Ho Chi Minh," in *Encyclopedia of the Vietnam War* ed. Stanley I. Kutler (New York: Charles Scribner's Sons, 1996), p. 230. Ho's speech announcing the formation of the Vietminh was addressed to a veritable panoply of possible Vietnamese audiences: "Elders! Prominent personalities! In-

tellectuals, peasants, workers, traders, and soldiers. Dear compatriots!" ("Call for the Revolutionary League for the Independence of Vietnam," in *Vietnam*, ed. Steven Cohen, p. 14). About the only folks left out of this plea were turncoat lackeys who worked for the French opium monopoly!

23. Lacouture, *Ho Chi Minh*, pp. 81–82.

24. Robert D. Schulzinger, *A Time for War: The United States and Vietnam, 1941–1975* (New York: Oxford University Press, 1997), p. 18.

25. Ibid.

26. Ibid., pp. 18–19.

27. Buttinger, *Political History*, p. 210.

28. Lacouture, *Ho Chi Minh*, p. 104.

29. Olson and Roberts, *Domino*, p. 23.

30. Schulzinger, *A Time for War*, p. 19.

31. Duiker, "Ho Chi Minh," p. 232.

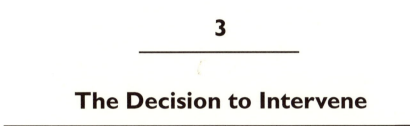

3

The Decision to Intervene

In the spring of 1950, the United States sent a new chargé d'affaires to Saigon. Edward Gullion was feeling pretty optimistic about France's prognosis in the war against the Vietminh if the United States would provide military aid to the French in Vietnam. Such a commitment would "bolster the confidence of the Vietnamese" who were supporting Emperor Bao Dai (not to mention the confidence of French forces in Vietnam).[1] Charles Ogburn, Jr., the Policy Information Officer of the State Department's Bureau of Far Eastern Affairs, was not so sanguine. "Maybe," he conjectured, such a delivery or weapons "would discourage Ho Chi-minh's followers and shoot so much adrenalin into the Bao Dai government as to bring about a fundamental change in prospects. Maybe it wouldn't." In a prescient passage, Ogburn went on to lay out his scenario in Indochina: "Ho Chi-minh's cohorts," he was convinced, would not be much affected psychologically by the presence of American military assistance, given their "blazing hatred for France and the French." Ogburn granted that Ho "might give way under the *physical* impact of American weapons—if we send enough." However, even in this circumstance, Ogburn predicted that "should things get too hot for them, they will . . . go underground until a more propitious occasion presented itself." Only if the French were prepared "to police Vietnam indefinitely" or "to kill off a hundred thousand or more" Vietminh could there be any whiff of military victory—and this was a faint hope indeed, according to Ogburn.[2]

President Harry S Truman accepted Gullion's hopeful paradigm rather than Ogburn's more pessimistic one and began a program of military aid to the French. In February 1950 a working group in the State Department advised that the United States should "furnish military aid in support of the anti-Communist nationalist governments of Indochina," aid that would naturally be funneled through the French. In March, Secretary of State Dean Acheson urged Truman to allocate $15 million of a foreign military aid program to the French in Indochina. A month later, the National Security Council adopted NSC 64, a position paper on Indochina. The Council saw Ho's war in Vietnam as "one phase of anticipated communist plans to seize all of Southeast Asia" and recommended that the United States take "all practicable measures to prevent further communist expansion in Southeast Asia."[3] Although Truman did not officially sign the military aid legislation that legitimized military assistance to France, in late June eight C-47 cargo aircraft carried equipment to Indochina. Just so did America take a major step toward intervention.

This opening thrust in American military intervention very much set the tone for the first phase of American involvement in Vietnam: to stop communism with American money and guns but without a major American intervention that would include combat troops. American policymakers much preferred to rely on surrogates—in this case the French and anticommunist Vietnamese—to hold back the Red tide in Asia than to commit U.S. military forces.

With some important variations, this was the main theme in American intervention from 1950 until the fateful summer of 1964 when Lyndon Johnson ordered retaliatory air strikes against the North Vietnamese. Under Truman, the United States increased its economic and military assistance, including a handful of American advisors. President Dwight D. Eisenhower followed much the same policy, although in 1954 he considered approving an American air strike (and perhaps even combat troops) to help the French in their major battle at Dienbienphu. He decided against this option largely because the British were reluctant to support an American intervention that might torpedo the upcoming Geneva Conference on Indochina.[4] From 1954 to 1961, after the Geneva Accords ended the French War and temporarily divided Vietnam into a communist North and a noncommunist South (See map 2), Eisenhower supported the South Vietnamese government of Ngo Dinh Diem with money and additional American advisors, as well as placing the South under the umbrella of the Southeast Asia Treaty Organization, a NATO-like security arrangement.

John F. Kennedy brought to the presidency a deep commitment to the anticommunist paradigm. Indeed, his campaign in 1960 focused on the failure of the Eisenhower administration to develop flexible means to prevent communist advances, especially in "wars of liberation." And although the situation in Vietnam did not become a major focus of Kennedy's foreign policy until 1963, his public rhetoric about stemming the communist tide certainly helped prepare the U.S. public for deeper American involvement in Vietnam.

Kennedy greatly altered the quantity of American assistance to South Vietnam, while still remaining within the basic pattern established by Truman and Eisenhower. He radically increased the number of American military advisors from around nine hundred to more than sixteen thousand, in addition to providing the South Vietnamese with American helicopters, light aircraft, and transport planes, all flown by American servicemen. Although American advisors were involved in combat as they counseled South Vietnamese units, Kennedy resisted calls from the Chairman of the Joint Chiefs, Maxwell Taylor, and the Deputy National Security Advisor, Walt Rostow, to introduce official American combat troops into the war. Nor was he willing to launch American air attacks against North Vietnam. Rather than risk a wider war or political fallout in the 1964 election, he decided, in essence, to make haste slowly, hoping that "a little more" would do the job.

Ironically, America's major intervention under Kennedy came when his administration encouraged a coup against the government of Ngo Dinh Diem, the putative ally of the United States in the struggle to contain communism in Vietnam. In the eyes of most U.S. officials, the South Vietnamese head of state had begun to lose touch with the South Vietnamese people and was ineffective in prosecuting the war. Unable to pressure him to become more conciliatory towards internal opponents like the Buddhists and more aggressive against the Vietcong, the United States watched as he was overthrown and, along with his brother Ngo Dinh Nhu, executed in November 1963.

Kennedy's own death three weeks after that of the Ngos left new president, Lyndon Johnson, with a problematic legacy in Vietnam. The United States was deeply committed to stemming the expansion of communism into South Vietnam but without using American combat troops. Instead, the United States would rely on the South Vietnamese to shoulder the brunt of the conflict. (Indeed, as late as September 1963, Kennedy had publicly asserted, "In the final analysis it is their [South Vietnamese] war. They are the ones who have to win it or lose it. We can help them, we can give them equipment, we can send our men out there as advisors, but they have to win it."[5])

Johnson pledged to carry out the policies of the Kennedy administration. His commitment was based partly on a desire to honor a fallen president. But more important was Johnson's own vision of America's role in the world. As historian Charles DeBenedetti has pointed out, the new president had an extraordinary "faith in the American national mission to secure world peace through military strength and demonstrated toughness." Communist activity in Vietnam threatened that mission and required American action. Johnson's view of Vietnam was also colored by his personal sense of manhood. According to columnist Hugh Sidey, the president fretted that failure to win in Vietnam would cause people to view him as "a coward. An unmanly man. A man without a spine."[6]

Initially, Johnson's policy sought to prevent the fall of South Vietnam to communism through reliance on the South Vietnamese to take on the bulk of the fighting. Unfortunately, the new South Vietnamese government under General Duong Van Minh seemed confused and ineffective. In January 1964, some of Johnson's more militant advisors, especially Walt Rostow and Maxwell Taylor (both holdovers from the Kennedy administration), believed that the conflict had reached a stage of "definitive crisis" and argued, as Taylor put it, for "bolder actions which may embody greater risks."[7] But Johnson was not convinced, at least in part because of his political instincts. Facing an election in 1964, he certainly had no intention of appearing to "quit Saigon," in the words of McGeorge Bundy.[8] But neither did he want an Americanized war confronting uncertain voters. In addition, he clearly did not want the war to detract from his legislative initiatives, especially the Civil Rights Act of 1964. Ideally, he hoped to bury the war and focus on a strong domestic program. As historian Michael Beschloss notes, Johnson wanted "to defer irrevocable decisions on the war in Southeast Asia until the 1964 presidential election [was] over." This meant that he wanted "to appear neither soft on Communism nor frighteningly ready to take the nation into a war of unimaginable cost."[9]

In a sense, Johnson was fortunate in his opponent in that election. Senator Barry Goldwater (R-Ariz.) was a Cold War hawk who consistently criticized the president for not doing enough in Vietnam. As Johnson noted in a telephone conversation with his friend, Senator Richard Russell (D-Ga.), Goldwater was one of "those politicians" who "got to raising hell . . . saying . . . let's move [invade the] North."[10] This kind of extreme approach allowed Johnson to paint himself as the more moderate, thoughtful candidate on the war issue.

Nonetheless, Johnson was concerned enough with maintaining his options to escalate that in the spring of 1964 he listened to advisors who wanted to introduce a congressional resolution authorizing the president to "use all measures, including the use of armed forces" if such a response was needed to stop communism in Vietnam.[11] Johnson decided not to submit such a resolution at that time, fearing that without some direct and clear hostile action on the part of the enemy, he might have trouble explaining to Congress the necessity for the resolution. Just such an incident, however, occurred in the Gulf of Tonkin, off the coast of North Vietnam in early August 1964.

In the early morning of August 2, 1964, three North Vietnamese torpedo boats attacked an American destroyer in the Gulf of Tonkin off the coast of North Vietnam. The *Maddox*, supported by U.S. aircraft, managed to fight off the attack, damaging the boats and wounding six men and killing four. Secretary of Defense Robert McNamara claimed that the attack was unprovoked and that "the *Maddox* was operating in international waters [and] was carrying out a routine patrol."[12] President Johnson ordered the *Maddox* to continue patrolling, joined by another destroyer, the *Turner Joy*. According to administration officials, on the night of August 4, enemy boats again attacked American ships in international waters. This provocation, then, led the president to order reprisal air attacks against selected targets in North Vietnam—the first U.S. combat air missions against the North.

This bare-bones "official" account leaves a great deal out. In fact, the *Maddox* was on an electronic surveillance mission (code-named "Desoto") designed to gather information about North Vietnamese radar and radio communications. Moreover, it did operate within the twelve-mile territorial limit claimed by North Vietnam. Finally, the American destroyer was maneuvering at roughly the same time that South Vietnamese boats were staging raids against the North Vietnamese coast as part of top secret mission OPLAN-34A, and the captain of the *Maddox* was aware of these raids. According to historian Edwin Moise, it would be perfectly understandable if the North Vietnamese saw the *Maddox* as connected to OPLAN 34A: "The available DRV [North Vietnamese] accounts suggest that the North Vietnamese . . . assumed that it [the destroyer] was what it appeared to be: a warship whose main working tools were five-inch guns." For such a ship, the "most plausible missions . . . were intimidation, support of the vessels making raids against the coast, or actual shelling of the coast."[13] Thus, U.S. officials were simply not telling the whole truth—and in some cases lying—about an incident for which the United States was partly responsible.

At least the August 2 incident took place. We now know that the August 4 one almost certainly did not. In all likelihood, no North Vietnamese torpedo boats attacked the American ships. People aboard both destroyers did see radar blips that they thought indicated PT boats, and the sonar operator on the *Maddox* reported underwater sounds consistent with torpedos being fired. However, as Captain John J. Herrick of the *Maddox* reported shortly after the alleged attacks, "Freak weather effects and overeager sonarman may have accounted for many reports. No actual visual sightings by *Maddox*."[14] According to Undersecretary of State George Ball, "within the next two or three days [after August 4], even President Johnson began to doubt the occurrence of a second attack. With disgust he said to me at one point, 'Hell, those dumb, stupid sailors were just shooting at flying fish!' "[15] Moise concludes in his authoritative account of the "incident" that, based on both his interviews with participants and documentary evidence, "the weight of evidence is overwhelming: no attack occurred."[16]

What we know now neither Johnson nor McNamara knew on August 4, 1964. Admiral U.S. Grant Sharp, Commander in Chief of the Pacific Forces, was convinced on the basis of intercepts of enemy radio messages that an attack had taken place and so informed his superiors. On August 5, the president ordered air strikes against selected North Vietnamese naval forces and a petroleum storage area in Vinh. Codenamed "Pierce Arrow," the retaliatory strike included sixty-four sorties by carrier-based aircraft. Two American planes were shot down, with one pilot killed and one captured.

Although Pierce Arrow set an important precedent as the first American air attack on North Vietnam, the most crucial result of the Gulf of Tonkin incident was the congressional resolution passed on August 7. The language of the resolution was actually hammered out in an August 4 meeting between representatives of the administration and key members of Congress as they worked on a draft prepared by Secretary of State Dean Rusk.

The resolution first established a context: The attacks on American ships in the Gulf of Tonkin not only violated international law, they were part of a "deliberate and systematic campaign of aggression that the Communist regime in North Vietnam has been waging against its neighbors." The United States had pledged to help noncommunist countries like South Vietnam "protect their freedom," with, of course, no American "territorial, military or political ambitions." The heart of the document stated that "the Congress approves and supports the determination of the President as Commander in Chief to take all necessary measures to repel any armed attack against the forces of the United States and to prevent further aggression." Among those "necessary measures" was "the use of armed force."[17]

The Johnson administration immediately pulled on board William Fulbright (D-Ark.), the influential Chairman of the Senate Foreign Relations Committee, to be the major spokesman for the resolution. Based on what Johnson and others told him, Fulbright was convinced that the president did not plan to use the resolution to launch full-scale war but rather employ it gingerly with only selective use of force. Whether the administration deceived Fulbright and Congress in the way it presented the need for the resolution has been a matter of dispute. What is known is that as early as June 10,

1964, when Johnson officials were discussing such a resolution, they brought up possible congressional queries. To one mock question, "Does this resolution imply a blank check for the President to go to war over Southeast Asia?" the following mock response was proposed: "[H]ostilities on a wider scale are not envisioned, and in any case any large escalation would require a call-up of the Reserves and thus a further appeal to the Congress."[18] Reserves were never called up, and Congress was never asked for any further general authorization of the use of military force. And, as is known, Johnson did use the resolution as a kind of blank check to escalate the war. In fact, as Johnson later joked, the Gulf of Tonkin Resolution was "like grandma's nightshirt—it covered everything."[19]

Based partly on Fulbright's support, Congress overwhelmingly passed the Gulf of Tonkin resolution on August 7, 1964, unanimously in the House and with only two dissenting votes in the Senate. Johnson had his statement of approval, along with a rousing boost in the public opinion polls.[20] The combination of air strikes and congressional approbation would appear to have strengthened the president's hand immensely as he dealt with the war.

Some analysts have downplayed the importance of the incident and the resolution. Military historian and strategist Colonel Harry G. Summers, Jr., for example, argues that "the causes of war were already present" in August 1964 no matter what the "truth" of the second incident. Moreover, he notes that in August 1967, Johnson "repudiated the Gulf of Tonkin Resolution as the legal basis for the war . . . and fell back on his authority . . . as Commander-in-Chief of the Armed Forces."[21] Summers underestimates the importance of Tonkin both as a precedent for attacks on the North and a legal justification that Johnson used to escalate the war enormously between 1965 and 1967. Moreover, the way the incidents were explained to both Congress and the public helped establish a pattern of official dissimulation that continued throughout the conflict.

Even with the precedent set by Pierce Arrow and the legal underpinning provided by Congress, Johnson was still left with a dilemma. As journalist-historian Stanley Karnow asserts about the president, "Given his view of America's position in the world, Johnson could not envisage anything less in Vietnam than an outcome that stopped communist 'aggression.' "[22] And yet he wanted to avoid "a wider war," clearly preferring not to use American combat troops. Indeed, he had consistently stated during the 1964 presidential campaign that "we are not about to send American boys nine or ten thousand miles away from home to do what Asian boys ought to be doing for themselves."[23]

The success of Johnson's determination to keep American involvement limited depended on the Vietnamese. Either the North Vietnamese had to negotiate a settlement that agreed to keep the South noncommunist, or South Vietnam had to be stable and aggressive enough to fight the war successfully without American combat troops. In the eight months after the Gulf of Tonkin incident, neither of these alternatives appeared likely. North Vietnam showed no interest in negotiating except on its terms, which, to the Americans, meant the capitulation of the South. And South Vietnam seemed anything but stable. The government that had overthrown Diem was itself overthrown in early 1964 by ARVN military officer General Nguyen Khanh. Although Johnson at first seemed to admire Khanh, calling him "my American boy," the general's mercurial personality and dictatorial tendencies turned the South into a confusing cauldron of coups and countercoups over the next year.[24]

With North Vietnam hardly forthcoming and the South in shambles, Johnson moved slowly but inexorably toward deeper American involvement. The Gulf of Tonkin incident helped remove the Vietnam issue from the 1964 election, with Republican nominee Goldwater supporting Johnson's reprisal strike and the congressional resolution. But the president was taking no chances of appearing to be a warmonger. When a Vietcong mortar attack on October 31 killed four American servicemen at Ben Hoa airfield, Johnson declined to retaliate. He did not want "a wider war" to interfere with the election.

Even after his overwhelming victory in the election, Johnson seemed reluctant to retaliate against Vietcong provocations by attacking North Vietnam. On December 1, he argued that until the South Vietnamese government was more stable, there was "no point in hitting the North." Such action might send a signal to the South to strike the North, which would be like sending a "widow woman to slap Jack Dempsey."[25] When a Christmas Eve attack against the Brinks Hotel in Saigon killed two Americans, Maxwell Taylor, the American Ambassador to South Vietnam, recommended reprisal air assaults against North Vietnamese military barracks, but Johnson declined.

This did not mean that the president had permanently rejected escalation. Indeed, on December 2, 1964, he approved a National Security Council contingency plan calling for air strikes against the North along with continued pressure on the South to reform. And in late 1964, he approved attacks against North Vietnamese supply trains on the Ho Chi Minh Trail in Laos (Operation Barrel Roll). Then, in early 1965, the administration reluctantly reached the conclusion that the war was on the verge of being lost, and when a Vietcong attack at Pleiku left several American Marines dead and wounded, Johnson ordered sustained air strikes against North Vietnam. Code-named "Rolling Thunder," the operation began on February 13, 1965, as an eight-week exercise but ultimately continued until April 1968. Eight days later, William Westmoreland, U.S. commander in Vietnam, requested two Marine battalions to protect the American air base at Danang, and in spite of Ambassador Taylor's objection, Johnson agreed, fearing for the safety of American planes and pilots.

The 3,500 marines who stormed ashore at Danang in March of 1965 were supposed to take up defensive positions. In April, however, Johnson permitted limited offensive actions by the Marines. Over the next two months, additional American troops were deployed in the South, adopting an enclave strategy that expanded offensive operations to within fifty miles of major cities and bases. Continued ARVN defeats, however, led Westmoreland to call for more troops and a clear and enhanced offensive mission. In June 1965 the commander indicated that the 23,000 advisors, 8,600 Marines, 20,000 logistical and engineering personnel, and 40,000 new troops already promised would not be enough to stave off the enemy and requested an additional 100,000 men. After a long series of discussions with his major advisors, Johnson agreed to the request. Significantly, he downplayed this major escalation and change of mission in a low-keyed noon press conference on July 28. The precedent of the Gulf of Tonkin and the legal force of the resolution had been used to Americanize the war. As historian Robert Schulzinger argues, at this point "the U.S. passed the point of no return in Vietnam."[26]

Why did Lyndon Johnson move America's commitment from providing advisors and military supplies to a full combat role? Clearly, he had misgivings about escalation. During the July 1965 meetings, he worried that America's allies would fail to help in the military effort in Vietnam, wanting to make sure the United States "had wrung every single soldier out of every country we can." He also prodded Joint Chiefs of Staff Chair General Earle Wheeler about the need for additional troops in the future, asking, prophetically, "What will happen if we put in 100,000 more men and then two, three years later you tell me we need 500,000 more? . . . And what makes you think that Ho Chi Minh won't put in another 100,000 and match us every bit of the way?" (Wheeler's response to this last query is instructive: More troops from the North would just make "greater bodies of men . . . which will allow us to cream them"—an early statement of the attrition strategy later adopted by the military.[27]) And two trusted advisors, Clark Clifford and George Ball, expressed thoughtful opposition to massive escalation, complicating Johnson's decision.

The president rejected the advice of Ball and Clifford and muted his own doubts for a number of reasons. Undoubtedly, some old-fashioned macho competition was involved, as Johnson saw Ho Chi Minh as almost a personal adversary in a schoolyard brawl. Significantly, for example, on learning of the successful deployment of Marines at Danang in March 1965, he "smiled broadly and remarked to an associate, 'Now I have Ho Chi Minh's pecker in my pocket.' "[28] More importantly, he was apprehensive that the loss of South Vietnam might cause a right-wing counterreaction in the United States comparable to the McCarthyism of the 1950s—another " 'mean and destructive debate' that would 'shatter my presidency . . . and damage our democracy.' " In a related matter, Johnson feared that if he "left the war and let the communists take over Vietnam," he would be seen as an appeaser and would be unable to accomplish major domestic goals.[29]

But the overarching reason Johnson escalated was simply that he, like most Americans, was a prisoner of the Cold War. He firmly believed in the domino theory and the danger to America of the spread of communism. As he put it once in a typically earthy parable, "If you let a bully come into your front yard one day, the next day he'll be up on your porch, and the day after that he'll rape your wife in your own bed."[30] The loss of South Vietnam to communism would send a signal to the communists that their wars of national liberation could work and to our allies that our word was not to be trusted. Put simply, without the Cold War, there would have been no Vietnam War. Does anyone imagine for a moment that the president would have sent one Marine to Vietnam had Ho Chi Minh not been a communist but rather just another tinhorn authoritarian thug?

Unwilling to opt for a declaration of war and an invasion of North Vietnam for fear of starting World War III, Johnson chose gradual escalation as the best of a series of options fraught with risk. As Robert Schulzinger argues, "Every alternative seemed unpalatable. . . . [But] most important [American] decision-makers firmly believed that the costs to the U.S. position in the Cold War competition with the Soviets and China of a communist victory in South Vietnam far exceeded the costs of greater U.S. involvement in the war."[31] Johnson had persuaded himself that this was the only alternative and that his plight was inevitable. As he told his friend and advisor Bill Moyers, trying to justify himself, "I feel like a hitchhiker caught in a hailstorm on a Texas highway. I can't run. I can't hide. And I can't make it stop."[32]

NOTES

1. Robert D. Schulzinger, *Time for War: The United States and Vietnam, 1941–1975* (New York: Oxford University Press, 1977), p. 47.

2. Memorandum, Ogburn to Assistant Secretary of State for Far Eastern Affairs, 21 March 1950, *Foreign Relations of the United States, 1950:6* (Washington, D.C.: U.S. Government Printing Office, 1976), pp. 766–67.

3. Schulzinger, *Time for War*, p. 47.

4. See David Anderson, *Trapped by Success: The Eisenhower Administration and Vietnam, 1953–61* (New York: Columbia University Press, 1991), pp. 28–35. Eisenhower reopened the slim possibility of American intervention after the fall of Dienbienphu to the Vietminh, but only if the war was "internationalized," that is, included troops from other nations, including Australia and New Zealand, and only if France guaranteed the independence of the Indochinese states of Vietnam, Cambodia, and Laos. A war-weary France declined help under these conditions (pp. 35–36).

5. John F. Kennedy, "Interview with Walter Cronkite," September 2, 1963, quoted in John M. Newman, *Deception, Intrigue, and the Struggle for Power* (New York: Warner Books, 1992), p. 365.

6. Charles DeBenedetti, "Johnson and the Antiwar Opposition," in *The Johnson Years*. Volume Two: *Vietnam, the Environment, and Science*, ed. Robert A. Divine (Lawrence, Kans.: University Press of Kansas, 1987), p. 30.

7. Schulzinger, *Time for War*, p. 134.

8. Ibid.

9. Michael Beschloss, ed., *Taking Charge: The Johnson White House Tapes, 1963–1964* (New York: Simon and Schuster, 1997), p. 256.

10. "Telephone Conversation," Lyndon Johnson and Richard Russell, May 27, 1964. Ibid., p. 368.

11. Schulzinger, *Time for War*, p. 145.

12. Edwin E. Moise, *Tonkin Gulf and the Escalation of the Vietnam War* (Chapel Hill: University of North Carolina Press, 1996), p. 86.

13. Ibid., p. 67.

14. Joseph C. Goulden, *Truth Is the First Casualty: The Gulf of Tonkin Affair—Illusion and Reality* (Chicago: Rand McNally, 1969), p. 152. Based on personal communication with the Captain, Edwin Moise says that Herrick "eventually concluded . . . that it was *unlikely* that any torpedos were fired at any time on the night of August 4 . . . [and] unlikely in fact that any enemy vessel came within 10,000 yards of the *Maddox* on that night" (Moise, *Tonkin Gulf*, p. 207). The most compelling evidence of North Vietnamese attacks was a series of radio intercepts of North Vietnamese messages. Looked at in raw form, they seemingly suggested that enemy boats were preparing to attack the two destroyers. Moise concludes, however, that many of these messages referred to "DRV preparations to defend against [a scheduled August 5 OPLAN-34A] raids" rather than instructions to attack the *Maddox* and the *Turner Joy* (Ibid., p. 102).

15. George Ball, *The Past Has Another Pattern: Memoirs* (New York: W. W. Norton, 1982), p. 379.

16. Moise, *Tonkin*, p. 204.

17. "To Promote the Maintenance of International Peace and Security in Southeast Asia," in *A Vietnam Reader: Sources and Essays*, ed. George Donelson Moss (Englewood Cliffs, N.J.: Prentice-Hall, 1991), p. 74.

18. Moise, *Tonkin*, p. 227.

19. Stanley Karnow, *Vietnam: A History* (New York: Viking Press, 1983), p. 374.

20. Harris Poll, *Washington Post*, August 10, 1964, pp. A1, A4.

21. Col. Harry G. Summers, Jr., ed., *Vietnam War Almanac* (New York: Facts on File, 1985), p. 342.

22. Karnow, *Vietnam*, p. 396.

23. Lyndon Johnson, "Campaign Speech," Akron, Ohio, October 21, 1964, in Moss, *Vietnam Reader*, p. 78.

24. James S. Olson and Randy Roberts, *Where the Domino Fell: America and Vietnam, 1945–1995*, 2nd ed. (New York: St. Martin's Press, 1996), p. 122. Given the confusion of coups during 1964–1965, one wonders if the South Vietnamese flag shouldn't have been a revolving door. Johnson became almost apoplectic at the coup parade in the South: "I don't want to hear any more of this coup ————," he yelled at his aides in early 1965 (Schulzinger, *Time for War*, p. 170). By the time Khanh was ousted for good in February 1965, the United States had already begun the Rolling Thunder air campaign against the North.

25. Schulzinger, *Time for War*, p. 167.

26. Ibid., p. 154.

27. Ibid., p. 176.

28. Olson and Roberts, *Domino*, p. 128.

29. Karnow, *Vietnam*, p. 320.

30. Ibid., p. 321.

31. Schulzinger, *Time for War*, p. 162.

32. Karnow, *Vietnam*, p. 396.

4

Fighting the War: 1965–1968

Colonel Harry Summers, Jr., recalls the following exchange with a North Vietnamese colonel in April 1975:

"You know you never defeated us on the battlefield," said the American colonel [Summers].

The North Vietnamese colonel pondered this remark a moment. "That may be so," he replied, "but it is also irrelevant."[1]

In one sense, Summers is largely correct. Americans killed and wounded more North Vietnamese and Vietcong, expended more ammunition, dropped more bombs, and spent more money than the enemy did. To be sure, American troops did not achieve their military objectives in some battles in the war, nor did their South Vietnamese allies, but by most statistical measurements, the United States should have achieved its central objective: keeping South Vietnam noncommunist.[2] But the United States failed to accomplish its major political goal in the war, as on April 30, 1975, North Vietnamese troops stormed Saigon and unified Vietnam under communist control. Was there a connection between the way America fought the war and the failure to achieve its central political objective? An examination of strategy and tactics can help answer this important question.

In the first place, there was no one single war in Vietnam. Strategy and tactics changed over time. Prior to 1965, the United States provided military aid and advisors to the South Vietnamese in an attempt to help them prevent a communist takeover. From 1961 to 1965, that assistance focused on "counterinsurgency," as American advisors, particularly Army Special Forces units, worked to change the "stereotyped and predictable" ARVN strategy that relied on what historian Vincent H. Demma calls "large sweeps or search and destroy operations that alerted the insurgents."[3] Small-group guerrilla training and pacification efforts like the Strategic Hamlet Program failed to turn back the enemy, largely because of internal instability and turn-over in South Vietnam's central government. Thus, the United States, fearing the collapse of the South, initiated air attacks on North Vietnam (Rolling Thunder) and introduced combat troops in early 1965.

Initially, American ground forces were to defend U.S. air bases and other crucial "enclaves" in South Vietnam. Within a few weeks of the initial Marine landing at Danang, however, President Johnson approved a change of mission to offensive probes out of the enclaves. North Vietnam responded to expanded American intervention by infiltrating additional regular units into the South, as the Vietcong increased guerrilla activity. Soon, it became apparent that the American troops would need to assume a more aggressive offensive posture. Thus, a strategy counterinsurgency escalated into a limited war.

Burgeoning communist activity and Johnson's decision in July 1965 to increase U.S. troop levels from 75,000 to 175,000 prompted William Westmoreland, commander of the America Military Assistance Command, Vietnam (MACV), to develop an extensive three-phase strategy to defeat NVA and Vietcong forces. In Phase I, which was already occurring, American and South Vietnamese forces would basically try to stem the tide of communist victories by securing cities and main bases.

In Phases II and III, the war would be taken to the enemy. Phase II, which depended on a large additional infusion of American combat troops, would seek to search out and destroy Vietcong and North Vietnamese main forces and start the pacification effort to separate the enemy from its rural base of support. Ideally, insurgent forces would be pushed into sparsely populated areas and then demolished with superior American firepower. During this phase, South Vietnamese units would be involved primarily in support of pacification efforts in areas cleared of enemy troops, providing security and "winning the hearts and minds" of South Vietnamese villagers. In Phase III, American forces would concentrate on wiping out remaining enemy units in remote bases, while the ARVN would eliminate NLF political cadres still operating in South Vietnamese villages. Gradually, the South Vietnamese would take over all responsibility for the war. During all three phases, Operation Rolling Thunder would continue to put pressure on North Vietnam by targeting supply lines and military bases. Air attacks on the North would also raise morale in the South.

Strategically, Westmoreland focused on one fundamental American strength: firepower—artillery and air support, to be precise. Put simply, he wanted his ground forces to make contact with the enemy, in essence flushing them out, and then destroy that enemy with the technical and mechanical superiority represented by weapons of large destruction. Ideally, he wanted to draw the communists into large-scale battles where that firepower could play the major role, and Americans would not die in great numbers. He also hoped to fight most of the battles away from heavily populated areas where civilian casualties and refugee problems would muddy the military issues.

Clustered around this central strategy were a group of less emphasized, often poorly supported, even contradictory ones, that generally fell under the rubric of "pacification." South Vietnamese, sometimes aided by Americans, were supposed to secure villagers' support for the GVN through nonmilitary interventions in village life, ranging from offering medical supplies to providing entertainment. Though sometimes successful, too often this policy was vitiated when ARVN troops and officials were inefficient or hostile toward villagers. During Operation Cedar Falls in 1967, for example, according to journalist Jonathan Schell, ARVN troops in the village of Ben Suc seemed to spend more time "tak[ing] food" from the villagers' houses and having "goosing matches" than they did helping the people.[4] Moreover, the enemy often employed effective countermeasures—for example, firing on Americans from supposedly pacified villages, which would result in American artillery and air strikes against the villages. The resultant damage often left villagers bitter and alienated.

Obviously, this grand strategy was not successful; nor did a variety of tactics achieve the central political and military goal of the war. South Vietnam "fell" to the communists. There is no consensus on the reasons for this strategic failure. Some, like Harry Summers, indicate that Westmoreland went after the wrong enemy in the wrong place. Rather than focus on the South, the United States should have declared war on North Vietnam, attacked communist sanctuaries in Laos and Cambodia early on, and provided enough combat personnel to defeat the real enemy, the DRV and the NVA.[5] Others, like military historian Vincent Demma, think the focus on the South might have worked were it not for restrictions imposed on the military for political reasons. For example, rules of engagement prevented hot pursuit of enemy forces into Laos and Cambodia. Demma also argues that failure to call up reserves so slowed the deployment of troops that Westmoreland was unable to implement his strategy in an effective fashion.[6]

Others, like historian Robert Schulzinger, point out that the Johnson administration had understandable and probably justifiable fears that a ground war expanded to areas outside the South might well draw communist China and even the Soviet Union directly into the conflict. LBJ did not want to fight a land war in Asia against the Chinese or risk a nuclear confrontation. Moreover, an emphasis on political restrictions on the American military as a cause for strategic failures overlooks the very real role of the Vietnamese in the equation. A combination of South Vietnamese instability, corruption, incompetence, and increasing dependence on American combat troops played a major role in the failure. So too did the determination and will of the Vietcong and the North Vietnamese. As Schulzinger concludes, "The ever-patient Vietnamese [revolutionary forces] believed that eventually Americans would tire of the war."[7]

Though not yet terminally tired, by 1967 America did have to face the fact that the war was largely a stalemate. Clearly, the Vietcong and NVA had not defeated the ARVN and their American allies; by the same token, the American-South Vietnamese effort had failed to convince the NLF to quit or the North Vietnamese to stop helping their southern comrades. The Tet Offensive of early 1968 would cause an agonizing reappraisal of both strategic and political thinking in the United States.

If strategy changed over time and was modified by circumstances, the military experience for American soldiers varied even more widely. Virtually the only commonality among the Americans who served in Vietnam was a limited tour of duty. All soldiers served for 365 days, except for Marines whose tour was thirteen months. There was no one Vietnam War for American troops; there were thousands. The nature of the war for those who served in it depended on a number of factors: one's Military Occupational Specialty (MOS); the time period when a soldier served; where he or she was stationed; the branch served in; one's race and gender; and sometimes sheer chance. For example, roughly 80 percent of Americans who served in Vietnam were technically posted to "rear" areas as clerks, supply personnel, cooks, statistical analysts, and a host of other positions. For the most part, they were not exposed to the same physical danger as were combat troops. Yet even here, we need to be careful. Certainly during the Tet Offensive in early 1968, major enemy attacks threatened many Americans in rear areas. And rear-echelon troops were always subject to the possibility of individual terrorist acts.

African Americans faced special difficulties. In the mid-1960s, blacks tended to serve mainly in combat units and suffered a disproportionate number of casualties, largely because African Americans tended to volunteer for military service at a higher rate than whites. Later in the war, ugly racial incidents between black and white troops, especially in the rear, began to erupt.

Even in combat, there were major distinctions. Soldiers on the ground faced an enemy who was sometimes hidden, sometimes within arm's length. On many occasions, an unseen enemy killed and died. However, confrontations were often very up-close and personally observed. Most pilots, on the other hand, never saw the results of their attacks. Death was more distant and impersonal.

In essence, there is simply no meaningful way to generalize about "the Vietnam experience" of the more than two million Americans who served in-country between 1964 and 1973.[8]

Because American strategy clearly focused on defeating the enemy militarily, an examination of the combat experience is central to understanding the human side of the war. Two particular incidents serve as symbols of two major kinds of combat in the war. The Battle of the Ia Drang Valley in 1965 represented the kind of combat American strategists hoped for—it involved relatively large units in a sparsely populated area with the effective use of superior American firepower. The second action was not even a battle. In early 1967 in the small village of Thuy Bo, American Marines experienced an incident far removed from the Ia Drang model. A minor search-and-destroy mission resulted in the death of both Americans and Vietnamese civilians and the disappearance of an enemy who seemed very difficult to find. This was the kind of combat Americans generally got.

The Battle of the Ia Drang Valley occurred in November 1965, only a few months after the initial landing of American combat troops in Vietnam. The battle featured a new kind of American combat unit—the Air Cavalry. As part of President Kennedy's attempt to beef up American ground warfare capacity, this new unit, called the 11th Air Assault (Test) Division, trained in unconventional tactics. It focused on the use of the helicopter to provide rapid mobility for ground combat units, as well as carefully calibrated air and artillery support. In July 1965 the unit was renamed the 1st Cavalry (Airmobile) and in August went to Vietnam as part of Johnson's summer escalation of the war.

The unit was based near An Khe in the central highlands between Qui Nhon and Pleiku—in the words of Hal Moore, Commander of the 1st battalion, "a fort in the middle of Indian country."[9] And one of the chief "Indians," General Chu Huy Man, commander of North Vietnamese units in the area, actually welcomed the arrival of Moore's men. Although the placement of the Air Cavalry changed enemy plans to capture parts of the central highlands, it provided an opportunity to learn. Hoang Phuong, who fought in the Ia Drang as a lieutenant colonel in the NVA, remembers that "our problem was that we had never fought Americans before. . . . We wanted to draw American units into contact for purposes of learning how to fight them." In the words of Chu Huy Man, "We wanted to lure the tiger out of the mountain."[10]

Phuong and Man would soon get their chance. Moore's battalion was tasked with conducting an assault in an area near Plei Me, which formed a part of the Ia (River) Drang Valley. On November 14, 1965, helicopters inserted a 450–man force within a few miles of two NVA regiments consisting of several thousand troops. Over the next three days, a fierce series of battles occurred. Although outnumbered, American troops fought courageously, sometimes in hand-to-hand combat. Colonel Moore describes part of the battle: "The bloody hole in the ground that was Captain Bob Edwards' Charlie Company command post was crowded with men," mostly the dead and the wounded. Edwards recalls, "We were laying there watching bullets kick dirt off the small parapet around the edge of the hole. . . . I didn't know how badly I had been hurt, only that I couldn't stand up. . . . I knew that my other two platoons were in bad shape and the enemy had penetrated to within hand grenade range of my command post." According to Moore,

the din of battle was unbelievable. Rifles and machine guns and mortars and grenades rattled, banged, and boomed. . . . Among my sergeants there were . . . men who had parachuted into Normandy on D Day and had survived the war in Korea—and those old veterans were shocked by the savagery and hellish noise of this battle. Choking clouds of smoke and dust obscured the killing ground. We were dry-mouthed and our bowels churned with fear, and still the enemy came on in waves.[11]

After four days of fighting, those waves were ultimately repulsed, in large measure because of overwhelming firepower as "every available fighter-bomber in South Vietnam was stacked overhead" and artillery firebases launched attacks on enemy units to help hold back and ultimately "defeat" the enemy. At least General Westmoreland saw the results as an American victory and a vindication of his basic tactic. After all, an estimated 3,561 North Vietnamese had died compared to "only" 305 Americans. U.S. forces drew the enemy out, then destroyed it with massive firepower, in a relatively unpopulated area. Westmoreland believed that American forces could simply wear the enemy out in the long haul by searching and destroying, and creating major confrontations with large enemy units.

The North Vietnamese also thought that they had won the battle, or at least fought to a draw. The casualties they suffered could be replaced, and their troops seemed to have withstood a high-tech assault. As General Vo

Nguyen Giap put it, "[W]e concluded that we could fight and win against the Cavalry troops." "In time," according to Colonel Moore, the communists "were certain the patience and perseverance that had worn down the French colonialists would also wear down the Americans."[12]

The North Vietnamese and Vietcong illustrated that patience over the next two years by largely avoiding the kind of traps that Westmoreland wanted to set. There simply were no major battles of the Ia Drang Valley type until the Tet Offensive temporarily reintroduced a kind of large-scale combat into the conflict. For the most part, both the PAVN and the PLAF tried to avoid major battles, preferring to initiate small-scale engagements at times and places of their own choosing.

Far more typical of the combat experience than the Battle of the Ia Drang Valley was a small firefight that took place in early 1967 at a village called Thuy Bo, a few miles south of Danang. Two companies of the 2nd Battalion, 1st Marine Division, under the command of Captain Edward Banks, planned to search the village for Vietcong. Although the sector to be investigated had been designated as "unfriendly," Banks did not expect major problems.[13] Private Jack Hill, an American participant, recalled that "ordinarily, you come through the village on a sweeping motion."[14] In this case, however, a substantial enemy force was waiting for the Marines. Hill remembered the horror: "Our guys were falling everywhere. . . . We were pinned down, all day and all night. It was raining something pitiful. . . . So we just lay there . . . hearing our partners dying and crying for their mothers. It was total chaos." After survivors had gone for over thirty-six hours without sleep, enemy fire slacked off, probably because of artillery strikes, and the Marines moved into the village.

What happened next is a matter of bitter dispute. According to several villagers who survived and were interviewed in the early 1980s, there was "a holocaust." Communist officials claimed "that the Marines slaughtered one hundred and forty-five civilians, including women and children." According to Nguyen Bay, who was a fourteen-year-old boy when the attack occurred, when the women and children in the village said they didn't know the whereabouts of the Vietcong, the Americans "shot at us anyway." Bay was wounded in the head. Another villager, Li Thi Ton, remembered that she peacefully greeted "four or five [American] soldiers" who came into her home. They responded by laughing and throwing a grenade, which killed everyone but Ton, who was wounded. Thuong Thi Mai said she witnessed the deaths of her three children at the hands of the Marines, who then burned the remains so that all she could collect was "a handful of bones."

The Americans saw the events quite differently. According to Captain Banks, the attack of the village took only between two and five minutes, and Marines were simply responding to continued enemy fire. Private Hill recalled that he heard enemy machine guns at the opposite end of the village and had to use grenades to convince Vietnamese to "come out of their holes." Banks concluded that "not more than fifteen peasants had been killed—'as if it had been a robbery and gunfight on a city street and several bystanders were hit.' " The precise "truth" of this one small but highly paradigmatic firefight may never be known.[15]

In some ways, this battle resembled the one in the Ia Drang Valley a year and a half earlier: The enemy attacked an American unit, which then called in heavy artillery to destroy the attackers. There was pain, suffering, and courage, and, perhaps, a technical "victory" for the Americans. But the enemy force was relatively small. Also, Thuy Bo was a village in which civilians were killed, and a firm body count of enemy dead was impossible to determine. Westmoreland's desire for a war outside populated areas simply did not happen, partly because of the lesson the enemy learned at Ia Drang— namely, avoid major confrontations. What the villagers seemed to learn from the battle was, at best, to hate the war and want it ended no matter who emerged victorious and at worst to blame the Americans for their woes.

Most American soldiers in Vietnam fought courageously and tried to respect the civilian population. Infamous American atrocities like My Lai were no doubt aberrations. Probably Ike Rice, who flew on Air Force reconaissance flights during the war, was symbolic of the best of American military personnel. For much of the time he was on the ground in Vietnam, he helped repair an orphanage that housed children who had been wounded and lost parents, some possibly to the Vietcong and the NVA, others perhaps to bombs dropped by planes that Rice helped direct to their targets.[16]

In many ways, then, U.S. involvement in Vietnam reads like a Greek tragedy. The United States entered the war to save the South Vietnamese from the horrors of communism and to use American technology and know-how to build a new Vietnam. Yet American technology, through enormous firepower, too often destroyed the very people the United States was trying to save. In a war in which civilians were hard to identify and the enemy used that fact to great effect, U.S. tactics inevitably caused the maiming and deaths of many who were not the enemy. And thus the image of Lyndon Johnson caught in that Texas hailstorm seemed transposed to the battlefields of the war he so hated. America could not run, could not hide, and could not make the bleeding stop.

NOTES

1. Harry G. Summers, Jr., *On Strategy* (Novato, Calif.: Presidio Press, 1982), p. 1. Summers and North Vietnamese Colonel Tu were counterparts on negotiating teams for the two countries.

2. For example, Americans surely "lost" the battle of Firebase Mary Ann. In March 1971 a Vietcong sapper squad entered this forward firebase of the 23rd U.S. Army Division, killing thirty soldiers and wounding eighty-two (Keith William Noland, *Sappers in the Wire: The Life and Death of Firebase Mary Ann* [College Station, Tex.: Texas A&M University Press, 1995]). Summers tells another bitter little story about using statistics like body counts and shells fired to determine the progress of war. He notes the following joke going around Washington, D.C. Allegedly, in 1969 some functionary in the Nixon administration fed all sorts of data about the war, especially damage to North Vietnam, into a Pentagon computer and asked the computer, "When will we win?" The computer replied, "You won in 1964" (Ibid., p. 18). Obviously, statistics can lie.

3. Vincent H. Demma, "Strategy and Tactics," in *Encyclopedia of the Vietnam War*, ed. Stanley I. Kutler (New York: Charles Scribner's Sons, 1996), p. 509.

4. Jonathan Schell, *The Village of Ben Suc* (New York: Vintage Books, 1968), pp. 45, 44.

5. Summers, *On Strategy*, passim.

6. Demma, "Strategy and Tactics," pp. 513–14.

7. Robert Schulzinger, Jr., *A Time for War: The United States and Vietnam, 1941–1975* (New York: Oxford University Press, 1997), p. 331.

8. For statistics on military service in Vietnam, see Lawrence M. Baskir and William A. Strauss, *Chance and Circumstance: The Draft, the War and the Vietnam Generation* (New York: Alfred A. Knopf, 1978), p. 53. According to Baskir and Strauss, 2,150,000 U.S. "servicemen [sic]" served in Vietnam between August 4, 1964, and March 28, 1973. Historian George Donelson Moss puts the number at 2,700,000 from 1964 to 1975 (George Donelson Moss, *Vietnam: An American Ordeal*, 2nd. ed. [Englewood Cliffs, N.J.: Prentice-Hall, 1994], p. 417).

9. Lt. General Harold G. Moore (Ret.) and Joseph L. Galloway, *We Were Soldiers Once . . . and Young: Ia Drang—the Battle that Changed the War in Vietnam* (New York: Random House, 1992), p. 26.

10. Ibid., p. 15.

11. Ibid., pp. 3, 8.

12. Ibid., pp. 338, 339.

13. Stanley Karnow, *Vietnam: A History* (New York: Viking Press, 1983), p. 468.

14. *Vietnam, A Television History*, Episode 5 (Public Broadcasting System, 1983). The details of this battle are taken from this episode and Karnow, *Vietnam*, pp. 468–69.

15. The villagers were interviewed in the early 1980s by Americans while Vietnamese officials translated and watched. Did the "victims" feel pressured to

exaggerate the horrors? Perhaps it was a communist propaganda exercise designed to demonize the "American imperialists" long after the event. An almost offhand comment by Private Hill, however, suggests that something terrible did happen that day. Hill noted that "half the guys in my squad didn't shoot no women and kids," perhaps unconsciously admitting that the other half did commit atrocities. At the end of his interview, Hill poignantly notes that "when you got an angry eighteen-year old kid behind a gun and he just seen his buddy get killed, he's not gonna have no remorse of who's on the receiving end of that 60 caliber machine gun." Perhaps civilians were killed, in part in anger because of "three days of blood and guts and the mud," as Private Hill concluded. "The way I seen it," Hill said, "it was war" (*Vietnam: A Television History*, Episode 5).

16. Ira "Ike" Rice, interview by Anthony Edmonds, September 2, 1997.

5

The Tet Offensive, the Media, and the War

At 2:45 on the morning of January 30, 1968 (Saigon time), a squad of nineteen Vietcong commandoes, riding in a Peugeot truck and a taxicab, attacked the U.S. embassy in Saigon. As the raiders blew a hole in the embassy wall and rushed through, two American military policemen began firing at the invaders. One of them, Specialist Fourth Class Charles L. Daniel, screamed into his radio, "They're coming in! They're coming in! Help me! Help me!" Later Daniel and his fellow soldier were found dead.[1] At about the same time, Associated Press correspondent Peter Arnett was awakened by gunfire. After "shoving" his wife and two children into the bathroom of his apartment (it had "the thickest walls"), he ran to his office where he began covering the biggest story of the war—the communist Tet Offensive and its aftermath.[2]

This major enemy attack on thirty-six of forty-four provincial capitals, five major South Vietnamese cities, and sixty-four district capitals provides a powerful lens through which to view both a crucial political turning point in the conflict and the controversial role the press played in that war.

The size, timing, and scope of the communist offensive caught American military leaders by surprise. Intelligence information suggested that some sort of enemy offensive was in the offing early in 1968, although most U.S. leaders thought that the target would be Khe Sanh, a besieged Marine base in the northwest corner of South Vietnam. (Even when the wide scope of the offensive became clear, General Earle Wheeler, Chairman of the Joint Chiefs of Staff, told congressional leaders "that Hanoi's military purpose [during the offensive] was to draw [American] forces away from the Khe Sanh area.")[3]

In fact, the capture of Khe Sanh was not a crucial goal of "Tet Mau Than," as the North Vietnamese called the series of Tet attacks. Rather, the major purposes were "to achieve a popular uprising against the GVN [Government of South Vietnam] . . . and to show the American public that the very notion of security was null and void."[4] Clearly, the first of these objectives was not met. The South Vietnamese failed to rise up against their government, as American and ARVN troops quickly defeated communist forces in every major area except the old imperial capital of Hue (which took three weeks to recapture). As communist general Tran Do admitted, "In all honesty, we didn't achieve our main objective, which was to spur uprisings throughout the south."[5] Additionally, in the eyes of most analysts, the enemy suffered a considerable military defeat in terms of casualties—as many as 40,000 killed in action. In a war of attrition, these are formidable numbers, especially when contrasted with American and ARVN deaths of roughly 1,100 and 2,300 for the South Vietnamese.[6]

Yet, in another, perhaps more fundamental sense, the Tet Offensive became an inadvertent psychological victory for the communists. If there was no uprising in South Vietnam, at least there was a psychological "impact on the United States," according to General Do, one that "had not been our [North Vietnamese] intention—but it turned out to be a fortunate result."[7] Initially, however, Tet's impact on Americans seemed to harden public attitudes: In February 1968, for example, one public opinion poll showed that 53 percent of those questioned actually favored stronger military action against the communists, even at the risk of conflict with China or the Soviet Union.[8] But by March, 78 percent of Americans polled on that question felt that the United States was not making any progress in the war, and only 26 percent approved of President Johnson's handling of the war.[9]

More importantly, a number of key figures—those whom journalist-historian Stanley Karnow has dubbed "the vocal elements of the population"—were becoming increasingly critical of the war: "Johnson was being abandoned by . . . the media commentators, business executives, educators, clergymen, and other 'elites,' whose voices resonated more forcefully in Washington than did those of Middle America."[10] In his syndicated column on February 6, 1968, for example, Art Buchwald featured a confident George Armstrong Custer proudly announcing " 'The battle of Little Big-horn had just turned the corner,' and the Sioux were 'on the run' "—an obvious slam at the president's initial attempt to put the Tet Offensive in a positive light.[11] Far more influential than Buchwald's barbs was the defection of CBS television news anchorman and correspondent Walter Cronkite. Generally perceived as America's "most respected newsman," Cronkite, in a February 27, 1968, special documentary on Tet and the war, concluded that the war seemed "certain . . . to end in a stalemate" and pleaded with the president to disengage America from the war, "not as victors but as an honorable people who lived up to their pledge to defend democracy, and did the best they could."[12] A stunned Johnson reportedly exclaimed, "If I've lost Cronkite, I've lost middle America."[13]

To add to Johnson's confusion, some of his military advisors were telling him privately that the Tet Offensive was in fact a "near thing," that the communists had come dangerously close to winning a military victory as well as a psychological one. In addition, General William Westmoreland, commander of American forces in Vietnam, contradicted himself. On the one hand, he said the offensive was a military failure for the communists. In the same message, however, he reported to Chairman of the Joint Chiefs Earle Wheeler, "We must accept the fact that the enemy has dealt the GVN a severe blow." As a result, he was not optimistic, noting that the South Vietnamese government faced a " 'tremendous challenge' to restore stability" in the post-Tet period.[14]

When in late February Westmoreland, under prodding from Wheeler, asked for an additional 206,000 troops, Johnson ordered Clark Clifford, his new Secretary of Defense, to study the request with the charge, "Give me the lesser of evils."[15] After extensive conversations with both civilians and military personnel, Clifford recommended that the request be rejected. By late March, Clifford had, in essence, turned against the war. Concerned about an economic crisis involving a run on the American gold supply, as well as growing disenchantment with the war among the business and legal elite, Clifford wanted to see a winching down strategy that would lead to "step-by-step deescalation."[16] Working with White House aide Harry McPherson and former Secretary of State Dean Acheson, Clifford sought to convince the president.

To secure additional advice, Johnson reconvened his circle of unofficial advisors known as the "Wise Men," including Acheson. Although members of the group disagreed on details, there was a general consensus that, in the words of Acheson, the United States could "no longer do the job we set out to do in the time we have left and we must begin to take steps to disengage."[17]

Although Johnson did not wholeheartedly subscribe to the advice of the Wise Men—"The establishment bastards have bailed out," he bitterly noted—nonetheless he adopted the basic tenor of their advice in a speech to the nation on March 31, 1968.[18] Instead of beginning, "I want to talk to you tonight about the war in Vietnam," as he had originally intended, he began, "I want to talk to you tonight about peace in Vietnam."[19] He not only instituted a partial bombing halt, he called for peace talks at any place, any time and named experienced diplomat W. Averell Harriman as his personal representative to prospective talks. Finally, he announced that he would not seek another term as president.

Johnson's surprising speech did not signal the end of the war; American involvement would go on almost five more years. Nonetheless, it did mark a sea change. As historian George Herring notes, "[T]he circumstances in which the March decisions were made and the conciliatory tone of Johnson's speech made it difficult, if not impossible, for him to change course. March 31, 1968, brought an inglorious end to the policy of gradual escalation."[20]

For William Westmoreland, the blame for the "inglorious end" that Tet's psychological defeat brought to American strategy could be laid largely at the feet of the media. In his memoir, he states clearly that "the general tone of press and television comment was critical, particularly following the Tet offensive of 1968." He goes on to paraphrase favorably Australian journalist Denis Warner, who noted that "there are those who say that it was the first war in history lost in the columns of the New York *Times*.[21] Criticism of the media in the Tet Offensive opens up the whole question of the role of print journalism and television in the war. Did a combination of reportage biased against the war and violence-filled television coverage sour Americans on the conflict? The truth of the matter is a good deal more complicated than a simple "yes" or "no."

In the first place, journalists in the 1960s were as much a part of the Cold War consensus as were politicians. Moreover, Presidents Kennedy and Johnson successfully cultivated media support. Although there was some grumbling about "managed news" under Kennedy and a growing "credibility gap" with Johnson, by and large members of the media were supportive of the two presidents. For much of the war, journalists tended to approve America's commitment to South Vietnam. For example, most of the reporters in the field in the early 1960s strongly championed the American effort. *New York Times* correspondent David Halberstam believed that South Vietnam "was one of the five or six nations in the world truly vital to the interests of the United States." He argued that America did "have something to offer these emerging nations. We can get things done."[22] What irritated Halberstam and colleagues like Peter Arnett and Neil Sheehan of the Associated Press was that Americans and their South Vietnamese allies simply weren't getting the job done under the government of Ngo Dinh Diem. Thus, many in the press were highly critical of the Diem regime—not of the overall goal of American policy.

Press criticism of Diem in the early 1960s and the corrupt South Vietnamese governments that followed Diem's assassination did lead to considerable bad blood between journalists and the government, however. Admiral Harry Felt once urged Malcolm Browne to "get on the team" after the young Associated Press reporter had launched a barbed criticism of the war effort; and President Kennedy actually pressured the *Times* to recall Halberstam from his post.[23] In response, some journalists accused the administration of managing the news and worried about a credibility gap between the American government and its citizens. In a little ditty based on "Twinkle, Twinkle Little Star," reporters pilloried the veracity of American officials who claimed that the war against the Vietcong was being won: "We are winning;/This I know./General Harkins told me so./If you doubt me,/Who are you?/McNamara says so too."[24]

Hoping to avoid such clashes, the Johnson administration tried to follow a policy of "Maximum Candor" with the press. Pushed especially by James L. Greenfield, Assistant Secretary of State for Public Affairs, this policy emphasized frequent press briefings that would be as open and honest as possible within the bounds of military security. It also posited extremely light official restrictions on the press as well as offering journalists considerable assistance in getting to combat areas where important stories were breaking. In return, reporters agreed to follow a set of ground rules that basically forbade them from revealing details about specific military operations.

Some tension continued to exist, of course, usually when the government departed from this policy and tried to hide information that reporters felt they had a right to know. For example, in the spring and summer of 1965, journalists grumbled when severe restrictions were placed on their mobility in and around Danang, the major embarkation point for U.S. troops. Reporters were denied access to pilots who had flown missions outside of Vietnam, for example; several reporters trying to look at the main airfield in Danang were taken into custody by military police. (Correspondents also complained about spartan facilities: As one reporter said of the Danang press office, "This is the only press center in the world without a phone."[25]) A more serious case of bad communication came in the continuing debate over body counts. Because of the strategy of attrition followed for much of the war, the number of enemy dead and maimed became the key statistical measure of American success. And many reporters were convinced that these figures were inflated in official briefings to the press. For example, *Time* magazine's Charles Mohr observed in 1965, " 'So great is the pressure for body count figures' that troops began 'to joke about Saigon's request for the "W.E.G.," or "wild-eyed guess." ' "[26] Thus, as one State Department official put it, *"The Maximum Candor policy pays off in Viet-Nam*. Nearly all problems with the press result from departures from this policy" (italics in original).[27]

Among the most mobile and effective of the journalists in Vietnam were photojournalists. Whereas print reporters were able to spend time interviewing personnel in noncombat areas, photographers like Larry Burrows and Eddie Adams needed to be where the action was. Some of the visual images to come out of the war—the self-immolation of Buddhist monk Thich Quang Duc in 1963, the My Lai Massacre in 1968, the Vietnamese girl running down a road after a napalm attack, and, especially Eddie Adams's famous picture of South Vietnamese General Nguyen Ngoc Loan executing a Vietcong suspect during the Tet Offensive—have all become visual icons of the war. As print journalist David Halberstam points out, photojournalists "held a special place in our [reporters'] esteem. We deferred to them, reporter to photographer, in [Vietnam] as we did in few others."[28]

In some ways like photojournalism, television reporting formed a special case in the debate over the media's role in the war. Critics of this newest medium argued, in the words of historian George Donelson Moss, that "nightly coverage of martial blood and gore" helped turn the American people away from support of the war. Moreover, "television reporters, cameramen, and anchormen, those who opposed the war, contrived to present stories and make editorial comments casting the U.S. war effort in an unfavorable light." Finally, television "provided extensive coverage to the vocal antiwar movement that . . . inflated its appeal." In sum, "a powerful adversarial medium worked in various ways to undermine public support for the American military effort in Vietnam."[29]

There is some truth to the assertions of these critics. Witness the power of Eddie Adams's famous footage of the execution of a Vietcong suspect during the Tet Offensive, or Walter Cronkite's pontifications about the war during the same period. But critics of television's role may well be exaggerating the medium's power during the war.

In the first place, relatively few Americans even watched television news during the 1960s. Although some influential Americans may have been deeply affected by a Walter Cronkite, yearly studies done by the Simmons Market Research Bureau show that Americans relied on newspapers far more than television during this period. On an average day in 1969, for example, only 24 percent of the adult population watched a television news show, but 78 percent read a newspaper. And the number of households that watched network newsprograms regularly was "miniscule."[30] Moreover, according to a 1967 Harris Poll, for those few who did watch television news, the experience was actually more likely to increase their support for the war, with only 31 percent indicating that television news made them more likely to oppose the war.[31] Indeed, what people saw probably tended to reinforce what they already believed.

Moreover, critics of television have exaggerated the amount of "blood and gore" footage shown on news programs. To be sure, there were shots of American soldiers being inserted into landing zones or coming out of the bush, but few of these portrayed actual fighting. In fact, as early as 1966, the Department of Defense, in a memorandum to American news outlets, called for "restraint in their use of images of dead and wounded GIs."[32] And the media generally abided by these guidelines. As Moss points out, "Only one in five combat stories depicted live action, and many of these live-action stories showed only scattered small arms fire or an airstrike in the distance." Indeed, "remarkably little American blood got spilled on the tube."[33]

Finally, most television reporters and their editors tended to support the American position throughout much of the war. They were part of a Cold War consensus that saw Vietnam as worth fighting for, and they saw the communists as cruel and dangerous adversaries. Content analysis, for example, illustrates that television news provided far more coverage of atrocities committed by the enemy than ones allegedly committed by Americans. This hardly suggests an anti-American bias.

Critics of the media see press and television coverage of the Tet Offensive as the paradigmatic case of an out-of-control medium that showed excessively violent images, failed to tell the truth, and used skewed commentaries to change public opinion. There is some truth to these charges. Correspondent Peter Braestrup takes his fellow journalists to task for failing to tell a balanced story. They were late in changing early reports that the American embassy building had been occupied by Vietcong, whereas in fact only part of the embassy grounds had ever been controlled by the enemy. Certainly, newspapers and television stations gave wide play to Eddie Adams's gruesome Loan execution picture, with some suggestion that this symbolized the futility of the war. Worse, they simply did not pay enough attention to official statements that emphasized an American military victory. Braestrup tells one chilling story of an NBC News producer's rejection of a three-part series suggesting that Tet had been a military victory for the United States because "Tet was already established 'in the public's mind as a defeat, and therefore it was an American defeat.' " Braestrup concludes that "[a]t Tet, the press shouted that the patient was dying, then weeks later began to whisper that he somehow seemed to be recovering—whispers apparently not heard amid the clamorous domestic reaction to the initial shouts."[34]

In fact, we simply do not know precisely how Americans reacted to violent footage like the General Loan execution. NBC News received a large number of letters about this sequence, most of which accused the network of bad taste in showing such gore, especially since children might have been watching. There was no indication that the scene changed anyone's mind about the war. Moreover, although there was evidence of skewed media coverage, especially of the attack on the American embassy, even Peter Braestrup does not claim that these stories were the result of bias. He concludes, in fact, that "no empirical data exist to link news coverage with changes in public opinion."[35] Nor is there any clear correlation between critiques like Walter Cronkite's famous "stalemate" commentary and changes in public opinion.

If many in the public and in Washington saw Tet as a blow to the U.S. effort in Vietnam, the blame lay not with media distortion but with earlier bursts of optimism from the highest levels of government. According to most official reports prior to early 1968, the United States had been winning the war. Indeed, in November 1967, Westmoreland, Ellsworth Bunker (American Ambassador to Vietnam), and even Vice President Hubert Humphrey had launched a public relations blitz filled with optimistic prognostications about the war's progress. In a November 21 speech before the National Press Club, for example, Westmoreland claimed that "whereas in 1965 the enemy was winning, today he is certainly losing." In fact, he flatly said that the communists' " hopes are bankrupt."[36] Of course, the media dutifully reported these sanguine predictions. The ease with which the communists launched the Tet Offensive called into serious question Westmoreland's bold assertion, even if Tet was some sort of "military victory" for the United States. Thus, the conjunction of official optimism, the fact of the Tet Offensive, and growing insider discontent with the war had much more to do with Johnson's March 31 decision than did media exaggeration or mendacity.

During the heart of "Johnson's war" from 1965 to 1968, then, both print and television journalists tended to be basically fair in their accounts of the war. As Army public affairs officer Winnant Sidle attested, "Most reporting of the war was either advantageous to government policy or . . . a reasonable approximation of what was happening in the field."[37] Historian William Hammond concludes that "throughout much of the war, the American news media . . . tended to give both their government and the U.S. soldier the benefit of the doubt."[38]

Negative coverage on television did appear more frequently after 1969, however, but primarily in the sense that more congressional doves and other opponents of the war were featured on newscasts. In other words, as congressional and public opinion turned increasingly against the war, that change was reflected in television coverage, which expanded to include negative points of view more frequently.

Moreover, the extent of media coverage of the war changed after 1968. With troop withdrawals and a diminution of ground combat involving Americans ordered by President Richard Nixon, the media paid less attention to Vietnam. The number of *New York Times* editorials on the war, for example, declined from 130 a year between 1966 and 1968 to fewer than seventy a year between 1969 and 1971. A similar trend occurred in television. Except for increased airtime during the U.S. incursion into Cambodia in 1970 and the South Vietnamese attack on Laos in 1971, television news coverage of the war declined by about 20 percent after 1968.[39]

To be sure, even this reduced attention to the war irritated President Nixon, who increasingly saw the media as his enemy. Convinced that biased reportage was turning Americans against his policy in Vietnam, in late 1969 Nixon authorized Vice President Spiro Agnew to unleash an attack on the media, especially television. But there is no evidence that negative reporting caused the public to turn against Nixon's handling of the war. Opinion polls show that throughout the period between 1969 and 1973, more Americans supported his policies than opposed them.[40] Moreover, there is no evidence that Nixon was influenced to take America out of Vietnam because of pressure from the media. We must conclude, finally, that those who somehow blame the media for losing the Vietnam War are in all likelihood simply wrong.

NOTES

1. Don Oberdorfer, *Tet: The Turning Point in the Vietnam War* (reprint ed., New York: Da Capo, 1984 [1971]), p. 8.

2. The offensive derives its name from the fact that it occurred during "Tet," the annual Vietnamese festival celebrating the lunar new year.

3. Larry Berman, "The Tet Offensive," in *The Tet Offensive*, ed. Marc Jason Gilbert and William Head (Westport, Conn.: Praeger, 1996), p. 23.

4. Ibid., p. 21.

5. Stanley Karnow, *Vietnam: A History* (New York: Viking Press, 1983), p. 545.

6. Casualty figures come from Charles Dobbs, "Tet Offensive," in *Dictionary of the Vietnam War*, ed. James Olson (New York: Peter Bedrick Books, 1987), p. 442.

7. Karnow, *Vietnam*, p. 545. Political scientist Bernard Brodie observed that the Tet Offensive was "probably unique in that the side that lost completely in a

tactical sense came away with an overwhelming psychological and hence political victory" (quoted in George Herring, *America's Longest War: The United States and Vietnam, 1950–1975*, 3rd ed. [New York: McGraw-Hill, 1996], pp. 203–4).

8. Karnow, *Vietnam*, p. 546.

9. Herring, *Longest War*, pp. 219, 220.

10. Karnow, p. 546.

11. Ibid., p. 547.

12. George Donelson Moss, "News or Nemesis: Did Television Lose the Vietnam War?" in *A Vietnam Reader: Sources and Essays*, ed. George Moss (Englewood Cliffs, N.J.: Prentice-Hall, 1991), p. 274.

13. Robert Buzzanco, "The Myth of Tet: American Failure and the Politics of War," in Gilbert and Head, *Tet*, p. 231. Cronkite's influence may have been considerably less than Johnson assumed. Historian George D. Moss concludes that "[i]t was apparently not true that popular celebrity-anchormen such as Walter Cronkite built up large personal followings during the Vietnam war era" (Moss, "News or Nemesis," p. 254). Nonetheless, Johnson apparently believed in Cronkite's influence, and that belief may well have been part of his reasons for de-escalating the war.

14. Buzzanco, "The Myth of Tet," pp. 234–35.

15. Herring, *Longest War*, p. 213. Robert Buzzanco argues that Wheeler assumed that Johnson would turn down the request. Therefore, if the war went badly, military leaders could blame "politics" for the failure and relieve themselves of culpability (Buzzanco, "Myth of Tet," 231–49 and passim).

16. Herring, *Longest War*, p. 224.

17. Ibid., pp. 225–26.

18. Ibid., p. 226.

19. *Vietnam, A Television History*, Episode 7 (Public Broadcasting System, 1983). In an interview for this PBS series, presidential aide Harry McPherson was surprised and delighted with the substitution of "peace" for "war," believing that this change in wording marked a major change in Johnson's thinking.

20. Herring, *Longest War*, p. 227.

21. William Westmoreland, *A Soldier Reports* (New York: Dell, 1980), p. 556.

22. William M. Hammond, "Media and the War," in *Encyclopedia of the Vietnam War*, ed. Stanley I. Kutler (New York: Charles Scribner's Sons, 1996), p. 309.

23. Clarence Wyatt, *Paper Soldiers: The American Press and the Vietnam War* (New York: W. W. Norton and Co., 1993), p. 127.

24. Ibid., p. 104.

25. Ibid., p. 162.

26. Ibid.

27. Ibid., p. 160.

28. David Halberstam, "Introduction," in *Requiem: By the Photographers Who Died in Vietnam and Indochina*, ed. Horst Faas and Tim Page (New York: Random House, 1997), p. 9.

29. Moss, "News or Nemesis," p. 249. The charge that the media's focus on the antiwar movement helped "lose" the war is discussed in chapter 6.

30. Ibid., 254.

31. Wyatt, *Paper Soldiers*, p. 148.

32. Susan D. Moeller, *Shooting War: Photography and the American Experience of Combat* (New York: Basic Books, 1989), p. 365.

33. Moss, "News or Nemesis," p. 266.

34. Peter Braestrup, *Big Story*, abridged version (Garden City, N.Y.: Anchor Books, 1978), pp. 75–118, 509, 517.

35. Peter Braestrup, "The Tet Offensive, Another Press Controversy: II," in *Vietnam Reconsidered: Lessons from a War*, ed. Harrison E. Salisbury (New York: Harper & Row, 1984), p. 170.

36. Braestrup, *Big Story*, p. 51.

37. Hammond, "Media and the War," p. 314.

38. Ibid.

39. Ibid., p. 320.

40. George H. Gallup, *The Gallup Poll: Public Opinion, 1935–1971*, Vol. 3 (New York: Random House, 1972), pp. 2184–338 and passim.

6

Richard Nixon, the Antiwar Movement, and the End of the American War in Vietnam

In a particularly poignant moment in his presidential administration, Richard Nixon tried to talk informally to antiwar protestors. In early May 1970, thousands of college students and other demonstrators descended on Washington to condemn the recent American military assault on Cambodia and mourn the deaths of four students killed by National Guardsmen at Kent State University. At around 4:00 A.M. on May 10, a restless president awakened his valet, Manolo Sanchez, and asked him if he had ever seen the Lincoln Memorial at night. When Sanchez said that he had not, the president took him. At the site, Nixon engaged some sleepy and very surprised student protesters in conversation. According to advisor Bud Krogh, who accompanied the president, Nixon talked mainly about sports and travel, very little about "the war thing." A Syracuse University student at the scene told a reporter, "I hope it was because he was tired, but most of what he was saying was absurd. Here we had come from a university that's completely uptight, on strike, and when we told him where we were from, he talked about the football team." Krogh concluded that "[i]t was a surreal experience."[1]

If Richard Nixon thought he was somehow communicating with "the" American antiwar movement on that May night, he was sadly mistaken—and not just because what he said was goofy. Simply put, there was no one antiwar movement in America at any time during the war. As historian Charles DeBenedetti accurately points out, because the antiwar impulse was "too diverse and fractious to sustain an ongoing movement, antiwar critics improvised an opposition that involved an unusually broad range of disaffected citizens." Opposition to the war, then, was "a multilayered, many-sided phenomenon."[2] Although some critics of the antiwar movement claimed that it was controlled by "Communists and extremist elements"—"Vietniks," in the phrase coined by *Time* magazine in late 1965—in fact, according to historian Robert Schulzinger, "The movement to oppose U.S. involvement in Vietnam was far too amorphous to be controlled by anyone."[3]

To try to make some analytical sense out of this buzzing confusion, we can identify at least five "bases" of opposition to the war, to use DeBenedetti's word. These bases often overlapped both chronologically and philosophically, with shifting memberships and more than occasional arguments over goals and tactics. One rather small but influential core was found among "dissident members of the nation's policy shaping elite," men like journalist Walter Lippmann and Senator William Fulbright (D-Ark.). In the late 1960s, some business leaders like Baltimore insurance executive Henry Niles, who founded Business Executives Move for a Vietnam Peace (BEM) in 1966, joined this core. They generally saw America's oversized military commitment to Vietnam as contrary to "true" national security interests—especially improved relations with the Soviet Union. They also worried that an ever-escalating conflict would unnecessarily provoke communist China. Thus, as DeBenedetti notes, "Fundamentally, they saw Vietnam as irrelevant to America."[4] As the war went on, an increasing number of influential Americans in politics, the media, and the professions became advocates of this position.

A larger, more amorphous group comprised what DeBenedetti labels "peace liberals." Composed of a mélange of internationalists, pacifists, and Christian socialists, ranging from Norman Cousins, editor of the influential literary magazine, *Saturday Review*, to Dorothy Day, editor of the *Catholic Worker*, to housewife Dagmar Wilson, these peace liberals were deeply disturbed by escalation of American military involvement in the war. Through letter-writing, petitions, lobbying, and peaceful demonstrations, they wanted to change U.S. policy away from a military approach and toward a more political one that would enable a pluralist South Vietnam to negotiate its own peace with the North.

A third, much smaller group of more-militant pacifists saw the war as profoundly immoral. Catholic priests Daniel and Phillip Berrigan, for example, were convinced that the United States had no moral right to intervene in any way in Vietnamese life. Through aggressive nonviolent civil disobedience, ranging from individual draft-card burning to destruction of draft records, the Berrigans and groups like the War Resisters League wanted to stir the conscience of America and its leaders to effect immediate and total withdrawal from an immoral overseas adventure. Given the dramatic nature of its protests, this group received substantial media attention, far outweighing its numbers and supporters in the general population.

The fourth rough grouping was made up of various traditional and "new" leftist organizations, including the rather miniscule pro-Soviet Communist party, the Maoist Progressive Labor party, the Trotskyite Socialist Workers party, and, preeminently, the most visible of the New Left organizations, the Students for a Democratic Society (SDS). Propounding varieties of Marxist analyses, these groups generally placed the Vietnam War in a larger framework of American imperialism and were quite sympathetic to the Vietcong and North Vietnamese (as well as other Third-World socialist regimes like Castro's Cuba.) They also saw the war not as some kind of foreign policy aberration but rather as a symptom of a corrupt capitalist polity that needed to be radically altered. Although most rejected violence, some, like the Weather Underground, an offshoot of the SDS, reveled in the power of violent confrontation, as did more localized groups like the New Year's Gang in Madison, Wisconsin.

Finally, there were an untold number of Americans upset with the war, increasing as it dragged on, who belonged to no antiwar group and probably never protested against the war in any sort of demonstration. These were citizens who simply wanted the war to end. As DeBenedetti points out, "[T]hroughout the war years, public-opinion pollsters reported consistently high levels of support for peace negotiations," and significantly, this was the stance propounded by "the broadest range of antiwar critics."[5] Thus, there was an inchoate, often untapped mass of vaguely antiwar sentiment throughout the country.

Of course, membership in these groups often overlapped, and elements of each group were active during all phases of the war. Nonetheless, at certain time periods, particular approaches to protesting against the war seemed to dominate.

Prior to 1965, opposition to the war was sporadic at best and located primarily among a few old-line radical pacifists. As early as 1963, for example, the War Resisters League (WRL), led by David Dellinger, protested the growing American advisory presence in Vietnam. On May 16, 1964, the WRL sponsored a demonstration in New York City in which several young men burned their draft cards, and in December it led the first national demonstration against the war. In October 1964 veteran pacifist A. J. Muste and his Fellowship of Reconciliation similarly issued a public call to resist the draft as a protest against the growing number of American military advisors being sent to Vietnam.[6]

Such early demonstrations of discontent sparked little interest and won few adherents. After the introduction of American combat troops in March 1965, however, a small but growing number of college students began to protest against the war through a series of educational forums popularly known as "teach-ins." These students partly were concerned about the possibility of being drafted to fight in the war. They were also very much influenced by the earlier protests of the 1960s, from the civil rights movement in the South to the Free Speech Movement at the University of California at Berkeley in 1965. The first teach-in took place at the University of Michigan at Ann Arbor on March 24–25, 1965, when almost three thousand students and faculty spent much of the night of the 24th listening to lectures and debates on the war. During the next day around six hundred persons stayed to protest against military escalation in Vietnam. By the end of the academic year, some 120 campuses witnessed this cross between education and demonstration, culminating in a thirty-six hour-teach-in at the University of California at Berkeley. A minority of student activists there, including Jerry Rubin, called for a " 'do-it-yourself' revolution" as the best way to end the war. Most teach-in participants, however, would have agreed with Socialist Party leader Norman Thomas, who said, " 'I am interested in peace' in Vietnam, 'and peace does not require us to hate America.' " Or, as WRL member Robert Pickus put it, such a call to revolution was "so much pure crap."[7]

On a more somber note, 1965 ended with two lone suicides by self-immolation, one by Quaker Norman Morrison, the other by *Catholic Worker* pacifist Roger Laporte. Both men saw their acts as sacrifices to call attention to the horrors of the war. They seemed to have no lasting impact, however. Indeed, they actually provided rhetorical fuel for opponents of the antiwar impulse. A few days after Morrison's death, some antiwar demonstrators were burning their draft cards in New York. A mob of hecklers shouted, "Burn yourselves, not your cards."[8]

The small antiwar movement's quest to educate Americans about the war's stupidity received a boost in 1966, when William Fulbright, Chair of the Senate Foreign Relations Committee, opened hearings on American involvement in Vietnam. The nationally televised inquiry naturally featured administration spokesmen like Dean Rusk, but these proponents of administration policy faced probing and critical questions from Fulbright, who was becoming increasingly disillusioned by the war. The hearings also gave a forum to critics of escalation like George Kennan, the intellectual father of the very containment policy that the Vietnam War was supposedly reflecting.

That same year, a New York-based coalition of antiwar groups calling itself the Spring Mobilization Committee to End the War in Vietnam staged a daylong peaceful protest against the war, which drew fifty thousand people and set the pattern for future demonstrations in major American cities. On a few college campuses, some young white radicals, especially those associated with SDS, sought to inspire demonstrators with the rhetoric of revolution, but for the most part antiwar activists stuck to traditional means of making their dissenting views known: letter writing, public vigils, and trying to encourage antiwar sentiment in Congress.

This latter tactic seemed to have borne fruit by late 1967, as liberal Democratic senators like Eugene McCarthy (D-Minn.) and Robert Kennedy (D-NY) began to speak out openly against the war and in favor of a negotiated settlement even if it meant shared power with the communists. This surge of "establishment" antiwar sentiment culminated in December 1967 with Senator McCarthy's decision to challenge President Johnson for the Democratic nomination.

During 1967 more "radical" confrontational activity increased, including antidraft rallies and sit-ins against corporate and military recruiters. This more militant strain peaked with a march on Washington in late October. More than one hundred thousand protestors gathered at the Lincoln Memorial to listen to speakers condemn the war. About half of them split off later to protest at the Pentagon, where some placed flowers in the barrels of rifles carried by soldiers protecting the building, while others joined with poet Allen Ginsburg in trying to levitate the Pentagon through Tibetan chants. A few militants, dubbing themselves the SDS Revolutionary Contingent, tried to breach an off-limits area and were repelled by military police using tear gas.

The two basic approaches represented by McCarthy on the one hand and the Pentagon demonstration on the other carried into the turbulent year 1968. Thousands of volunteers, many of them antiwar college students, worked in the McCarthy campaign to win the Democratic nomination. Thousands more joined the effort of Senator Robert Kennedy, who also later ran as an antiwar Democrat. Still firmly committed to the possibility of peaceful change within the existing political system, these politicians and their supporters wanted a quick end to the war through honest negotiation and compromise.

On the other hand, polarization and confrontational tactics also blossomed in 1968. If peace liberals flocked to the McCarthy and Kennedy banners, more-radical activists, in the words of Charles DeBenedetti, "denounced McCarthy's candidacy as a trap and a diversion from the prior need for disruptive direct action in the streets. It was a time, they said, for deeds, not words."[9] That spring, hundreds of college campuses erupted in demonstrations, most of them related to antiwar protest and some witnessing demonstrator occupation of campus offices and violent confrontations with authorities. An April protest at Columbia University, for example, ended with a police action against students who occupied buildings on campus, resulting in numerous arrests and injuries.

The two broad streams of protest met at the Chicago Democratic Convention in August. The death of Robert Kennedy in June and growing party-insider support for Vice President Hubert Humphrey caused considerable disarray among peace liberals. With little hope that McCarthy or Senator George McGovern (D-S.D.), who inherited some of Kennedy's support, could win the nomination, antiwar forces within the party fought for a strong antiwar plank in the party platform. When that failed, attention focused on another group who opposed the war. Some ten thousand demonstrators of various tactical persuasions had poured into Chicago. Although most were peaceful, a considerable minority planned confrontational tactics to draw public attention to the war. Some followed leaders like Abbie Hoffman and Jerry Rubin, whose "Yippie Party" nominated a pig (named Pigasus) for president and threatened (jokingly) to seed the Chicago water supply with LSD. Others sought to create sympathy by raising Vietcong flags in Grant Park; still others threw rocks, bags of feces, and imprecations at Chicago policemen. Some just watched, marched, and sang.

When the police responded to the demonstrators with mass arrests and violence, especially during the night of Hubert Humphrey's nomination, many Americans shared an uneasy sense that the country was falling apart and desperately needed new leadership to bring it together. The fact that millions saw the events on television heightened their impact. Republican presidential nominee Richard Nixon took advantage of this feeling as he ran on a pledge to end the war through a "secret plan"—although he never quite said how—and restore domestic tranquillity by dealing firmly with radical antiwar activists. His election victory in 1968 seemed to confirm public distaste for both the war and many of those who opposed it.[10]

Neither the war nor the antiwar movement ended with Nixon's election. His secret plan turned out to be a warmed over version of a McNamara proposal to turn more of the fighting over to the Vietnamese. He also began a program of phased American troop withdrawals, while increasing American military aid to the South. In addition, Vietnamization included stepped up bombing attacks in the South and initiated a top-secret (and legally questionable) series of bombing attacks on suspected communist positions in neutral Cambodia. Clearly, the Nixon administration still hoped to keep the South noncommunist; as Robert Schulzinger points out, Nixon and his chief foreign policy advisor, Henry Kissinger, "like officials of every previous administration . . . believed U.S. credibility was at stake in Vietnam" and that "a forced departure . . . would embolden American rivals elsewhere in the world."[11]

The other great purpose of Vietnamization, according to Schulzinger, "was to turn the public's attention away from the war."[12] In this Nixon was not very successful, at least initially. In fact, the largest nationwide demonstrations against the conflict occurred in 1969 only a few months after the first troop withdrawal was announced. The October and November "Moratoriums" against the war, organized by peace liberals, attracted millions of protestors, many of them, according to historian George Herring, "sober, middle-class citizens."[13] On October 15, one hundred thousand people gathered on the Boston Commons, while some ten thousand came out in Minneapolis, including Hubert Humphrey. The Moratorium even reached Muncie, Indiana, the famed "Middletown" analyzed in dozens of sociological studies. This alleged "average" American town in the heart of the Midwest saw several hundred people, mainly students and faculty at Ball State University, congregate that October 15 in front of the campus administration building to hear the solemn reading of the names of dead soldiers. During the November Moratorium, another two hundred or so marched down the main street of Muncie, singing "Give Peace a Chance," before adjourning to a local park to hear speeches. The Moratorium was important, then, because, as Charles DeBenedetti notes, its "main force . . . was the willingness of ordinary and respectable citizens to conduct collective actions that indicated their wish 'to have done with Vietnam' and to restore domestic harmony."[14]

The massive demonstrations seemed to have no effect on the Nixon administration. In fact, the president made a point of noting that he planned to spend the afternoon of the October Moratorium watching college football on television. And as if to underline the disparate approaches to protest (and the difficulty of restoring "domestic harmony"), a week before the peaceful October 15 protest, a small group of militant Weathermen launched an orgy of vandalism on Chicago's Gold Coast, thus bringing down a spate of bad publicity on the movement as a whole. Finally, the peaceful Moratoriums, although larger than any previous antiwar protest, hardly included a majority of Americans. In fact, at Ball State, more students participated in a series of panty and jockstrap raids during October than bothered to join in antiwar activity. Moreover, some three thousand Ball State students actually signed a petition supporting President Nixon's policy in Vietnam—far more than ever marched against the war.[15]

By the early spring of 1970, the momentum generated by the Moratorium seemed to be dissipating. At that juncture, Nixon's decision to send American troops into Cambodia in late April gave new energy to the movement. Viewing the "incursion" as a clear expansion of a war that was supposed to be contracting, thousands of students on hundreds of campuses reacted by protesting against all aspects of the war. In the aftermath of the burning of the ROTC building at Kent State University, four students were killed by National Guardsmen, unleashing the largest number of campus upheavals in American history. Robert Schulzinger estimates that "demonstrations took place at 1,350 campuses, and more than four million people took part."[16] Even at usually quiet Ball State, there was a major demonstration, as six thousand red arm bands were distributed, and over a thousand people attended a teach-in on the campus's main quadrangle. The demonstrations culminated when more than one hundred thousand people descended on Washington D.C., demanding an end to the war. It was some of those demonstrators who were shocked to see Richard Nixon wandering around the Lincoln Memorial at 4:30 one May morning.

Hindsight tells us that the Cambodia/Kent State protests represented the high-water mark of the antiwar movement. To be sure, some continued to demonstrate, especially members of the Vietnam Veterans Against the War. Their protest in Washington, D.C., in April 1971 provided telling evidence that some Americans who experienced the war found it to be wrong. Never again would so many people so publicly protest against the war, however, as did during the Cambodia/Kent State demonstrations. The draft lottery, which had actually been instituted in December 1969, and the continued withdrawal of American troops from Vietnam took much of the wind out of the sails of the antiwar movement, especially its college-age members. Discontent did continue to spread, however, especially in Congress. Increasingly, senators and representatives grew weary of the war. In late 1970 the Gulf of Tonkin Resolution was repealed, and by 1971 the House Democratic Caucus had adopted a resolution calling for a termination of the war by the end of 1972. When Vietnam War veteran John Kerry testified before Congress in April 1971 as an antiwar advocate, people listened. In addition, the president saw the war as a growing impediment to his grand design in foreign policy: establishing links with the People's Republic of China, pursuing détente with the Soviet Union, and playing the two communist powers against each other. With Nixon's domestic political support wavering, he and his chief negotiator Henry Kissinger reached an agreement with the North in January 1973. All American troops would be coming home as the American war in Vietnam ended.[17]

Did the antiwar movement in fact help end the war? Although the jury is still out, the tentative answer is a resounding "maybe not, maybe so." Certainly, Presidents Johnson and Nixon claimed not to be influenced by opponents of the war. Just as clearly, public opinion polls indicated that a majority of Americans polled consistently had negative feelings toward antiwar protesters. Shortly after the October 1967 march on Washington, for example, opinion polls showed that by a three to one margin, Americans believed that antiwar protests put the lives of U.S. soldiers at risk, and 70 percent felt that such protests encouraged the communist enemy.[18] Three years later, another poll asked people to rate a set of political groups and leaders along a positive-negative scale. Respondents placed antiwar protestors in the most negative category. Significantly, over half of those responding so negatively to the demonstrators actually favored immediate withdrawal of American forces from Vietnam, and thus could be viewed as antiwar themselves.[19] Symbolic of this venom against the protesters was the fact that many Americans were hostile toward the demonstrators at Kent State in the spring of 1970—even the four students who were killed. At a memorial service for the students held in Toledo, Ohio, for example, one woman carried a sign reading "The Kent State four/Should have studied more"; the mother of three Kent State students told an interviewer that "[a]nyone who appears on the streets of a city like Kent with long hair, dirty clothes, or barefooted deserves to be shot."[20] In a poll conducted a few weeks after the Kent State shootings, more of those polled considered "campus unrest" America's "most important problem" than saw the Vietnam War as the nation's most crucial issue.[21]

Part of the explanation for this public hostility probably lies in the fact that media, especially television, tended to focus on the more radical, militant aspects of antiwar protest, thus helping create stereotypes of drug-crazed, fanatical anarchists tearing America down. Such images also might explain the overwhelming defeat suffered by antiwar Democratic party nominee George McGovern in the presidential election of 1972.

On the other hand, it may be, as former activist Todd Gitlin argues, that at least the movement kept Johnson and especially Nixon from "ratcheting up the war."[22] The antiwar agitation also might have had an impact on Congress and presidential advisors, leading them to be more suspicious of the war and desirous of seeing it over. If people are alive who would be dead were it not for opponents of the war, then perhaps the antiwar movement was a positive influence in the Vietnam era.

NOTES

1. This account of Nixon's wanderings comes from Tom Wells, *The War Within: America's Battle over Vietnam* (Berkeley, Calif.: University of California Press, 1994), p. 439. The president's travels that night didn't end at the Lincoln

Memorial. He took his valet to the House of Representatives' chamber in the Capitol building, sat him in the speaker's chair, and lectured him on how the House functions. Later over breakfast at the Mayflower Hotel, H. R. Haldeman, Nixon's Chief of Staff, joined the party. Haldeman noted that the president's mood was "kind of strange." One anonymous administration official referred to the whole episode as "King Lear Act VI" (ibid., pp. 440, 441).

2. Charles DeBenedetti, "Johnson and the Antiwar Opposition," in *The Johnson Years,* Volume Two: *Vietnam, the Environment, and Science,* ed. Robert A. Divine (Lawrence, Kans.: University Press of Kansas, 1987), p. 24.

3. Robert D. Schulzinger, Jr., *A Time for War: The United States and Vietnam, 1941–1975* (New York: Oxford University Press, 1997), p. 231.

4. DeBenedetti, "Johnson and the Antiwar Opposition," pp. 24–25. Fulbright was actually a firm supporter of the war in 1964, helping to shepherd the Gulf of Tonkin Resolution through the Senate. By early 1966, however, he had come to oppose the war on national security grounds.

5. Ibid., p. 27.

6. This information comes from Randy Roberts and James S. Olson, "Antiwar Movement," in *Encyclopedia of the Vietnam War,* ed. Stanley I. Kutler (New York: Charles Scribner's Sons, 1996), p. 31.

7. Charles DeBenedetti, with assisting author Charles Chatfield, *An American Ordeal: The Antiwar Movement in the Vietnam Era* (Syracuse, N.Y.: Syracuse University Press, 1990), pp. 115–16.

8. Schulzinger, *Time for War,* p. 234.

9. DeBenedetti, "Johnson and the Antiwar Opposition," p. 29.

10. In a speech to supporters the day after the election, Nixon recalled a touching incident during the campaign. In a small Ohio town, he saw a teenager holding up a sign that read "Bring Us Together." Claiming to be moved by the sentiment, Nixon promised that "that will be the great objective of this administration at the outset, to bring the American people together" (Richard M. Nixon, *RN: The Memoirs of Richard Nixon* [New York: Grosset and Dunlap, 1978], p. 335).

11. Schulzinger, *Time for Peace,* p. 276.

12. Ibid.

13. George Herring, *America's Longest War: The United States and Vietnam, 1950–1975,* 3rd ed. (New York: McGraw-Hill, 1996), p. 252.

14. DeBenedetti, *American Ordeal,* pp. 256–57.

15. Marie Kingsbury, "Residents' Letter Supports Nixon's Policy," Ball State *Daily News,* October 17, 1968, p. 1.

16. Schulzinger, *Time for War,* pp. 287–288.

17. Some of the details of the Paris Agreement ending American involvement will be discussed in the next chapter.

18. DeBenedetti, *American Ordeal,* pp. 198–99.

19. Ibid., p. 284.

20. James Michener, *Kent State: What Happened and Why* (New York: Random House, 1971), pp. 453, 454. This same mother also indicated that she would want her sons shot if they ever went barefooted (p. 454).

21. George E. Gallup, ed., *The Gallup Poll, Public Opinion, 1935–1971*, vol. 3 (New York: Random House, 1972), p. 2252.

22. Todd Gitlin, "Foreword," in Tom Wells, *The War Within: America; Battle over Vietnam* (Berkeley: University of California Press, 1994), p. xiv.

7

Legacies of the War

Those who think the Vietnam War ended in April 1975 when North Vietnamese troops stormed the Presidential Palace in Saigon should take a trip on the World Wide Web. A simple "Vietnam War" punched into the Alta Vista Search Engine on November 15, 1997, turned up over three million "hits" involving the war. They ranged from individual veterans' home pages to commercials for books to moving accounts of the plight of Vietnamese since 1975. Moreover, books and films about the war have proliferated in the past decade and a half, as have college and high school courses and units dealing with the conflict. The world seems fascinated with what was America's longest war and Vietnam's most destructive one.

For the Vietnamese, the legacies of the war include a reunified country and the expansion of a communist political economic system into the south. But, as journalist Arnold Isaacs writes, "The Vietnamese [have] had their darkness" in the more than two decades since their reunification.[1] Part of that darkness lay in the sheer human and physical devastation caused by the war. Between 1.5 and 2 million Vietnamese died, and some three hundred thousand were left permanently injured. In the war's aftermath, another million emigrated. And, in stark contrast to the few American soldiers who remained missing in action, some three hundred thousand missing Vietnamese have never been found.

Added to this human cost were the millions of acres of land poisoned or destroyed, villages and hamlets turned to rubble, and an economy left in shambles. Although communist leaders tried to create a kind of mythic glory around the war, in fact, as Isaacs notes, "Tragic memories remained just beneath the surface, like . . . the litter of unexploded shells, bombs, and mines lying hidden and still deadly in Vietnam's earth."[2] To an observer from another planet, it would have seemed that the North Vietnamese had lost the war.

To be sure, this devastation and America's refusal to recognize the new government or provide economic aid laid the groundwork for the difficulties faced by Vietnam. But the government's own economic and political policies exacerbated the situation. In an attempt to impose Ho Chi Minh's vision of a socialist economic order on the South, communist cadres expropriated private property, collectivized farms, and forced over a million city dwellers to farm "New Economic Zones" in abandoned areas in the South. The country sank into an economic morass; by 1980 the average worker made three hundred Vietnamese dong a month while a pair of cotton pants cost four hundred and a new bicycle twenty thousand. Within a few years, "the ideology of communism," according to historians James Olson and Randy Roberts, had "transformed Vietnam into one of the poorest countries in the world."[3]

Economic difficulties were paralleled by political ones. Thousands of southerners, especially those who had fought in the ARVN or worked for the Americans, were sent to "re-education camps," where many were tortured and died. In addition, North Vietnamese officials began to replace members of the Southern National Liberation Front in key roles in southern political life, as Hanoi exercised increasing bureaucratic control over the nation. An expensive invasion of Kampuchea in 1978, followed by a Chinese attack on Vietnam in 1979, added to the pressures on the economic and political structure. Soviet aid was just enough to keep the nation afloat but too little to promote meaningful economic growth. Finally, hundreds of thousands of Vietnamese simply left the country, most illegally. The migration stripped Vietnam of much of its professional and managerial class, adding to the country's economic headaches.

In 1986 Vietnamese leaders recognized the vast failure and committed the nation to radical change, especially in economic structures. In some ways this change was part of the almost tectonic shifts in the communist world, especially in the Soviet Union, as Premier Mikhail Gorbachev sought to "open" the Soviet system through his program of perestroika. Nguyen Van Linh, who had been appointed secretary-general of the Vietnamese Communist party in 1985, reduced the authority of central planners and encouraged the creation of small private businesses. Calling this change in policy *doi moi*, or "renovation," the party also worked to establish contacts with the capitalist world to attract foreign investment.

This change in economic policy has caused a boom in Vietnam. Between 1988 and 1996, for example, foreign firms have invested more than $21 billion in over a thousand major projects.[4] Tourism has become a major industry, as thousands of non-Vietnamese journey to what is arguably one of the most beautiful countries in the world. And all things American are immensely popular now, including Americans.[5] One of Saigon's most popular clubs, for example, is called "The Apocalypse Now," after the movie of the same name, where patrons are entertained by the sound-track voice of comedian Robin Williams, blasting out: "GOOOOOD MOOOORNNINNG, VEE-YET-NAMMMM," the traditional American Armed Forces Radio wake-up call during the war (and also the title of a commercial film about the war).[6]

In spite of these signs of change, Vietnam is hardly a bastion of widespread wealth and universal democratic freedoms. Most Vietnamese remain poor in a nation with an average per capita annual income of slightly more than $200. And the record on political and cultural repression is ambiguous at best, with some "enemies of the state" still imprisoned and others being set free. In 1993 singer-poet Trinh So Con noted, "There were still 'forbidden zones' for artists . . . but there was not an obvious or explicit climate of repression."[7] At the same time, the state legal system continued to protect the privileged position of the Communist party in Vietnam, as a new criminal code's list of crimes against national security included " 'anti-socialist propaganda' and 'undermining the policy of unity.' "[8]

Obviously, we can hardly predict how the legacy of the war will play out in Vietnam. But, as Arnold Isaacs rightly notes, a new generation of leaders will have to face the probability that "greater economic freedom and material prosperity [will] inevitably give rise to greater demands for political freedom as well." If a kind of democratic capitalism does become the legacy of the war in Vietnam, then in a curious and belated sense, America might have won its longest war after all.

In 1975, however, loss, not victory, hovered in the air around America's Vietnam experience as North Vietnamese troops surged into Saigon. If the impact of the war remains powerful in Vietnam, its legacy is perhaps even more profound in the United States. To be sure, Americans did not die in the same numbers as did Vietnamese, nor was the American landscape scarred and obliterated. But the United States did, arguably, lose that war. America did not achieve its central goal—to prevent the fall of South Vietnam to communist forces. This fact has colored the legacy of the war in the United States over the past two decades.

The defeat in Vietnam had a major impact on American foreign and defense policies. As historian George Moss notes, "The specter of Vietnam lurked in the background of every American foreign policy debate of the 1970s, 1980s, and 1990s."[9] Put simply, the nation became considerably more cautious about intervening militarily, especially in Third World countries, for fear of "another Vietnam." Indeed, the War Powers Resolution, passed by Congress in November 1973, was designed to make such interventions more difficult without congressional approval. Absent the Vietnam War, the United States might well have sent troops to Angola in the late 1970s to counter Cuban influence there. President Jimmy Carter's relatively mild response to the Soviet invasion of Afghanistan in 1980—a boycott of the Moscow Olympics, a curtailment of grain sales to the Soviet Union, and the deep-sixing of a nuclear weapons treaty—was partly the result of fears of another Vietnam. Debates over President Ronald Reagan's policy in Nicaragua and El Salvador in the 1980s echoed arguments over Vietnam, as both proponents and opponents of aid to anticommunist forces employed the Vietnam example. (Significantly, the use of U.S. combat troops was never seriously considered by President Reagan. Indeed, in 1988 when some conservatives "made a last ditch appeal for U.S. military aid to continue the Nicaraguan war, [he] told his chief of staff, 'Those sonsofbitches won't be happy until we have 25,000 troops in Managua, and I'm not going to have it.' "[10]) In fact, Reagan's one major military excursion, the invasion of Grenada in October 1983, was premised on avoiding the alleged mistakes of Vietnam: It had limited goals, could be finished rapidly, and could be won easily.

The Persian Gulf War of 1990–1991 was perhaps the paradigmatic case of the impact of the Vietnam War on foreign policy and military strategy. When Iraq invaded Kuwait and threatened Saudi Arabia in late 1990, President George Bush consciously and very publicly used Vietnam as the perfect foil to his approach to Saddam Hussein and the Gulf. Rather than commence military action in relative isolation, he worked through the United Nations and cobbled together a military coalition of several interested states. He involved Congress in a thorough airing of the issues before launching an attack on Iraq. He largely left military strategy to the Joint Chiefs of Staff and theater commander General Norman Schwartzkopf. Finally, the basic strategy of the war was simple: Hit hard from the air, then hit hard from the ground, achieve the central objective, and end the war—a direct contrast to the strategy of gradual escalation as practiced in Vietnam. America was simply not going to get involved in another conflict unless it could have reasonable assurance of a quick victory with clear military and political goals.

Of course, there were enormous differences between circumstances in the Gulf in early 1991 and in Vietnam in the 1960s and 1970s. In Vietnam, America intervened in what was at least partially a civil war, whereas in the Gulf, one nation was clearly invaded by another. Ho Chi Minh was certainly more respected in South Vietnam than Saddam was in Kuwait, and America's economic interests in the Gulf were clearly more vital than they were in Vietnam. In Vietnam, the enemy was often difficult to identify and fought primarily a guerrilla war, whereas in the Gulf, the identity of the "bad guys" was clear, and the war was conventional in nature. But in the final analysis, most Americans were not concerned with these distinctions. To them, as political scientist Steve Yetiv argues, "The Persian Gulf War erased post-Vietnam doubts about American resolve."[11]

The events surrounding the Gulf War also illustrated two other legacies of the Vietnam War: the virtual disappearance of the antiwar impulse and tight controls on media reporting of American military actions. To be sure, many anti–Vietnam War advocates achieved considerable success and even fame in the years after 1975. Jerry Rubin became a successful businessman; Jane Fonda made a lot of money with her exercise videos; Tom Hayden, the founder of Students for a Democratic Society (SDS), is a member of the California General Assembly. But the "movement" that organized antiwar sentiment virtually disappeared. Aside from some protests against nuclear weapons and South African apartheid, the movement was hardly heard from in the decades following the fall of Saigon. During the Gulf War, a few sporadic antiwar demonstrations did occur, but the American public overwhelmingly supported the American position.

Although the media hardly disappeared during the Gulf War, the military did place severe restrictions on the mobility of journalists. Earlier during the invasion of Grenada, reporters weren't even allowed on the island until it had been secured. Although journalists did go to Saudi Arabia shortly after the Iraqi invasion of Kuwait, during the Gulf War itself, a system of "pool reporting" allowed only a few to accompany troops. Believing that the media had somehow helped lose the Vietnam War, American officials wanted to avoid any such possibility in the Gulf.

Not so easily dampened was another legacy of the war: a deepening public cynicism about national leaders and institutions, including America's economic resilience. The so-called credibility gap, beginning under President John F. Kennedy, widening under President Lyndon Johnson, and becoming a gaping maw with President Richard Nixon's Watergate scandal, led many Americans simply not to believe what their leaders told them. And although the nation's economy seems to have rebounded from the "stagflation" of the 1970s, the economic drain of the war was certainly substantial.

Symbolic of this public distrust is the continuing prominence of the POW/MIA issue. In spite of consistent government denials that any American prisoners of war still are being held in Southeast Asia, as of 1992, public opinion polls indicate that roughly two-thirds of all Americans polled believe that such prisoners are alive.[12] A veritable cottage industry has grown up around the POW issue, conflating it with the fact that around two thousand Americans have been classified as Missing in Action (MIA) or Body not Recovered (BNR). The National League of Families, a lobbying group representing relatives of soldiers still considered missing, has been immensely effective in keeping the issue on the public agenda and probably helped delay American diplomatic recognition of communist Vietnam. And certainly the popularity of POW rescue films like *Rambo: First Blood, Part II* (1985) and *Missing in Action* (1984) illustrate Americans' fascination with the POW/MIA issue.

Obviously, a substantial number of Americans sincerely believe that some of their countrymen remain alive in Vietnam and that the Vietnamese government is dragging its heels in providing information about those missing in action. Many MIA family members feel this way. In spite of numerous reports of "sightings" of live Americans, however, as Arnold Isaacs points out, "none ever led to an actual prisoner, or to any convincing proof that there were (or ever had been) any prisoners to be found." Moreover, he argues that beyond any reasonable doubt, "the vast majority of MIAs had . . . been killed at the time they disappeared; that it was virtually inconceivable that any were still alive." Perhaps, as Isaacs concludes, many Americans have hung on to the myth of the missing so long precisely because they "desperately wanted to recover something we [had lost]" during that war.[13]

Those for whom the legacy of the Vietnam War has been most compelling are those who directly experienced it and its effects. Over 2,000,000 Americans saw military service in Vietnam between 1964 and 1975. Of those, 58,209 died, over 300,000 were wounded, around 2,000 are MIA/BNR, and roughly 750,000 have suffered from some form of Post–Traumatic Stress Disorder (PTSD). Millions of other Americans actively opposed the war, some suffering exile, prison terms, injury, and death for their beliefs. And hundreds of thousands of Vietnamese immigrated to the United States after the war. For people in these categories, the war's impact was immediate and long-lasting.

For many veterans, the war's most immediate legacy was a sense of dissonance when they returned to "the World." Because of the fixed tour of duty—thirteen months for Marines, one year for other military personnel—veterans came home singly rather than in large units as happened after World War II. The trip home was usually a rapid twenty-four- to thirty-six-hour flight rather than a more leisurely week or more by ship. There was little time or opportunity for bonding or reflection.

Although many veterans returned from Vietnam to understanding families and a grateful community and adjusted rather quickly to civilian life, a number of them felt they were met with either hostility or, more often, indifference on their return. Some reported being spit on by antiwar protestors. Frederick H. Giese from Arlington Heights, Illinois, recalls standing in line at a restaurant at the San Francisco Airport with family members who had come to meet him:

[T]his middle-aged lady walked up to me with a bowl of potato salad in her hand. She threw the salad smack in the middle of my chest and spat what she had in her mouth in my face. Then she proceeded to call me a "baby killer," "war monger" and a lot of other vile names.[14]

Probably more common was the experience of an anonymous veteran who participated in a support group formed by Boston psychiatrist Jonathan Shay. The veteran recalled a clear and powerful incident of what Shay refers to as the "social process of silencing the survivor." He describes a dinner given by his wife's parents shortly after he returned from Vietnam:

And after dinner we were all sitting in the living room and her father said, "So tell us what it was like." And I started to tell them, and I told them. And do you know within five minutes the room was empty. They were all gone except my wife. After that, I didn't tell anybody I had been in Vietnam.[15]

Perhaps as upsetting to veterans as either the disdain of antiwar advocates or the apathy of much of the public was the negative portrayal of veterans in popular culture in the 1960s and 1970s. Except for John Wayne's celebratory *Green Berets* (1968), during this period most films about Vietnam focused on the "crazed," violent vet who, like Robert DeNiro in *Taxi Driver* (1976), came unhinged because of the war. And countless television dramas in the 1970s featured a stock Vietnam vet who unleashed horrors on the landscape.

The culmination of veteran angst probably occurred in January 1981, when the American hostages held in Iran were released and came home to "an extravagant outpouring of sympathy and concern," in the words of Arnold Isaacs. Although many Vietnam veterans, like Ron Zaczek, did not begrudge the hostages their parade, nonetheless Zaczek couldn't help being "rankled": "I've never forgotten how it was for us [Vietnam War veterans]. Nothing seems to make up for that."[16] Former Army nurse Lily Lee Adams was more than just rankled at the hostages' reception; she was furious:

I remember seeing them [former hostages] getting into cars and seeing all the yellow ribbons. . . . Then in the middle of all this, I said: "Wait a minute. What the —— did they do? They sat around for four hundred and some odd days reading magazines, and I worked my ass off three hundred and sixty-five days saving lives."[17]

This nadir, however, might also have represented a turning point in the American attitude toward Vietnam veterans. Veteran Bobby Muller, head of the Vietnam Veterans of America (VVA), remembers that when the hostages were welcomed home with a ticker-tape parade in New York City, a number of people made unsolicited calls to the VVA office, indicating heartfelt support for veterans of the war.[18] And two years later, the Vietnam Veterans Memorial was dedicated, and the long-delayed process of reconciliation found its most important symbol.

The memorial was not built without considerable anguish and controversy. Spearheaded by veteran Jan Scruggs, the effort to build a memorial raised more than $5 million in private funds and convinced Congress to provide land between the Washington Monument and Lincoln Memorial for the project. The design finally chosen from over 1,400 entries was submitted by Maya Yin, a twenty-one-year-old Yale University architecture student. It was a stark, V-shaped black granite wall, which would contain the names of all Americans who died in the war in the chronological order of their deaths. A number of veterans and their supporters complained that the design was insufficiently heroic. (One called it "a black gash of shame."[19]) In response to the complaints, and in spite of Lin's objections, authorities commissioned a more traditional statue of three American soldiers near the Wall. In 1993 a bronze statue honoring women who had served in the war was installed.

Since the dedication ceremony opening the memorial on Veterans Day in 1982, the Wall has become one of the most frequently visited public spaces in Washington. Visitors there often leave mementos near the names of loved ones—letters, money, cans of beer, even childhood teddy bears. When people look at the names on the Wall, they see themselves reflected in the black granite, making all Americans a part of the war and its pain. Thus the Wall has become a powerful emotional symbol that has tended to draw veterans and nonveterans together.

Of course, all is not love and forgiveness still in the legacies of the war. The effects of Agent Orange and other pesticides remain in both the United

States and Vietnam. PTSD still afflicts thousands of veterans, and complaints against Veterans Administration hospitals for red tape and inferior patronizing treatment abound. For many Americans, especially veterans and immigrants from Southeast Asia, the war will never be over as long as communist governments exist in Vietnam, Laos, and Cambodia. And the war remains very much alive to thousands of family members of those still labeled missing in action.

Nonetheless, in addition to the power of the Wall, there have been other signs that the agony of the war is being replaced by reconciliation. Some films about the war, such as *84 Charlie Mopic* (1989), are providing a more realistic portrait of the combat experience (although some, such as *Platoon* [1986] paint a more ambiguous portrait). Moreover, immigrants from Southeast Asia seem to be adjusting more successfully to the American environment. Most antiwar activists who fled the country have received amnesty. Recent, and seemingly successful, American interventions in Haiti and Bosnia open the possibility for such small actions in the future (although the "ghosts" of Vietnam still faintly haunt policy in such areas, which to some Americans are far removed from vital U.S. security interests). And most important, reestablishment of American diplomatic relations with Vietnam on July 11, 1995, contains the possibility of the ultimate reconciliation—one between the two powers who fought for so long against each other.

But those who speak with hope about healing and peace and reconciliation always seem to come back to the Vietnam War Memorial. Arnold Isaacs, who served as a journalist in southeast Asia, ends his fine work on the legacies of the war with this telling personal story. While visiting the Wall in November 1993, Isaacs noticed a small scrap of paper lying almost exactly at the crease where the two wings meet, "under the names of the very last dead and the carved date 1975—as if whoever put it there had walked along and read all 58,183 names, in order, and then bent down to leave [a] message at the very end." The note, Isaacs points out, "was written in pencil. It said only: 'I'm sorry.' "[20]

NOTES

1. Arnold R. Isaacs, *Vietnam Shadows: The War, Its Ghosts, and Its Shadows* (Baltimore: Johns Hopkins University Press, 1997), p. 166.

2. Ibid., p. 191.

3. James S. Olson and Randy Roberts, *Where the Domino Fell: America and Vietnam, 1945–1995*, 2nd ed. (New York: St. Martin's Press, 1996), p. 274.

4. "Investment by Country," *Vietnam Business Journal*, November/December 1996, p. 16.

5. When I traveled to Vietnam in 1994, I was struck by the distinct lack of hostility toward the Americans in our group. I especially recall chatting with a Vietnamese desk clerk in a hotel bar in Dalat. When she found out I was an American, she wanted to talk about Melville, Hawthorne, and Hemingway. As I got up to leave, she went to her desk, brought out a plastic-covered copy of John F. Kennedy's *A Nation of Immigrants*, and asked me to sign it!

6. Isaacs, *Vietnam Shadows*, p. 181.

7. Ibid., p. 187.

8. Ibid., p. 188. As an example of the combination of openness and repression in Vietnam today, in late 1997, the Vietnamese government granted licenses to Internet providers. However, according to the *Daily Yomiuri*, a Japanese newspaper, "authorities are determined to prevent access to 'undesirable' information on the Net." Said one Vietnamese official, "We are prepared to protect Internet users from untrustworthy information." (*Daily Yomiuri*, December 3, 1997, World Wide Web http://www.vinsight.org/1997news/1203.htm).

9. George Donelson Moss, *Vietnam: An American Ordeal*, 2nd ed. (Englewood Cliffs, N.J.: Prentice-Hall, 1994), p. 409.

10. Lou Cannon, *President Reagan: The Role of a Lifetime* (New York: Simon & Schuster, 1991), p. 337.

11. Steve A. Yetiv, *The Persian Gulf Crisis* (Westport, Conn.: Greenwood Press, 1997), p. 133.

12. Isaacs, *Vietnam Shadows*, p. 104.

13. Ibid., pp. 104, 129, 136.

14. Bob Greene, *Homecoming: When Soldiers Returned from Vietnam* (New York: G. P. Putnam's Sons, 1989), p. 24. Greene, a *Chicago Tribune* columnist, collected hundreds of such "return" stories in letters from his readers. Though some vets did report literal spitting incidents, some others commented on cases of warm, affirming "welcome homes." Most said that the spitting issue was irrelevant: "[T]hey were made to feel small and unwanted in so many other ways that it felt like being spat upon" (p. 12).

15. Jonathan Shay, *Achilles in Vietnam: Combat Trauma and the Undoing of Character* (New York: Atheneum, 1994), p. xxii.

16. Isaacs, *Vietnam Shadows*, p. 23.

17. Keith Walker, ed., *A Piece of My Heart: The Stories of Twenty-Six American Women Who Served in Vietnam* (Novato, Calif.: Presidio, 1985), pp. 330–31.

18. Isaacs, *Vietnam Shadows*, p. 23.

19. Kelly Evans-Pfeifer, "Vietnam Veterans Memorial," in *Encyclopedia of the Vietnam War*, ed. Stanley I. Kutler (New York: Charles Scribner's Sons, 1996), p. 614.

20. Isaacs, *Vietnam Shadows*, p. 199.

Official photograph of Ho Chi Minh. Date unknown. Official U.S. Army photo, courtesy of National Archives

Members of the 101st Airborne Division waiting for departure to a combat operation in April 1966. Official U.S. Air Force photo, courtesy of National Archives

Members of the 5th Regiment, 1st Marines struggle through elephant grass in November 1968. Photo by Cpl. S. L. McKenzie II, courtesy of the National Archives

Rifleman from the 9th Regiment, 3rd Marines takes a break from the war sometime in 1968. Photo by PFC E. E. Hildreth, courtesy of the National Archives

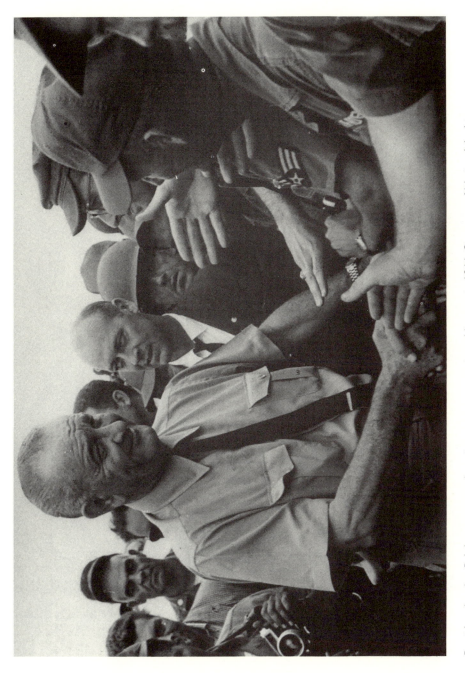

President Lyndon B. Johnson greets American troops on a trip to Vietnam in 1966. Courtesy of National Archives

General William Westmoreland congratulates troops of the First Cavalry Division in December 1966. Photo by PFC Freddie M. Duncan. Courtesy of National Archives

CBS News anchorman Walter Cronkite interviews a Marine battalion commander during the later stages of the Tet Offensive in Hue in February 1968. Official U.S. Marine Corps photo, courtesy of National Archives

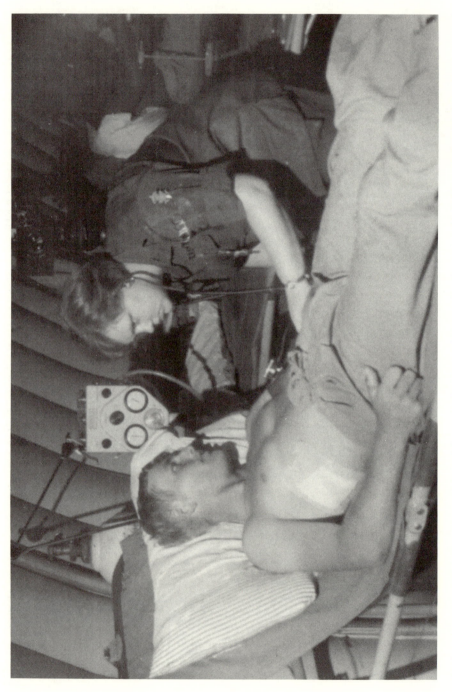

An American nurse ministers to a wounded soldier at the 2nd Surgical Hospital in September 1969. Photo by Ronald Delauria, courtesy of National Archives

March on Washington November 15. End the War. Get Out Now!

Stop the war!
Stop the war machine!
Stop the death machine!

November 13-15
March Against Death: A Vietnam Memorial.
Delegations from every state representing
American war dead and Vietnam
villages destroyed, walking in a 36 hour
single file procession from
Arlington National Cemetery to the Capitol.

November 15
Assemble: 9:00am, Mall area
just west of 3rd Street NW
March: begins at 11:00am
Rally and Concert: Continuous Rally
and Folk Rock Concert 1-5pm,
The Ellipse

November 16
continuing actions sponsored by
constituency groups.

For Information Contact:
New Mobilization Committee to End the War in Vietnam.
1029 Vermont Ave., NW, Suite 900, Wash., D.C. 20005
Phone (202) 737-8600

Advertisement for an anti-Vietnam War rally in November 1969. Courtesy of the Library of Congress

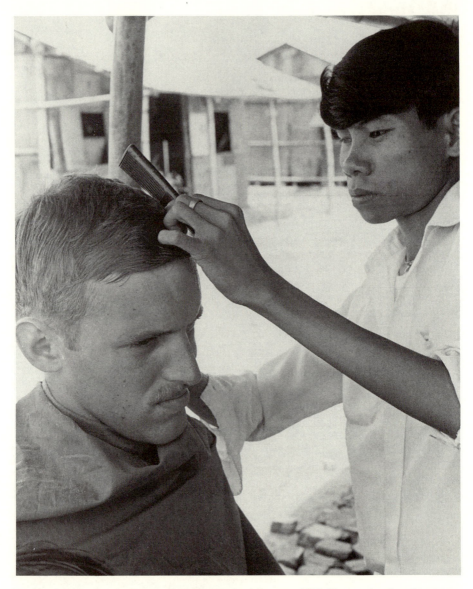

Lt. Jerry Waite gets a haircut on Go Noi Island in I Corps in 1970. Two weeks after this picture was taken, the "barber" was identified as a Vietcong soldier killed during an attack on the American installation. Courtesy of Jerry Waite

U.S. soldiers from the 101st Airborne Division teach Vietnamese children baseball during a goodwill visit to a village in January 1970. Photo by 2nd Lt. Roger I. Pinnell, courtesy of National Archives

Two marine officers pose with a Vietnamese woman jokingly "entered" in the 1969 Miss Universe contest. Photo by Sgt. John K. Mullins, courtesy of the National Archives

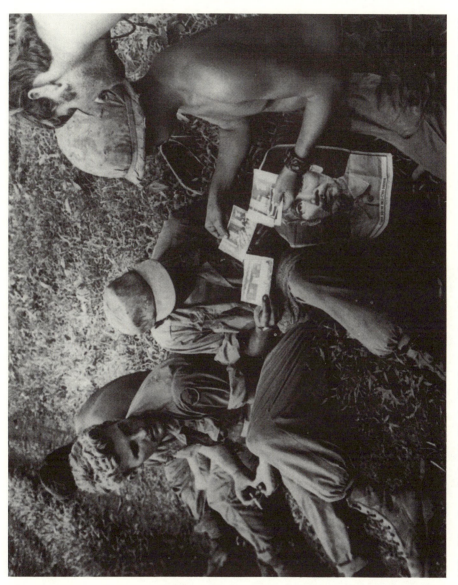

U.S. soldiers from the 1st Air Cavalry division examine pictures found in an enemy bunker on May 7, 1970. Official U.S. Army photo, courtesy of National Archives

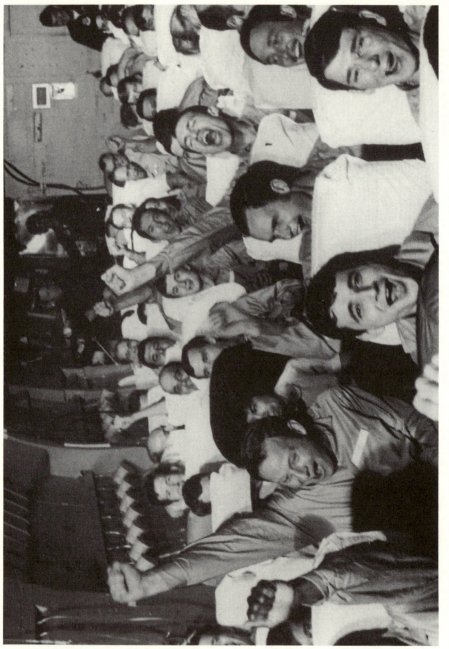

Former U.S. prisoners of war rejoice as their plane takes off from Hanoi in January 1973. Marine photograph, courtesy of the National Archives

Biographies: The Personalities Behind the War

Creighton W. Abrams (1914–1974)

Creighton Abrams, a general in the U.S. Army, was the commander of American forces in Vietnam from 1968 to 1972. He became Chief of Staff of the U.S. Army in 1972, a post he held until his death in 1974.

Born in Springfield, Massachusetts, on September 16, 1914, Abrams graduated from the U.S. Military Academy at West Point in 1936. He served under General George Patton in World War II, gaining a reputation as a first-rate combat officer. He was a staff officer in Washington during the early 1960s, and in 1967 President Lyndon Johnson appointed him deputy commander of U.S. forces under General William Westmoreland. In this role, he focused on modernizing the South Vietnamese army (ARVN).

He became commander of U.S. forces in 1968 when Westmoreland was named Chairman of the Joint Chiefs. Abrams' central task was to oversee President Richard Nixon's policy of Vietnamization. Thus, as the ARVN took over more of the fighting, America's role was largely limited to relatively small-scale operations rather than the massive search-and-destroy missions mounted under Westmoreland. Abrams also tried to stem a growing tide of low morale, drug use, and racial problems among American troops.

As Army Chief of Staff after the withdrawal of American troops in 1973, Abrams had the unenviable task of restoring morale and reorganizing a peacetime military force. His problems were compounded by the end of the draft and introduction of an all-volunteer army. He died in Washington, D.C., in 1974.

Viewed by his colleagues as a "soldier's soldier," the gruff, combative Abrams was described by one reporter as "an unmade bed smoking a cigar."[1] Yet he was probably one of the most subtle thinkers in the military, a deeply analytical man who loved classical music. He was underappreciated by the larger public, given the fact that he led American troops in Vietnam during a period when the war became increasingly unpopular. Abrams died on September 4, 1974.

Note

1. Quoted in K. E. Hamburger, "Abrams, Creighton," in *Encyclopedia of the Vietnam War*, ed. Stanley I. Kutler (New York: Charles Scribner's Sons, 1996), p. 2.

Joan Baez (1941–   )

Joan Baez is a major American folksinger who became part of the anti–Vietnam War movement in the mid-1960s. She was born in Staten Island, New York, on January 9, 1941. In the 1950s, a self-described "highly neurotic teenager . . . feeling very lonesome," she discovered the folk music scene at Harvard University, where her father was teaching physics.[1] By the early 1960s, she had become a popular folksinger, whose clear soprano voice made her especially adept at ballads. During this same period, she was politicized as she confronted racism on a tour of the South. She also sang at a rally during the Free Speech Movement at the University of California, Berkeley, in 1964.

By 1966 she had become a vocal opponent of the Vietnam War. In that year she refused to pay her federal income taxes as a protest against the war. In 1967 she married draft resister David Harris and was arrested for picketing at a draft induction center in Oakland, California. She continued her antiwar activities during the late 1960s and early 1970s. On June 22, 1973, for example, she helped organize a protest in Washington "in which 2,500 women and children linked hands around the Capitol, encircling the building."[2] Her antiwar activities culminated in December, 1973, when she happened to be in Hanoi, North Vietnam, delivering Christmas messages to American POW's during the massive U.S. bombing of the city. She saw this event as the height of American arrogance and destructiveness in the war.

Interestingly, after the communist victory in 1975, she spoke out against the oppression of Vietnamese and Cambodians by their respective communist governments, thus illustrating her firm commitment to freedom and nonviolence.

Notes

1. "Interview with Joan Baez," n.d., World Wide Web, http://interferenza.com/bcs/articles/baez.htm [,] p. 1.

2. Tom Wells, *The War Within: America's Battle Over Vietnam* (Berkeley: University of California Press, 1994), p. 550.

George Wildman Ball (1909–1964)

George Ball, a lawyer and public official, was Undersecretary of State from late 1961 until September 1966, when he resigned to return to private practice. In his official position under both Presidents Kennedy and Johnson, he was best known as a kind of gadfly, consistently opposing the escalation of American involvement in the Vietnam War.

Born in Des Moines, Iowa, on December 21, 1909, he received both undergraduate and law degrees from Northwestern University. Between 1933 and 1944, he alternated between private practice and public service in the federal government. In 1944 he served as director of the U.S. Strategic Bombing Survey, which concluded that strategic bombing of German cities and industrial plants did not serve to break the will of the civilian population of Germany during World War II. For the next fifteen years, he practiced law in Washington, D.C., when, in January 1961, President John F. Kennedy appointed him to the State Department as Undersecretary for Economic Affairs. Ten months later he became Undersecretary of State, the second-ranking official in the department.

During the Kennedy years, he opposed the introduction of American combat troops into Vietnam, arguing that a land war in Asia simply was not in America's national interest. He held much the same position during his years in the Johnson administration. He was especially outspoken in his opposition to the bombing campaign directed against North Vietnam beginning in early 1965 (Operation Rolling Thunder). His experience heading the Strategic Bombing Survey had convinced him that bombing would probably only strengthen the resolve of the North Vietnamese. President Johnson used Ball as a devil's advocate/sounding board, although he probably never seriously considered following Ball's advice.

Ball clearly preferred a diplomatic solution to the conflict. But by the fall of 1966, he was convinced that "once we were engaged in all-out war, diplomacy moved into the shadows." To Ball, the search for a strategy to bring military victory was like "the writhings of a decapitated chicken." Since "withdrawal [from Vietnam] had become a dirty word," Ball himself withdrew, stepping down from his post in September 1966.[1] He returned to private practice.

Ball reappeared briefly in government in an unofficial position during the early spring of 1968. President Johnson named him a member of the so-called Wise Men, a group of current and former advisors, called together to counsel LBJ on the war after the Tet Offensive. Unsurprisingly, Ball agreed with the views of former Secretary of State Dean Acheson that "we could . . . not achieve our objective [in Vietnam] through military means."[2] The fact that the majority of the group concurred probably helped prod Johnson toward a de-escalation of the war and the quest for serious negotiations. Ball spent the remainder of his life as a lawyer and investment counselor. He died on May 26, 1994.

Notes

1. George W. Ball, *The Past Has Another Pattern: Memoirs* (New York: W. W. Norton, 1982), p. 424.

2. Ibid., p. 408.

McGeorge Bundy (1919–1996)

McGeorge Bundy served as Special Assistant to the President for National Security from 1961 to 1966. In that post, he was one of several crucial advisors counseling Presidents John F. Kennedy and Lyndon B. Johnson on American policy in Vietnam.

Born on March 30, 1919, in Boston, Bundy graduated first in his class from Yale University. During World War II, he served in the Army, helping in logistical planning for the invasions of Sicily and France. After the war, he was a consultant to the Marshall Plan implementation group in the State Department and to the Council on Foreign Relations. He was appointed a lecturer at Harvard in 1949 and rose meteorically to the position of Dean of Arts and Sciences there by 1953.

Impressed by his intelligence and savvy, President Kennedy named Bundy Special Assistant for National Security in 1961. Although committed to a noncommunist South Vietnam, Bundy advised Kennedy not to deploy American combat troops there, hoping rather to rely on a strong democratic South Vietnam to carry the brunt of the battle against the insurgent communists. In early 1965 Bundy changed his mind about the level of American involvement. He was in South Vietnam on February 7, when he learned of a major Vietcong attack on American barracks at Pleiku, leaving 8 Marines dead and 126 wounded. On his return to Washington, he argued that the Pleiku assault had " 'produced a practical point of departure' for a new, more assertive U.S. military policy in Vietnam."[1] As a result of this type of advice, President Johnson approved a sustained bombing campaign against North

Vietnam and the subsequent introduction of American combat troops. Bundy supported escalation until 1966, when growing doubts about the war led to his resignation.

He became head of the Ford Foundation in 1966 and in 1968 served with former and present advisors as part of the "Wise Men," whom Johnson asked for counsel after the 1968 Tet Offensive. Bundy joined with the majority of this group in urging de-escalation and negotiations to end the war. He stayed with the Ford Foundation until 1979, when he joined the faculty at New York University as a Professor of History. He joined the Carnegie Corporation of New York in 1990. When he died of a heart attack on September 16, 1996, he "was working on a book about the war whose main message was that Vietnam was a terrible mistake."[2]

Notes

1. Robert D. Schulzinger, *A Time for War: The United States and Vietnam, 1941–1975* (New York: Oxford University Press, 1997), p. 172.

2. James C. Thompson, Jr., "A Memory of McGeorge Bundy," *New York Times*, September 22, 1996, sec. 4, p. 3.

William L. Calley, Jr. (1943–   )

William Calley was a second lieutenant in the 23rd Division (Americal) of the U.S. Army from 1967 to 1969. He commanded a platoon involved in the infamous My Lai Massacre, in which American soldiers killed and wounded several hundred Vietnamese civilians. Calley was the only American convicted of a crime in the incident.

Calley was born in Miami, Florida, on June 8, 1943. After flunking out of junior college and working at a series of temporary jobs, he enlisted in the Army and arrived in Vietnam in December 1967. On the morning of March 16, 1968, his platoon was part of a sweep of hamlets in Quang Ngai Province, including one labeled My Lai 4 on American military maps. The troops were told to expect Vietcong in the hamlet. Over the next few hours, Calley and many men in his platoon killed and wounded several hundred Vietnamese civilians, sometimes herding them into groups before opening fire.

The killings were covered up until April 1969 when Ron Ridenour, a soldier who had heard stories of the incident, wrote public officials demanding an investigation. In the next few months, Calley, his commanding officer (Ernest Medina), and several of his men were arrested and charged with premeditated murder. In his trial, Calley claimed that Medina had ordered him "to destroy and kill everything in the hamlet . . . because 'they were all enemy.' "[1] Medina denied the allegation, and Calley was ultimately convicted of murder and sentenced to life imprisonment.

The Calley case led to a public outcry, with many supporters of the war defending him for doing his best in a nasty war in which troops often could not distinguish friends from enemies. Opponents of the war thought that although guilty, Calley was a scapegoat and that others involved in the incident and its cover-up should be brought to trial. Georgia Governor Jimmy Carter, a defender of Calley, went so far as to organize an " 'American Fighting Men's Day,' exhorting the citizens of Georgia to drive with their headlights on and 'honor the flag as [Calley] had done.' "[2]

Calley served only a few years of his sentence, receiving a full parole in 1975, after President Nixon had earlier reduced his sentence. William Calley lives in Columbus, Georgia, where he works in his father-in-law's jewelry store.

William Calley and the My Lai Massacre were enormously controversial at the time and remain so. Many, like Colonel Harry Summers, see the atrocities committed at My Lai as an aberration. For Summers, "the overwhelming majority of American combat soldiers . . . risked their lives to protect—not harm the men, women, and children of South Vietnam."[3] To others, like historian Christian Appy, the My Lai massacre, "though exceptional in its scale . . . reflected the patterns and psychology of brutalization that were at the heart of American military operations in South Vietnam."[4] Although Summers's view is probably closer to the truth than Appy's, the actions of William Calley in Vietnam certainly represent the horror and divisiveness of the conflict.

Notes

1. Sally Smith, "Calley, William Laws, Jr.," in *Dictionary of the Vietnam War*, ed. James Olson (New York: Peter Bedrick Books, 1988), p. 61.

2. Michael Bilton and Kevin Sim, *Four Hours at My Lai* (New York: Viking, 1992), p. 340.

3. Harry G. Summers, Jr., *Vietnam War Almanac* (New York: Facts on File, 1985), p. 258.

4. Christian G. Appy, *Working Man's War: American Combat Soldiers and Vietnam* (Chapel Hill: University of North Carolina Press, 1993), p. 277.

Ngo Dinh Diem (1901–1963)

Ngo Dinh Diem was prime minister of the Republic of Vietnam (South Vietnam) from 1954 to 1955 and its president from 1955 to 1963. He was a fiercely anticommunist nationalist who hated both the French and the communist North Vietnamese and communist insurgents in the south. He provided a degree of stability in South Vietnam from 1954 to 1961, but in his last two years as president, he became increasingly isolated and authoritarian.

Diem was born on January 3, 1901, and christened a Catholic in the old imperial capital of Hue. The son of an advisor to Emperor Thanh Thai, Diem was both well connected and quite intelligent. After completing the civil service curriculum at a French college in Hanoi, Diem worked in the national administration, rising to the position of Minister of the Interior in 1933. He resigned that post when he became convinced that France would never liberalize its administrative structure. His anti-French passion actually led him to negotiate, unsuccessfully, with the Japanese to become prime minister of a Vietnamese client state in 1945. He was also fiercely anticommunist, a position that intensified when he became convinced that Vietminh killed his brother. Thus, he refused Ho Chi Minh's offer in 1945 to become interior minister in the newly independent Democratic Republic of Vietnam.

Between 1951 and 1953, Diem, a devout Catholic, lived and studied at Maryknoll Seminary in the United States. Several important American Catholic political and religious figures, like Senators John F. Kennedy and Mike Mansfield and Francis Cardinal Spellman, became Diem's friends and patrons, promoting his cause of anticommunist nationalism in Washington. When the French surrendered at Dienbienphu in May 1954, Diem became Emperor Bao Dai's prime minister, in essence ruling over the part of Vietnam south of the 17th parallel. In the confusing days after the Geneva Accords, few American observers gave Diem much of a chance to create order out of the chaos existing in South Vietnam. But with the counsel of CIA operative Edward Lansdale, some well-placed bribes, and a small but loyal military force, Diem was able to neutralize his major political opponents. In 1955, in a clearly rigged election in which Diem received over 98 percent of the vote, he defeated Bao Dai for the presidency of the Republic of Vietnam. With the blessing of the administration of U.S. President Dwight Eisenhower, Diem also refused to take part in the reunification election mandated in the Geneva Accords.

During the next four years, Diem consolidated his power in South Vietnam. Deeply suspicious of any opposition, he carefully picked relatives and friends, many of whom were fiercely anticommunist Catholic refugees from North Vietnam, for major and minor government posts. Especially influential were his brother, Ngo Dinh Nhu, and his brother's wife, Madame Nhu, both of whom became deeply involved in local political intrigues. Diem's attempts to root out communist influence in the countryside included the appointment of political cronies as village leaders and a tendency to reward large landholders. His "agroville" program tried to resettle recalcitrant peasants in "new" secure villages.

These policies tended to alienate many rural Vietnamese and may well have helped local recruiters for the procommunist Vietcong who were working to undermine Diem's government. By 1960 these forces had coalesced into the National Liberation Front (NLF), which, with the support of North Vietnam, launched a guerrilla war against South Vietnam. The United States increased military aid to South Vietnam as NLF forces intensified their efforts. Diem became increasingly isolated and sensitive to opposition. He ordered his generals to be cautious, much to the dismay of gung-ho American advisors, who wanted to wage offensive war against the Vietcong. In fact, many of the South's crack troops found themselves protecting Diem against potential coups.

Anti-Diem sentiment came to a head in the summer of 1963 when a number of Buddhists objected to government restrictions on religious demonstrations. Although there was no doubt some communist infiltration of the Buddhist movement, it was largely a sincere protest against perceived oppression. The symbolic apogee of the Buddhist movement came on June 11, 1963, when a bonze (monk) publically burned himself to death as a protest against the Diem government. In demonstrations that followed, a number of protesters were killed, wounded, and arrested, and Diem's stock dropped precipitously in American political circles. By the fall of 1963, President John F. Kennedy indicated that he would not oppose a coup against Diem. On November 1, 1963, Diem and his brother Nhu were overthrown and murdered.

Though some, including then Vice President Lyndon Johnson, defended Diem as the best alternative in South Vietnam, most historians have concluded that the Diem government was both excessively authoritarian and inefficient in carrying out the war. As historian Robert Schulzinger points out, "America wanted a popular government in Saigon, one which could foster nationalist, anticommunist fervor on the part of the largely rural and Buddhist population."[1] This Ngo Dinh Diem could not provide.

Note

1. Robert D. Schulzinger, *A Time for War: The United States and Vietnam, 1941–1975* (New York: Oxford University Press, 1997), p. 119.

Dwight David Eisenhower (1890–1969)

Dwight David Eisenhower was president of the United States from 1953 to 1961. During his administration, the United States made a commitment to support the existence of an anticommunist government in South Vietnam through financial and military aid, including a small number of American military advisors.

Born in Denison, Texas, on October 14, 1890, Eisenhower graduated from the United States Military Academy and commanded the Allied invasion of Europe during World War II. After the war, he served as Army Chief of Staff, president of Columbia University, and commander of the military forces under the North Atlantic Treaty Organization (NATO). In 1952 he was elected president of the United States as a Republican.

Eisenhower's views on foreign policy involved a mix of firm anticommunism and a deep desire to avoid unnecessary military conflict, especially a nuclear confrontation. Thus, from the outset of his presidency, he was committed to helping the French prevent a victory by the communist Ho Chi Minh. By the end of the French War in Indochina, the United States was paying for roughly 75 percent of the French effort. In 1954, when the French were in danger of losing the Battle of Dienbienphu, Eisenhower considered deeper American intervention, but he was reluctant to commit American combat troops or air power. Thus, he set conditions for intervention that he probably knew could not be met, including congressional approval, British participation, and a French willingness ultimately to grant independence to Indochinese states. Knowing that these conditions would not be met, he could then maintain America's generally anticolonial image.

By summer 1954 Eisenhower was resigned to the fact that the northern half of Vietnam would fall under communist control, but he was determined that the South would stay noncommunist. Thus, partly as a result of the urging of Secretary of State John Foster Dulles, who favored building anticommunist coalitions, the Eisenhower administration created the Southeast Asia Treaty Organization (SEATO), designed in part to provide military protection to South Vietnam. He also supported the efforts of Ngo Dinh Diem, a fiercely anticommunist nationalist, to establish a stable government in the South. Furthermore, Eisenhower agreed with Diem's rejection of reunification elections in 1956, fearing a communist victory. Although the American president was often frustrated with the failure of his South Vietnamese counterpart to implement meaningful economic and political reform, Eisenhower nonetheless saw Diem as America's best hope for a noncommunist South Vietnam. To assure Diem's success, the Eisenhower administration approved substantial American economic, military, and technical aid to South Vietnam.

After leaving office in 1961, Eisenhower retired to his farm in Gettysburg, Pennsylvania. He was consistently a hawk on the war who "grew increasingly disenchanted by [President Lyndon Johnson's] failure to 'swamp the enemy with overwhelming force.' "[1] Eisenhower died in Gettysburg on March 28, 1969.

Although Vietnam was "essentially a second-echelon issue" for Eisenhower, especially in his second administration, his steadfast support of an anticommunist South Vietnam confirmed and broadened President Harry Truman's containment policy in the area.[2] Moreover, in the most thorough study of Eisenhower and Vietnam, historian David Anderson concludes that Eisenhower's policy in Vietnam "oversimplified and over committed." By fostering excessive dependence on the United States, Eisenhower made increasingly problematic the possibility of a truly independent anticommunist South Vietnam.[3]

Notes

1. Leo P. Ribuffo, "Eisenhower, Dwight D.," in *Encyclopedia of the Vietnam War*, ed. Stanley I. Kutler (New York: Charles Scribner's Sons, 1996), p. 189.

2. David L. Anderson, *Trapped by Success: The Eisenhower Administration and Vietnam, 1953–61* (New York: Columbia University Press, 1991), p. 151.

3. Ibid., p. 208.

J. William Fulbright (1905–1995)

J. William Fulbright was a major figure in the United States Senate, where he represented Arkansas from 1945 to 1975. From the mid-1960s until the end of the Vietnam War, he became one of the leading "establishment" critics of the war, arguing that it illustrated a dangerous American "arrogance of power."[1] His stand against the war cost him a good deal of political support and the friendship of President Lyndon Johnson.

William Fulbright was born in Sumner, Missouri, on April 9, 1905. After graduating from the University of Arkansas and George Washington University Law School, he taught law at the two institutions, becoming president of the University of Arkansas in 1939. After serving in Congress from 1942 to 1944, he was elected to the U.S. Senate from Arkansas, an office he held until 1975.

Fulbright supported American involvement in Vietnam during the 1950s and early 1960s. As Chairman of the Senate Foreign Relations Committee, he helped move the Gulf of Tonkin Resolution rapidly through the Senate. Although he admitted later that "he should have been more critical and more skeptical," at the time he did not want to oppose his friend, Lyndon Johnson, and indirectly help Republican presidential nominee Barry Goldwater.[2]

By mid-1965, however, Fulbright began to worry that Johnson's policy of escalation might well lead to worse relations with the Soviet Union and possibly war with the Peoples Republic of China. In early 1966, the Senate Foreign Relations Committee started hearings on the war, featuring the testimony of such moderate opponents of escalation as George Kennan. The Senator's book, *The Arrogance of Power* (1967), helped crystalize his thoughts, as he wrote about the impossibility as well as the hubris inherent in America's attempting to be the world's policeman.

He continued his criticism of the war during the presidency of Richard Nixon, arguing strenuously against both Vietnamization and the 1970 incursion into Cambodia. He also supported the 1973 congressional resolution calling for the end of American bombing in Cambodia and was instrumental in shepherding the War Powers Resolution (1973) through the Senate, over the veto of President Nixon.

Defeated in the Arkansas Democratic senatorial primary in 1974, Fulbright stayed in Washington, D.C., to practice law. He died there on February 9, 1995.

Fulbright's opposition to the war was always couched in terms of American self-interest. He came to believe that whatever might be accomplished in Vietnam by the war, it was devastating the nation: "corrupting democratic values at home, undermining the Great Society, and endangering world peace." He came to the position, finally, that "a sound foreign policy" must be grounded in one central principle: that it protect "the domestic liberties and the well-being of the American people."[3] It was precisely this test that the Vietnam War failed.

Notes

1. William Fulbright, *The Arrogance of Power* (New York: Random House, 1966), passim.

2. William C. Berman, *William Fulbright and the Vietnam War: The Dissent of a Political Realist* (Kent, Ohio: Kent State University Press, 1988), p. 25.

3. William C. Berman, "Fulbright, William J.," in *Encyclopedia of the Vietnam War*, ed. Stanley I. Kutler (New York: Charles Scribner's Sons, 1996), pp. 203, 204.

Vo Nguyen Giap (1911–)

General Vo Nguyen Giap was commander of the People's Army of Vietnam (PAVN), known to the Americans as the North Vietnamese army (NVA) during the Vietnam War. He was also a member of the Communist Party (Lao Dong) Politburo from 1951 to 1976 and Minister of National Defense from 1946 to 1980.

Giap was born in Quan Binh province on August 25, 1911, to a profoundly anti-French family. He became an ardent communist in 1926 after reading *Colonialism on Trial* by Nguyen Ai Quoc (Ho Chi Minh). In 1933 he read law at the University of Hanoi, where he continued his study of communist writers. After the French outlawed the Communist party in 1939, Giap went to China where he became one of Ho Chi Minh's close friends and deputies.

Ho appointed Giap to head the military wing of the Vietnam Independence League (Vietminh) in its struggles against the Japanese and then the French. He is probably most famous for his leadership in the Vietminh victory over the French at Dienbienphu in spring 1954. The French assumed that the Vietminh could never move sufficient artillery to threaten the French strong points at Dienbienphu. Giap showed extraordinary dedication and logistical skill by inspiring his forces to move artillery and supplies across the mountain passes to hills surrounding the French fortress. Although he lost many soldiers in mass attacks, his ultimate plan of artillery bombardments and slow advance through trench building led to the French defeat.

The war in the South after 1954 was more complicated. From 1954 to 1959, Giap generally favored the Soviet model of building strength in North Vietnam and not engaging in military activity in the South. But by 1959, communist guerrilla forces in South Vietnam and their supporters in the Politburo in the North were pleading for a more interventionist policy, including increased military assistance from the North. As Giap's latest biographer, Cecil Currey, notes, "Giap, despite his own misgivings, was forced into a position where he had to provide more active help to the South."[1] This increased communist activity elicited a growing American response, as both sides escalated militarily.

Giap preferred a strategy of guerrilla warfare and expansion of the communist political base in the South, especially after North Vietnamese troops were defeated in the battle of the Ia Drang Valley in 1965. In the mid-1960s, however, Ho opted for a more conventional, aggressive warfare, as urged by Giap's chief rival, Nguyen Chi Thanh. After the North Vietnamese suffered several major defeats using Thanh's strategy, and the death of Thanh in 1967, Giap regained favor in Hanoi. He planned a major guerrilla assault throughout South Vietnam for early 1968, hoping for a general uprising. Even though his "people's offensive" during Tet 1968 failed militarily, the psychological effects in the United States were ultimately devastating to the U.S. cause. From 1969 to 1972, Giap successfully directed small-scale guerrilla warfare against American and ARVN forces. The Easter Offensive, his conventional attack in northern South Vietnam in early 1972, failed largely because of massive American air power. Giap was replaced as commander of North Vietnamese military forces in 1973, probably for reasons of health. He remains an immensely popular war hero in Vietnam.

Some students of military affairs think Giap's reputation as a military leader is exaggerated. Colonel Harry Summers, Jr., for example, focuses on Giap's military failures at the Ia Drang, during Tet 1968, and in the 1972 conventional attacks.[2] Cecil Currey, however, sees Giap as a master strategist, tactician, and logistics expert. His great achievement was to combine the political and the military, convincing millions of Vietnamese peasants to support his cause. As Giap himself argued, "We hold that our war strategy does not embrace purely military affairs. . . . War must be a comprehensive and combined strategy. The political goals are basic. The army must not only fight but educate the masses."[3] By implementing this strategy and by patiently outlasting his enemies, Giap's forces emerged victorious in what Vietnamese call the French War and the American War in Vietnam.

Notes

1. Cecil B. Currey, *Victory at Any Cost: The Genius of Viet Nam's Gen. Vo Nguyen Giap* (Washington, D.C.: Brassey's, Inc., 1997), p. 235.

2. Harry G. Summers, Jr., *Vietnam War Almanac* (New York: Facts on File, 1985), p. 179.

3. Currey, *Victory at Any Cost*, p. 320.

Abbie Hoffman (1936–1989)

Abbie Hoffman was one of the most prominent figures in the American anti-Vietnam War movement in the 1960s and early 1970s. He is probably most famous for organizing and participating in a major antiwar demonstration at the Chicago Democratic Convention in 1968.

Born Abbott Hoffman in Worcester, Massachusetts, on November 30, 1936, Hoffman received a B.A. from Brandeis University and a masters at the University of California, Berkeley. After some involvement in the black civil rights struggle in the early 1960s, he became increasingly active in opposing the Vietnam War. His radicalism always combined elements of serious protest and manically comic guerrilla theater. On one occasion, for example, he was part of a group who threw dollar bills on the floor of the New York Stock Exchange, delighting as frenetic traders scrambled after the cash. He was also known to attempt publicly to exorcise the Pentagon!

In 1968 Hoffman, along with fellow radicals Jerry Rubin, Ed Sanders, and Paul Krassner, formed the "Yippie Party," designed as a semiserious attempt to protest against both the war and repression in American society. After overseeing the nomination of a pig named Pigasus for president in 1968, Hoffman joined thousands of others to stage a mass demonstration at the Democratic Convention in Chicago. He was arrested, and along with seven others, charged with conspiring to disrupt the convention. After a lengthy and highly visible trial in 1969, the members of the so-called Chicago 8 were acquitted. For the next four years, Hoffman wrote and became part of the college lecture circuit, continuing to speak out against the war. Arrested for selling cocaine in 1973, he "went underground" for the next seven years. In 1980 he turned himself in and was sentenced to participate in a work-release program. After completing his sentence, he protested against what he saw as evils in American society, including CIA recruitment on campus. Increasingly suffering bouts of depression in the late 1980s, Hoffman died on April 12, 1989, in Solebury, Pennsylvania. The coroner concluded that suicide by drug overdose was the cause of death.

Hoffman's antiwar activity, especially his use of theatrical methods to bring attention to antiwar protests, garnered abundant publicity, much of it negative. Because he was seen by many Americans as quite simply loony, even dangerous, some have argued that his approach to opposing the war might well have alienated more people than the war itself did. Hoffman thought he was melding together political and cultural radicalism. As he once phrased it, "A semi-freak among the love children, I was determined to bring the hippie movement into a broader protest."[1] At the very least, as a kind of lapdog of the Left, he added a bit of puckish black humor to otherwise grim and dirty business.

Note

1. John T. McQuiston, "Abbie Hoffman, Antiwar Activist and Puckish Protestor, Dies at 52," *New York Times*, April 13, 1989, sec. B, p. 13.

Lyndon Baines Johnson (1908–1973)

Lyndon Johnson was President John F. Kennedy's vice president from 1961 to 1963 and served as president of the United States from 1963 to 1969. As president, he was responsible for the massive escalation of America's role in the Vietnam War, introducing American combat troops and approving a bombing campaign against North Vietnam.

Born in the hill country of Texas on August 27, 1908, Johnson first entered public service in the 1930s as an assistant to Richard M. Kleberg, a Democratic congressman from Texas. After he served as the director of the National Youth Administration in Texas, Johnson's political career blossomed. He successively was elected to the House of Representatives in 1938 and the Senate in 1948. In 1953 he became Senate Minority Leader, and two years later, Majority Leader when the Democrats regained control of the Senate.

His first experience with Vietnam came in 1954, when, as Senate Minority Leader, he advised President Dwight D. Eisenhower not to intervene militarily in Vietnam to help the French at Dienbienphu unless such intervention was supported by America's allies and the French offered independence to Vietnam. Ironically, when the communists took control of the northern part of the country, he castigated Eisenhower, claiming that "American foreign policy [had] never in all its history suffered such a stunning reversal."[1]

As vice president, Johnson traveled to Vietnam in 1961, at Kennedy's behest, to assure South Vietnamese President Diem of continuing American support. Publicly he called Diem the "George Washington, the Father of your country," but privately he simply noted that Diem was "the only boy we got out there."[2] Because he was generally out of the Kennedy administration's loop in foreign policy matters, Johnson seldom was asked his opinion of the war. He did attend a meeting of Kennedy advisors on August 31, 1963, in which he spoke out against the coup that ultimately toppled the Diem government, although he offered no alternative to Diem.

With the assassination of President Kennedy on November 22, 1963, Lyndon Johnson became the thirty-sixth president of the United States. He was firmly committed to carrying out the Kennedy program in Vietnam while enlarging it at home. And when he won a landslide election victory over Republican Barry Goldwater in 1964, he could be president in his own right. After his election, he believed that Kennedy's strategy of money, weapons, and advisors was simply not getting the job done in Vietnam. Thus, Johnson gradually escalated American involvement from a few thousand military advisors to bombing attacks on North Vietnam to the introduction of American combat troops, whose numbers ultimately topped 540,000.

With growing opposition to the war at home, the psychological impact of the Tet Offensive, and increasing signs that the war had become a stalemate, Johnson chose not to run for president in 1968. In 1969 he retired to his Texas ranch, where he died on January 22, 1973, three days before the signing of the Paris Accords, ending American military involvement in the war.

Johnson's Vietnam policy has been pilloried by critics from all parts of the political spectrum. Antiwar advocates screamed, "Hey, hey, LBJ, how many kids did you kill today," likening the president to a war criminal. Conservative revisionists have blamed Johnson for losing the war through a combination of micromanagement and failure to exploit the full arsenal of American military might. Even middle-of-the-road liberals have attacked his strategy for focusing excessively on military solutions and not enough on political ones.

From the president's own perspective, the conflict in Vietnam was like a nightmare from which he could not awake. He was absolutely convinced that America could not "run" from its commitments to Vietnam. Almost all of his advisors said so. As a member of the World War II generation, he deeply feared the message that capitulation would send out, that he would be like British Prime Minister Neville Chamberlain appeasing the Germans at Munich in 1938: He'd "be giving a big fat reward to aggression." Johnson seemed to care little for Vietnam itself—indeed, he privately referred to it as a "little piss-ant country."[3] But it was a crucial symbol of American credibility. Losing in Vietnam would encourage communists in more strategically important places. Yet Johnson also feared that a total American commitment could lead to the outbreak of a general war, a risk he was unwilling to take in a world bristling with nuclear weapons. As a fervent New Deal liberal, finally, Johnson had some rather naive hopes that he could actually convince Ho Chi Minh to quit the war and accept American largesse to rebuild the nation. As he suggested in his speech at Johns Hopkins University in April 1965, with American help, the Mekong River could become another TVA.

As with all nightmares, there was a darker side to this one. Underlying Johnson's geopolitical concerns were more intensely personal ones. He feared for his own political life should he "lose" Vietnam the way President Harry Truman allegedly "lost" China to communism. Oddly, he also feared Robert Kennedy's wrath—that the dead president's brother would tell "everyone that I had betrayed John Kennedy's commitment. . . . That I was a coward. An unmanly man. A man without a spine. Oh, I could see it coming alright."[4] This strange combination of motives, then, helps define the life of the man perhaps most responsible for America's longest war.

Notes

1. Jeff Shesol, *Mutual Contempt: Lyndon Johnson, Robert Kennedy, and the Feud That Defined a Decade* (New York: Norton, 1997), p. 259.

2. James S. Olson and Randy Roberts, *Where the Domino Fell: America and Vietnam, 1945–1995*, 2nd ed. (New York: St. Martin's Press, 1996), p. 84.

3. Shesol, *Mutual Contempt*, p. 261.

4. Ibid.

John F. Kennedy (1917–1963)

John F. Kennedy was president of the United States from 1961 to 1963. Under his leadership, the United States significantly broadened and deepened its economic and military commitment to South Vietnam in an effort to stem the communist insurgency there. Although he did not authorize bombing North Vietnam or the introduction of American combat troops, Kennedy was a staunch defender of America's containment policy as applied to southeast Asia. Indeed, he argued that if South Vietnam fell to communism, the

United States would suffer "a severe blow to [its] worldwide prestige and credibility."[1]

John F. Kennedy was born in Brookline, Massachusetts, on May 29, 1917, into a wealthy and influential Catholic family. His millionaire father, Joseph Kennedy, was Chairman of the Security and Exchange Commission and Ambassador to Great Britain in the 1930s. "Joe" Kennedy used his wealth and contacts to smooth the way for his children politically. John, his second son, graduated from Harvard in 1940 and served in the Navy during World War II. He was elected to Congress from Massachusetts in 1946 and to the U.S. Senate in 1962. He was elected president in 1960.

Kennedy's interest in Vietnam began in the 1950s when as a senator he urged President Eisenhower to support an anticommunist South Vietnam, calling it "the cornerstone of the free world in Asia."[2] As a candidate for president, he said virtually nothing about southeast Asia but certainly argued that America had lost power and prestige under the Eisenhower administration. His inaugural address clearly trumpeted America's determination to stand up to communist threats. He promised that the United States would "pay any price, bear any burden, meet any hardship, support any friend, oppose any foe to assure the survival and the success of liberty."[3] Shortly after that stirring speech, the new president was reading a report on Vietnam from General Edward Lansdale, which prompted Kennedy to say to his advisor Walt Rostow, "This is the worst one we've got, isn't it?"[4]

Crises involving Cuba, Berlin, and Laos, however, captured most of Kennedy's attention during the first two years of his administration. But Vietnam remained a concern. The president sought to use American power to stop the communist insurgency without committing American combat troops. Kennedy was especially enamored of the concept of counterinsurgency warfare. Thus, he pushed for the development of U.S. Special Forces, known as "Green Berets," and ordered a number of such units sent to Vietnam to advise the South Vietnamese army. Indeed, Kennedy's basic strategy was to increase the number of American advisors and the amount of military aid but to rely on South Vietnamese to do the fighting.

That strategy ran afoul of growing discontent with the government of South Vietnamese President Ngo Dinh Diem. His authoritarian rule alienated important segments of the population, especially many Buddhists. A combination of Diem's harsh responses to antigovernment demonstrations and the growing strength of the communist insurgency convinced many in the Kennedy administration that the war could not be prosecuted successfully under the Diem regime. After considerable waffling, Kennedy ultimately indicated that the United States would not try to prevent a coup against Diem. Anti-Diem generals took this as a green light and launched a successful revolt on November 1, 1963. The deaths of Diem and his brother Ngo Dinh Nhu apparently stunned Kennedy, as American policy would face the challenges of a new and untested government in South Vietnam.

Of course, Kennedy would not live to respond to those challenges. His death at the hands of an assassin on November 22, 1963, has left a number of unanswered questions about his Vietnam policy, most notably his intentions about America's continued commitment there. Some, like historian John Newman, are convinced that Kennedy saw American involvement in Vietnam as a mistake and planned to terminate that commitment after the 1964 presidential election. (In his *JFK*, filmmaker Oliver Stone fantasized that this determination led to Kennedy's assassination on the orders of American military and intelligence leaders who wanted deeper American involvement in the war.) There is some evidence that the president was becoming increasingly skeptical about American policy in Vietnam. He did call for a small reduction in the number of American advisors there and apparently told some of his own advisors that he wanted to pull out all American troops after the election. More concretely, on October 4, 1963, Maxwell Taylor, Chairman of the Joint Chiefs of Staff, drafted an important discussion paper for consideration by the Chiefs. In it he ordered that "[a]ll planning will be directed toward preparing RVN (South Vietnam) forces for the withdrawal of all U.S. special assistance units and personnel by the end of calendar year 1965."[5] Unfortunately, there is no public record of the Chiefs' reaction. Nonetheless, there is still no evidence that John Kennedy ever changed his mind about the importance of keeping South Vietnam noncommunist. As historian Robert Schulzinger notes, "Throughout his presidency . . . [Kennedy] perceived the stakes in Vietnam as high and growing."[6] In all likelihood, had he lived and served a second term, John Kennedy would have pursued much the same policy that his successor did.

Notes

1. Robert J. McMahon, "Kennedy, John F.," in *Encyclopedia of the Vietnam War*, ed. Stanley I. Kutler (New York: Charles Scribner's Sons, 1996), p. 259.

2. Ibid.

3. John F. Kennedy, "Inaugural Address," *Congressional Record*, 87th Congress, 1st Session, Vol. 107, Part 1 (Washington, D.C.: Government Printing Office, 1961), p. 1012.

4. John Newman, *JFK and Vietnam: Deception, Intrigue, and the Struggle for Power* (New York: Warner Books, 1992), p. 3.

5. "Document Reopens Debate on JFK's Vietnam Plans," CNN Interactive, http://www.cnn.com/us/971222/vietnam/kennedy.ap/index.html [.]

6. Robert Schulzinger, *A Time for War: The United States and Vietnam, 1941–1975* (New York: Oxford University Press, 1997), p. 123.

Edward G. Lansdale (1908–1987)

Edward Lansdale was a general in the United States Air Force who served in and advised about Vietnam in various official and unofficial capacities, including that of operative for the Central Intelligence Agency and a Special Assistant to the U.S. Ambassador to South Vietnam.

Born in Detroit, Michigan, on February 6, 1908, Lansdale graduated from the University of California, after which he worked for an advertising agency in San Francisco. During World War II, he served in the Office of Strategic Services. He joined the Central Intelligence Agency in 1947, and after successfully helping thwart a communist-led rebellion in the Philippines, he became a CIA operative in Saigon in 1954. After the signing of the Geneva Accords in July 1954, which allowed for the movement of population between the northern and southern parts of Vietnam, Lansdale was authorized to carry out both propaganda and sabotage initiatives in the North. For example, he started rumors of deals by Ho Chi Minh that would allow raping and pillaging Chinese troops back into Vietnam; at the same time, his agents tried to contaminate the oil supply in Hanoi and surrounding areas. Ultimately, a million northerners, many of them Catholics, trekked south between 1954 and 1955, forming a major part of the political strength of South Vietnamese leader and friend of Edward Lansdale, Ngo Dinh Diem.

Acting on Lansdale's advice, Diem in essence rigged an election pitting himself against former Emperor Bao Dai in 1955. Between 1954 and 1956 Diem also managed to subdue several hostile religious, political, and criminal groups within the south. Lansdale was Diem's confidante. He saw the South Vietnamese leader as a true anticommunist nationalist who could unify South Vietnam and successfully oppose the communists.

From 1957 to 1963, Lansdale served as a deputy director of the Office of Special Operations in the Department of Defense, working on counterinsurgency projects. When President John Kennedy sent him back to Vietnam in 1961 on a fact-finding tour, Lansdale not surprisingly recommended continued aid to Diem. In 1965 he became a special assistant to Ambassador Henry Cabot Lodge and later the U.S. representative to a committee of the South Vietnamese government seeking to garner peasant support for the government. He urged that American strategy be based on counterinsurgency principles, arguing that the conflict in Vietnam was more political than military. When he failed to convince military leaders to shift U.S. strategy toward pacification rather than racking up body counts, he departed Vietnam in

1968. After leaving government service, he spent his time lecturing, writing, and trying to assist Southeast Asian refugees. He died in McLean, Virginia, on February 24, 1987.

Edward Lansdale was often the object of scorn and parody. He was the model for the idealistic but naive American do-gooder in *The Quiet American* (1955), Graham Greene's important novel about the war. He was also the inspiration for Eugene Burdick's and William Lederer's title character in the *Ugly American* (1963), a well-meaning though bumbling air force officer in the early years of the conflict. Although his faith in Diem and the democratic potential of the South Vietnamese may have been misplaced, he was, along with John Paul Vann, one of the most articulate spokespersons for the pacification strategy during the war. Even after the war was over, he firmly believed that "the United States could still prevail in . . . third-world nations by exporting 'the American way' through a blend of economic aid and efforts at 'winning the hearts and minds of the people.' "[1]

Note

1. Eric Pace, "Edward Lansdale Dies at 79; Adviser of Guerrilla Warfare," *New York Times*, February 24, 1987, sec. A, p. 25.

Henry Cabot Lodge, Jr. (1902–1985)

Henry Cabot Lodge, Jr., was a distinguished American public servant who held a number of political and diplomatic positions in his lifetime. He served as a Republican from Massachusetts in the United States Senate (1936–1953); American delegate to the United Nations (1953–1960); Republican vice-presidential candidate (1960); and Ambassador to South Vietnam from 1963 to 1864 and again from 1965 to 1967.

Lodge was born in Nahant, Massachusetts, on July 5, 1902, to a respected family steeped in the tradition of public service. After graduating from Harvard University, he worked as a journalist, spending some time in French Indochina while writing about the French Empire in southeast Asia.

His public service related to Vietnam began in 1963, when President John F. Kennedy appointed him Ambassador to the Republic of Vietnam. The Democratic president probably hoped the appointment would deflect potential carping about his Vietnam policy by Republican critics. Shortly after Lodge arrived in-country in June 1963, he decided that the government of South Vietnam under President Ngo Dinh Diem was a disaster and, barring some unforeseen turnaround, should not be supported by the United States. Although he denied actively participating in or specifically approving the coup against Diem, Lodge certainly helped convince the Kennedy administration that the United States should do nothing to prevent any serious attempt to overthrow the South Vietnamese leader. A successful coup against Diem did occur on November 1, 1963.

Lodge stepped down as ambassador in 1964 and was replaced by blunt-speaking General Maxwell Taylor. Lodge took up the post again at Lyndon Johnson's insistence in August 1965, partly because the president "no longer wanted a tough Ambassador [like Taylor] in charge." With America increasingly taking over the war, someone "complacent" like Lodge would be "less likely to cause [General William] Westmoreland trouble than . . . Taylor."[1] During his second tour, Lodge's major concern was what he called "the unending governmental instability" in South Vietnam, as well as the increasing militarization of the war at the expense of pacification.[2] As the American military commitment grew and chances for a diplomatic settlement seemed to wane, Lodge, according to his political counselor, Phillip Habib, "had 'had enough' of the beleaguered post of Ambassador."[3] Lodge resigned on April 25, 1967.

After his resignation, Lodge served briefly as one of Johnson's "Wise Men." He also was the chief U.S. negotiator at the Paris peace talks in 1969 and a special presidential envoy to the Vatican until 1977. Lodge spent his last years in retirement. He died on February 27, 1985, in Beverly, Massachusetts.

Although Lodge certainly was crucial in recommending the replacement of Diem in 1963, he did become increasingly skeptical of the war. However, according to his biographer, historian Anne Blair, Lodge's deep sense of professional propriety prevented him from pushing his concerns on his superiors.

Notes

1. Robert D. Schulzinger, *A Time for War: The United States and Vietnam, 1941–1975* (New York: Oxford University Press, 1997), p. 184.

2. Anne Blair, *Lodge in Vietnam: A Patriot Abroad* (New Haven: Yale University Press, 1995), p. 151.

3. Ibid., p. 153.

Robert Strange McNamara (1916–)

Robert McNamara was Secretary of Defense from 1961 to 1968. He is considered by many to be the chief architect of the American war in Vietnam. In the words of historian Brian VanDeMark, "As defense secretary, McNamara shaped U. S. policy in Vietnam more than any other individual during these crucial years."[1] Moreover, his growing doubts about the conduct of the war ultimately led to his decision to resign, and he came to represent the sentiments of millions of Americans who saw the war as a tragic mistake. Ironically, McNamara never publicly condemned the war until he published his controversial memoir, *In Retrospect*, in 1995.

Born on June 9, 1916, in San Francisco, McNamara received his bachelor's degree from the University of California, Berkeley, and a master's degree from Harvard Business School. During World War II he served as a statistical analyst for the Army Air Corps, rising to the rank of lieutenant colonel. He and several of his colleagues became known as "the whiz kids" because of their skills in management and systems analysis and together joined the Ford Motor Company in 1946. Over the next sixteen years, McNamara's rise in the corporation was meteoric. In 1960 he was named president of the company at the age of forty-four, a position he left to become President John F. Kennedy's Secretary of Defense.

McNamara shared the Cold War consensus that saw the need to resist communist expansion in places like Vietnam. He was firmly convinced that by "committing its superior resources effectively," America could repel communist-inspired wars of national liberation.[2] In Vietnam specifically, he recommended to President Kennedy a judicious combination of economic and military aid to the South, supplemented by American military advisors and based on a counterinsurgency strategy. In spite of signs of growing communist strength, the Secretary remained optimistic that this policy would work. In 1963 he even suggested that by the end of 1965, the United States would be able to withdraw the bulk of its advisors.

With the growing strength and success of the communist insurgency in 1964–1965, however, McNamara advocated escalation. He supported the Gulf of Tonkin Resolution, Operation Rolling Thunder, and the introduction of several thousand American combat troops. In July 1965 he judged that a few troops would not be sufficient to achieve American goals in Vietnam. After returning from one of his innumerable trips to Vietnam, he offered President Johnson stark alternatives. To "cut losses and leave" South Vietnam would "almost certainly" damage America's "future effectiveness on the world scene." The second alternative, to keep American force levels constant at about seventy-five thousand "would make the U.S. position progressively weaker and 'would confront us later with a choice between withdrawal and an emergency expansion of forces, perhaps too late to do any good.' " McNamara pushed for, and President Johnson ultimately accepted, a middle course: to "[e]xpand promptly and substantially the U.S. military pressure against the Vietcong in the South and maintain military pressure against the North Vietnamese in the North."[3]

By pursuing this strategy over the next three years, the Johnson administration ultimately committed more than 540,000 American troops and billions of dollars to a war in which victory continued to be illusive. Indeed, almost as soon as he proffered this advice, McNamara began to question the effectiveness of gradual escalation. By spring 1967, the Secretary was advocating a cap on U.S. combat troops, limiting air attacks on the North, turning more of the actual fighting over to the South Vietnamese, and reducing U.S. political demands in negotiations. President Johnson became increasingly suspicious of McNamara's views, especially given the Secretary's close friendship with Johnson's political rival Robert Kennedy. Perhaps reading the handwriting on the wall, McNamara accepted Johnson's nomination to head the World Bank and left office in February 1968. He remained president of that organization until 1983, when he retired. Since then, he has been active in a number of causes, including the nuclear freeze movement.

For over two and a half decades after 1968, Robert McNamara remained silent about the war and his role in it, except for testimony in a libel trial brought by William Westmoreland against CBS in 1984. Finally, in 1995 he published his memoir, *In Retrospect*, which focused on his role in the war. In the preface, McNamara admitted that in spite of acting "according to what we thought were the principles and traditions of this nation," he and his colleagues "were wrong, terribly wrong" in their Vietnam War policies.[4] For many Americans, both opponents and proponents of the war, this realization came thirty years too late.

Notes

1. Brian VanDeMark, "McNamara, Robert," in *Encyclopedia of the Vietnam War*, ed. Stanley I. Kutler (New York: Charles Scribner's Sons, 1996), p. 297.

2. Ibid., p. 299.

3. Robert D. Schulzinger, *A Time for War: The United States and Vietnam, 1941–1975* (New York: Oxford University Press, 1997), pp. 174–75.

4. Robert McNamara, with Brian VanDeMark, *In Retrospect: The Tragedy and Lessons of Vietnam* (New York: Times Books, 1995), p. xvi.

Martha Raye (1916–1994)

Martha Raye was a professional entertainer who sang, danced, and acted on Broadway, in Hollywood, and on television. She was probably most famous for the shows she put on for American troops on location in three different wars—World War II, Korea, and Vietnam.

She was born Margie Yvonne Reed on August 27, 1916. Her parents were Irish immigrants who formed the vaudeville song and dance team, Reed and Hooper. As a show business child, Margie began her stage career at age three. By 1936 she was in her first film, and by 1940 was appearing in revues and on radio with stars like Al Jolson, Eddie Cantor, and Bob Hope.

She began entertaining troops during World War II as part of the USO program, a tradition she continued in the Korean and Vietnam wars. Over the course of nine years, she went to Vietnam a number of times, sometimes remaining for as long as six months. From her point of view, it was a labor of love. She said of the troops in Vietnam: "They ask so little and give so much. . . . The least we can do back home here is give them the love, the respect, and the dignity that they, our flag and our country deserve."[1]

The troops in Vietnam adored her. They affectionately dubbed her "Colonel Maggie"—she was a commissioned Lt. Colonel in the U.S. Army Special Forces Reserves—and flocked to her shows. One veteran, Sonny Hoffman, recalls spending an evening drinking and talking with her at a small camp near the Cambodian border. He remembers most vividly her spirited defense of the infantry soldier, the "grunt," when a Green Beret trooper said something disparaging about the common soldier. And common soldiers returned the affection. As Hoffman noted, "Whether we adopted her or she adopted us is moot. She was one of us, a revered member of the team."[2]

Martha Raye was awarded the Jean Hersholt Humanitarian Award by the Academy of Motion Picture Arts and Sciences in 1969 and received the Presidential Medal of Freedom in 1993. She died in Los Angeles on October 19, 1994.

Notes

1. Lawrence Van Gelder, "Martha Raye, Singer and Comic Actress, Dies," *New York Times*, October 20, 1994, sec. B, p. 16.

2. George "Sonny" Hoffman, "Grunt's Dream," unpublished mss. in author's possession, p. 1.

Walt Whitman Rostow (1916–   )

W. W. Rostow served the Kennedy and Johnson administrations in a number of capacities, most importantly as Special Assistant for National Security Affairs from 1961 to 1966 and National Security Advisor from 1966 to 1969. Rostow's advice on Vietnam was consistently hawkish, as he advocated a strong military response to the communist insurgency.

Rostow was born on October 7, 1916, in New York City and was educated at Yale and Oxford, England, as a Rhodes Scholar. After serving with the Office of Strategic Services during World War II, he was briefly in the State Department. In 1950 he became a Professor of Economic History at M.I.T.

Partly because of Rostow's pathbreaking book, *Stages of Economic Growth* (1960), President-elect Kennedy named him his Special Assistant for National Security Affairs. Based on his research on underdeveloped countries, Rostow concluded that any insurgency had to be stopped at the source. In the case of the Vietnam conflict, that meant using American power to prevent North Vietnam from supporting the Vietcong in the South. Thus, Rostow suggested bombing the North. Although President Kennedy rejected this counsel, his successor ultimately agreed.

Rostow was elevated by President Johnson to the post of National Security Advisor in 1966 and soon recommended "systematic and consistent bombing of North Vietnam's petroleum facilities."[1] When many of Johnson's advisors began to suggest de-escalation of the war after the 1968 Tet Offensive, Rostow remained optimistic and urged an intensification of the military effort.

Rostow left office in 1969. He took a position as Professor of Economics at the University of Texas, where he has continued to defend America's role in the Vietnam War. "History," he argues, "will salute us."[2]

Notes

1. Harry G. Summers, Jr., ed., *Vietnam War Almanac* (New York: Facts on File, 1985), p. 299.

2. Glen Gendzel, "Rostow, Walt Whitman," in *Encyclopedia of the Vietnam War,* ed. Stanley I. Kutler (New York: Charles Scribner's Sons, 1996), p. 481.

Dean Rusk (1909–1994)

Dean Rusk was the Secretary of State during the John F. Kennedy and Lyndon Johnson administrations. He was a consistent supporter of American military intervention in Vietnam, although he also sought to avoid provoking the Peoples Republic of China or the Soviet Union into a wider conflict.

Born on February 9, 1909, in Cherokee County, Georgia, Rusk graduated from Davidson College and studied at Oxford University on a Rhodes Scholarship. During World War II, he served as General Joseph Stillwell's chief of staff in the China-Burma-India Theater, thus beginning his lifelong interest in Asia. He joined the State Department in 1946 and was named Assistant Secretary for Far Eastern Affairs in 1950. In spite of some sympathy for growing anticolonial sentiments in the Far East, he became convinced of the dangers of communist expansion in Asia and supported aid to the French effort in Indochina. He left State in 1952 to head up the prestigious Rockefeller Foundation. He became Secretary of State under President John Kennedy in 1961.

Rusk's advice to Kennedy on Vietnam was consistent: The United States had an obligation to help prevent the fall of South Vietnam to communism. The Secretary hoped to accomplish the goal without using American combat troops in the conflict. Rather, Rusk pushed a program of incremental escalation.

His opposition to the use of American combat personnel dissolved in 1965 when it appeared that the communists were on the verge of winning the war. As President Lyndon Johnson's Secretary of State, Rusk fully supported the sustained air attacks on North Vietnam (Rolling Thunder) as well as the use of American troops to fight the war. He outlined his views on the importance of America's commitment to Vietnam in a July 1965 memorandum to Johnson: "The central objective of the United States in South Vietnam must be to insure that North Vietnam does not succeed in taking over or determining the future of South Vietnam by force."[1] Failure to achieve this goal would make America seem "unreliable" in living up to its commitments. From such a failure, the "communist world would draw conclusions that would lead to our ruin and almost certainly a catastrophic war."[2] Yet, Rusk also did not want to risk such a war by being excessively provocative. Thus he opposed any military actions against North Vietnam that might draw the Peoples Republic of China or the Soviet Union into a wider war. For example, he did not favor the bombing of Hanoi or Haiphong for fear of killing Chinese and Soviet personnel.

Even after he left office in 1969, he held steadfastly to his position on the war, continuing to believe that American intervention was justified. Rusk returned to Georgia in 1970, where he taught international law at the University of Georgia Law School until he retired in 1984. He died in Athens, Georgia, on December 20, 1994.

Notes

1. Robert J. McMahon, "Rusk, Dean" in *Encyclopedia of the Vietnam War,* ed. Stanley I. Kutler (New York: Charles Scribner's Sons, 1996), p. 485.
2. Ibid.

Harry S Truman (1884–1972)

Harry S Truman was the thirty-third president of the United States, serving from 1945 to 1953. During his administration the United States first gave military aid to the French to help defeat the forces of Ho Chi Minh and maintain a noncommunist Vietnam.

Born on May 8, 1884, in Lamar, Missouri, Truman studied law at night school and worked his way up in the Kansas City political machine of Tom Pendergast. Elected as a Democrat to the United States Senate from Missouri in 1934, he served in relative obscurity until he chaired a Senate committee investigating waste in defense spending. His careful honesty brought him to the attention of President Franklin Roosevelt, who made Truman his vice-presidential choice in the election of 1944. After that successful campaign, he became president on the death of Roosevelt in April 1945.

Roosevelt had told Truman virtually nothing about his foreign policy, including his general hostility toward French colonialism in Vietnam. Because of increased tension between the United States and the Soviet Union, Truman basically tilted toward the French in their attempts to reclaim Vietnam as a colony after the defeat of Japan in World War II. The State Department did not even forward to him letters from Ho Chi Minh pleading for the United States to support Vietnamese independence.

Truman's initial pro-French stance was based more on an attempt to keep France happy and anticommunist in Europe than fear of a communist Vietnam. However, with the fall of China to communism in 1949 and the communist North Korean invasion of South Korea in 1950, Truman increasingly saw Ho as a tool of international communism who needed to be thwarted. In 1950 Truman convinced Congress to appropriate military aid to assist the French in their fight against the Vietminh, thus broadening American interests in Vietnam. More importantly, writes one historian, Truman's portrayal of Ho Chi Minh's forces as "communist tools in the Cold War and his repeated references to containment and the domino theory ... established the ideological framework" for America's Vietnam policy for the next two decades.[1]

After leaving the presidency in 1953, Truman devoted the rest of his life to writing, speaking engagements, and advising his successors. He died in Kansas City, Missouri, on December 26, 1972, less than a month before the Paris Accords would end America's military role in Vietnam.

Note

1. Kelly Evans-Pfeifer, "Truman, Harry S.," in *Encyclopedia of the Vietnam War,* ed. Stanley I. Kutler (New York: Charles Scribner's Sons, 1996), p. 546.

John Paul Vann (1924–1972)

John Paul Vann was a lieutenant-colonel in the United States Army and a senior advisor to the Army of the Republic of Vietnam (ARVN) from 1962 to 1963. He retired from the service in 1963 but returned to Vietnam in 1965 as a civilian advisor for the pacification effort in the Saigon area. In 1971, even though Vann was a civilian, General Creighton Abrams, Commander of United States forces in Vietnam, named him commander—via military aides—of all U.S. forces in the central highlands of South Vietnam.

Born in Roanoke, Virginia, on July 20, 1924, Vann enlisted in the Air Force at eighteen, served in World War II and Korea, and received a masters degree in business administration in 1959. He volunteered to serve in Vietnam in 1962, where he became one of the most respected and outspoken advisors to the South Vietnamese army. He also was especially close to young American reporters like David Halberstam and Neil Sheehan. He was candid with them about his conviction that the government of South Vietnam was corrupt and refused to let its army fight an aggressive war against the enemy.

He was also deeply opposed to the large infusion of American heavy equipment, which he feared would lead to a more conventional ground war rather than a counterinsurgency one. He firmly thought that the war was largely political, a belief he acted on when he became an important civilian advisor in 1965. In his view, indiscriminate firepower only alienated the very civilian population the Americans and South Vietnamese were trying to convince to support the South Vietnamese government.

By 1972, however, Vann had come to recognize that it was too late for America to use counterinsurgency tactics, given the power of the North Vietnamese army. In his role as commander of American troops in the central highlands, Vann developed a growing sense of optimism. He even came to rely heavily on B-52 strikes, although he would carefully select targets to minimize civilian casualties. Vann was coordinating the South Vietnamese-American response to a major North Vietnamese offensive when he died in a helicopter crash on June 10, 1972.

According to his biographer, journalist Neil Sheehan, Vann's combination of toughness, dedication, and outspokenness represented the best of American military action in Vietnam. His growing obsession with the war, including his delusion that the United States was actually winning as of 1972, represented the worst aspects of U.S. involvement. One of Vann's colleagues, Colonel Dave Wilson, decided that "Vann had invested so much of John Vann in the war that he had talked himself into believing he had to be winning."[1] The same might be said of the United States.

Note

1. Neil Sheehan, *A Bright and Shining Lie: John Paul Vann and America in Vietnam* (New York: Random House, 1988), p. 745.

William Westmoreland (1914–   )

General William Westmoreland was commander of the United States Military Assistance Command, Vietnam (COMUSMACV) from 1964 to 1968. In that position, he was, in effect, the military leader of American forces in Vietnam during their expansion from a few thousand to over half a million. He was also the chief military strategist and tactician during the heart of the Vietnam War.

Born in Spartanburg, South Carolina, on March 26, 1914, Westmoreland graduated from the United States Military Academy in 1936. He served in World War II as a field artillery commander and later as Chief of Staff of the Ninth Infantry Division. By 1960 he had risen to be Superintendent of West Point and in 1964 was appointed Deputy Commander of MACV.

When he took over as commander from General Paul Harkins in June 1964, there were approximately sixteen thousand American advisors in Vietnam, no official combat units, and no air attacks occurring against North Vietnam. Within a few months, he oversaw a bombing campaign, the introduction and buildup of combat troops, and a change of mission from advising and defense to offensive action against the communist enemy, spearheaded by Americans.

Westmoreland's overall strategy was threefold: to stop the bleeding, by preventing further enemy successes; then to launch offensive operations against Vietcong and North Vietnamese forces in the field; and finally, to destroy enemy base camps. He would accomplish these goals largely by fighting a war of attrition against the Vietcong and North Vietnamese. To wear the enemy down, he argued successfully for increased numbers of American troops, who would then take on the main burden of the fighting. The use of helicopters would increase military mobility, and superior firepower would destroy the enemy at a sufficient rate to lead the communists to negotiate a settlement on American terms. At the same time, the South Vietnamese army would be further modernized and improved. It also would take primary responsibility for pacification, "winning hearts and minds" of South Vietnamese citizens.

After the 1968 Tet Offensive, it seemed clear to most political leaders that the strategy had failed—or at least, the Johnson administration was unwilling to accede to Westmoreland's request for additional American troops. Partly because Johnson perceived the request for troops as excessive, he replaced Westmoreland with General Creighton Abrams, naming the former MACV commander Chief of Staff of the Army in April 1968. Westmoreland served in this position until 1972, when he retired from the Army. His major public role since then came in 1985 when he sued CBS News. He claimed that the network's documentary, "The Uncounted Enemy: A Vietnam Deception," had libeled him when it claimed that he had lied about communist troop strength. The suit was settled out of court, with both sides claiming victory.

Westmoreland's role in the war has remained controversial. Critics claim that he relied too much on U.S. ground forces and slighted the development of the South Vietnamese army. He also used helicopters excessively. Moreover, his dependence on massive firepower and consequent civilian casualties alienated the very peasants that needed to rally to the side of the South Vietnamese government. Finally, his emphasis on military solutions relegated to a minor role what critics perceived to be the much more important political war for the loyalty of South Vietnamese villagers.

Even his critics have to admit, however, that the introduction of American combat troops and the use of air power, especially in combat support missions, achieved Westmoreland's first goal—to "stop the bleeding." By 1966 the communists were no longer "winning" the war. But obviously, the second and third phases of his strategy did not succeed. In his memoir of the war, *A Soldier Reports*, Westmoreland understandably places the blame for the fall of South Vietnam elsewhere than on his own shoulders. By Westmoreland's reckoning, the strategy of graduated response, failing to exploit the enemy's defeat during the Tet Offensive, waiting too long to attack enemy positions in Cambodia and Laos, and the media's tendency to be critical of the war all contributed to the defeat. Moreover, President Johnson's failure to level with the American people about the potential costs and duration of the war helped fuel discontent. But probably the fountainhead of all these errors, Westmoreland wrote, was the "strong control of the conduct of the war from Washington."[1] Micromanagement from the top led to crippling restrictions on the military conduct of the war.

Westmoreland ends his account of the Vietnam War on an upbeat note. After all, he writes, it was the South Vietnamese, not the Americans who "lost" the war in 1975. Besides, the United States can be proud of itself for fighting a just war: "[H]istory may judge that American aid to South Vietnam constituted one of man's more noble crusades . . . a strong nation helping an aspiring nation . . . to achieve and keep a degree of freedom and human dignity."[2] In the end, the American general most identified with the war and most vilified by those who opposed it saw the Vietnam War as the expression of American idealism.

Notes

1. William Westmoreland, *A Soldier Reports* (New York: Da Capo Press, 1989), p. 410.
2. Ibid., p. 422.

Primary Documents of the War

THE VIETNAMESE TRADITION OF REBELLION

Historically, most Vietnamese have chafed under foreign domination. Hatred of oppression often manifested itself through violent rebellion, from the Trung Sisters in the early first century through the PLAF during the American war in Vietnam. But resistance to foreign rule often was expressed in more subtle ways, especially through literature. Profoundly moved by poetry, Vietnamese looked to writers to express feelings of resentment against the French.

A case in point is Nguyen Khuyen, whose poetry reflected a patriotic hatred of French rule and an appreciation of countrymen who passively resisted the oppressor. A native of northern Vietnam, Khuyen served as a Vietnamese government official during the reign of Emperor Tu Duc. When the northern and central parts of the country were ceded to the French in 1884, he pretended that he had eye problems and refused to serve in the new French colonial administration. The brief poem presented here, written shortly after French authority was established, is based on a Vietnamese friend's decision to decline appointment to a post in the new administration by feigning deafness.

According to historian Neil L. Jamieson, men like Nguyen Khuyen and his friend "were doing much more than merely withholding their services from an administration of which they did not approve. They were communicating this disapproval in a highly effective way."[1] Thus, they became part of the broad Vietnamese tradition of rebellion—a tradition Americans would face in their own Vietnam War.

Document 1
THE MAN WHO FEIGNS DEAFNESS
Nguyen Khuyen

There's a man who pretends to be deaf.

"Huh? Huh? What say?" he stupidly asks.

Little does one suspect he stops and starts his ears like they were plow
buffaloes.

I'd certainly like to be deaf like that.

Amidst a chattering crowd he sits dumb as a block of wood.

But late at night and all alone he's lively as a monkey.

In the back garden, to the front pond, enjoy a pipe, then a chew of betel,

Six or seven cups of tea while playing with some lines from Kieu.

Who wouldn't want to be deaf like that?

But do you think it's easy?

Just ask him. "What say?" he'll reply.

Source: Xuan Dieu, ed., *Tho Van Nguyen Khuyen (The Poetry of Nguyen Khuyen)* (Hanoi:
Van Hoc, 1971), pp. 92–93.

Note

1. Neil L. Jamieson, *Understanding Vietnam* (Berkeley, Calif.: University of
California Press, 1993), pp. 51–52.

COMMUNIST PARTY OF INDOCHINA PROGRAM, 1930

In 1929 anti-French groups within Indochina were rent with factional-
ism, with at least three different entities calling themselves "Communist" parties. In the words of journalist David Halberstam, in
Vietnamese politics "one trusted himself and his family and very few
others."[1] Disturbed by this infighting, communist officials in Moscow
sent Ho Chi Minh to Hong Kong in early 1930, realizing that he was one
of the most respected of the nationalist/communist leaders among his
countrymen.

On February 3, Ho called together two delegates from each of the
splinter groups and hammered out an agreement that led to the formation of the unified Vietnamese Communist party (renamed the Indochinese Communist party in October). According to party sources, this
momentous meeting took place "in the stands of Hong Kong Stadium
during a soccer match."[2] The party's "Program" reflects a combination
of nationalism and communism. Vietnamese independence was the first
and most important goal of the party, but that independence was
couched in overtly Marxist terms. In fact, the ten points read very much

like *The Communist Manifesto.* Ho's commitment to both patriotism and communism never wavered; although, as the following documents illustrate, the precise mix of these two elements would change in changing circumstances.

Document 2
THE PROGRAM OF THE COMMUNIST PARTY
OF INDOCHINA
Ho Chi Minh

Workers, peasants, soldiers, youth, pupils!

Oppressed and exploited compatriots!

The Communist party of Indochina is founded. It is the party of the working class. It will help the proletarian class lead the revolution in order to struggle for all the oppressed and exploited people. From now on we must join the Party, help it and follow it in order to implement the following slogans:

1—To overthrow French imperialism, feudalism, and the reactionary Vietnamese capitalist class.

2—To make Indochina completely independent.

3—To establish a worker-peasant and soldier government.

4—To confiscate the banks and other enterprises belonging to the imperialists and put them under the control of the worker-peasant and soldier government.

5—To confiscate all of the plantations and property belonging to the imperialists and the Vietnamese reactionary capitalist class and distribute them to poor peasants.

6—To implement the eight hour working day.

7—To abolish public loans and poll tax. To waive unjust taxes hitting the poor people.

8—To bring back all freedoms to the masses.

9—To carry out universal education.

10—To implement equality between man and woman.

Source: Ho Chi Minh, *Ho Chi Minh: Selected Works*, vol. 2 (Hanoi: Foreign Language Publishing House, 1960), pp. 145–48.

Notes

1. David Halberstam, *Ho* (New York: Alfred A. Knopf, 1997), p. 51.

2. Jean Lacouture, *Ho Chi Minh: A Political Biography* (New York: Vintage Books, 1968), p. 57.

FOUNDING OF THE VIETNAM INDEPENDENCE LEAGUE (VIETMINH)

In 1941 Japan took over virtual control of French Indochina, basically leaving a puppet French government in place to handle routine administrative details. Thus Vietnam fell under a double yoke of oppression. Ho Chi Minh had sneaked back into Vietnam in early 1941—his first time on his native soil in thirty years. Determined to organize opposition to both the French and the Japanese, he broadened the rather narrow sectarian basis of the Indochinese Communist Party (ICP), which he had founded in 1930. In essence, he folded the ICP into a more inclusive super nationalist organization that he called the Viet Nam Doc Lap Dong Minh (Vietnam Independence League), later shortened to Vietminh.

In his stirring "call" for Vietnamese within the country to join the new organization, issued in June 1941, Ho wants to inspire all Vietnamese, not just workers and peasants as a dedicated communist might be expected to do. Moreover, his rhetorical strategy clearly emphasizes patriotism, with the vague concept of the "World's Revolution" appearing only briefly at the end of the document. He appeals to the Vietnamese sense of history, noting proudly the way his compatriots defeated the Mongols centuries ago and asking that fellow countrymen and women unite again, this time to throw out the modern hordes.

Document 3
CALL FOR THE REVOLUTIONARY LEAGUE FOR THE INDEPENDENCE OF VIETNAM
Ho Chi Minh

Elders! Prominent personalities! Intellectuals, peasants, workers, traders, and soldiers! Dear compatriots!

Since the French were defeated by the Germans, their forces have been completely disintegrated. However, with regard to our people, they continue to plunder us pitilessly, suck all our blood, and carry out a barbarous policy of all-out terrorism and massacre. Concerning their foreign policy, they bow their heads and kneel down, shamelessly cutting our land for Siam; without a single word of protest, they heartlessly offer our interests to Japan. As a result, our people suffer under a double yoke: they serve not only as buffaloes and horses to the French invaders but also as slaves to the Japanese plunderers. Alas! What sin have our people committed to be doomed to such a wretched plight!

Now, the opportunity has come for our liberation. France itself is unable to dominate our country. As to the Japanese, on the one hand they are bogged in China, on the other, they are hamstrung by the British and American forces, and certainly cannot use all their forces to contend with us. If our entire people are united and single-minded, we are certainly able to smash the picked French and Japanese armies.

Some hundreds of years ago, when our country was endangered by the Mongolian invasion, our elders under the Tran dynasty rose up indignantly and called on their sons and daughters throughout the country to rise as one in order to kill the enemy. Finally they saved their people from danger, and their good name will be carried into posterity for all time. The elders and prominent personalities of our country should follow the example set by our forefathers in the glorious task of national salvation.

Rich people, soldiers, workers, peasants, intellectuals, employees, traders, youth and women who warmly love your country! At the present time national liberation is the most important problem. Let us unite together! As one mind and strength we shall overthrow the Japanese and the French and their jackals in order to save people from the situation between boiling water and burning heat.

Dear compatriots! National salvation is the common cause to the whole of our people. Every Vietnamese must take part in it. He who has money will contribute his money, he who has strength will contribute his strength, he who has talent will contribute his talent. I pledge to use all my modest abilities to follow you, and am ready for the last sacrifice.

Revolutionary fighters! The hour has struck! Raise aloft the insurrectionary banner and guide the people throughout the country to overthrow the Japanese and French. The sacred call of the fatherland is resounding in your ears; the blood of our heroic predecessors who sacrificed their lives is stirring in your hearts! The fighting spirit of the people is displayed everywhere before you! Let us rise up quickly! Compatriots throughout the country, rise up quickly! Unite with each other, unify your action to overthrow the Japanese and the French. Victory to Vietnam's Revolution! Victory to the World's Revolution!

Source: Ho Chi Minh, "Call for the Revolutionary League for the Independence of Vietnam," in *Ho Chi Minh: Selected Works* (Hanoi: Foreign Language Publishing House, 1960), pp. 151–54.

VIETNAM DECLARES INDEPENDENCE, 2 SEPTEMBER 1945

The end of World War II in August 1945 left a power vacuum in Vietnam. The Japanese, who had occupied the country, were defeated. French forces, whom the Japanese had allowed to hold nominal control of Vietnam until March 1945, were in disarray, having been thrown out of power. By far the strongest of many pronationalist, anti-French groups in Vietnam was Ho Chi Minh's Vietminh, which had helped wage guerrilla war against the Japanese. Ho's forces were especially helpful to the Americans as they assisted in finding downed fliers, while American OSS agents helped train Ho's ragtag troops.

Clearly the most popular leader in Vietnam, Ho sought to fill that power vacuum by solidifying Vietminh control over the country. Given the fierceness of Vietnamese patriotism declaring independence from the French seemed a particularly savvy move. Additionally, Ho realized that he needed a friendly America in case France tried to reestablish control over its former colony. He also probably honestly respected the American example of a former European colony that had successfully broken free. Not surprisingly, then, he used America's own Declaration of Independence as a model for his own.

Notably, the focus of the document is on freedom and independence. Although there are a few passing allusions to economic exploitation and French "imperialism," there are no references to "communism" or "the dictatorship of the proletariat." Clearly, on September 2, 1945, when Ho read the Declaration to a crowd of thousands in Hanoi, he wanted to unify and inspire. Ho's more doctrinaire and ideological political and economic designs would come later.

Document 4
DECLARATION OF INDEPENDENCE OF THE DEMOCRATIC REPUBLIC OF VIETNAM
Ho Chi Minh

All men are created equal. They are endowed by their Creator with certain inalienable rights, among these are Life, Liberty, and the pursuit of Happiness.

This immortal statement was made in the Declaration of Independence of the United States of America in 1776. In a broader sense, this means: All the peoples on the earth are equal from birth, all the peoples have a right to live, to be happy and free.

The Declaration of the French Revolution made in 1791 on the Rights of Man and the Citizen also states: "All men are born free and with equal rights, and must always remain free and have equal rights."

Those are undeniable truths.

Nevertheless, for more than eighty years, the French imperialists, abusing the standard of Liberty, Equality and Fraternity, have violated our Fatherland and oppressed our fellow-citizens. They have acted contrary to the ideals of humanity and justice. . . .

A people who have courageously opposed French domination for more than eighty years, a people who have fought side by side with the Allies against the fascists during these last years, such a people must be free and independent.

For these reasons, we, members of the Provisional Government of the Democratic Republic of Viet Nam, solemnly declare to the world that Viet Nam has the right to be a free and independent country—and in fact it is so already. The entire Vietnamese people are determined to mobilize all their physical and mental strength, to sacrifice their lives and property in order to safeguard their independence and liberty.

Source: "Declaration of Independence of the Democratic Republic of Vietnam, September 2, 1945," in *Breaking Our Chains: Documents on the Vietnamese Revolution of August, 1945* (Hanoi: Foreign Language Publishing House, 1960), pp. 94–97.

THE GENEVA ACCORDS
AND THE AMERICAN RESPONSE

The Geneva Accords, signed on July 21, 1954, effectively ended the military conflict between the Vietminh and the French, while leaving the issue of Vietnamese reunification and governance unsettled. The Geneva Conference, which began deliberations in April 1954, was initially called to discuss problems involving Korea and Berlin. The convening nations—France, Great Britain, the Soviet Union, the People's Republic of China, and the United States—took up the issue of Indochina after the French defeat at Dienbienphu in May. Partly because of the participation of Communist China, which the United States did not recognize, American Secretary of State John Foster Dulles indicated that the United States would join the discussion of Indochina only as an "interested nation." In fact, neither the United States nor the State of Vietnam (South Vietnam) signed the Accords.[1]

After considerable negotiation and tension, France and the Vietminh agreed to a cease-fire. Under pressure from the Chinese and Soviets, Vietminh negotiators accepted a temporary division of the country at the 17th parallel, with the communists controlling the North and a noncommunist Vietnamese government in the South. The agreement also provided for free elections by 1956 to unify the nation.

Although not a signatory, the United States did "take note" of the Accords and promised "to refrain from the threat or the use of force to disturb them." However, American representative Walter Bedell Smith also indicated that the United States would see aggression in the area by other countries as a serious threat to peace, thus implying that American intervention was a possibility.

The free elections were never held, largely because both Ngo Dinh Diem, the South Vietnamese premier, and U.S. President Dwight D. Eisenhower feared a victory by Ho. Ultimately, the United States argued that North Vietnam had invaded the South, thus violating the Accords and justifying American intervention.

Document 5
FINAL DECLARATION OF THE GENEVA CONFERENCE, JULY 1954

Final declaration, dated the 21st July, 1954, of the Geneva Conference on the problem of restoring peace in Indo-China, in which the representatives of Cambodia, the Democratic Republic of Viet-Nam, France, Laos, the People's Republic of China, the State of Viet-Nam, the Union of Soviet Socialist Republics, the United Kingdom, and the United States of America took part.

1. The Conference takes note of the agreements ending hostilities in Cambodia, Laos and Viet-Nam and organizing international control and the supervision of the execution of the provisions of these agreements. . . .

4. The Conference takes note of the clauses in the agreement on the cessation of hostilities in Viet-Nam prohibiting the introduction into Viet-Nam of foreign troops and military personnel as well as of all kinds of arms and munitions. The Conference also takes note of the declarations made by the Governments of Cambodia and Laos of their resolution not to request foreign aid, whether in war material, in personnel or in instructors except for the purpose of the effective defence of their territory and, in the case of Laos, to the extent defined by the agreements on the cessation of hostilities in Laos.

5. The Conference takes note of the clauses in the agreement on the cessation of hostilities in Viet-Nam to the effect that no military base under the control of a foreign State may be established in the regrouping zones of the two parties, the latter having the obligation to see that the zones allotted to them shall not constitute part of any military alliance and shall not be utilized for the resumption of hostilities or in the service of an aggressive policy. . . .

6. The Conference recognizes that the essential purpose of the agreement relating to Viet-Nam is to settle military questions with a view to ending hostilities and that the military demarcation line is provisional and should not in any way be interpreted as constituting a political or territorial boundary. The Conference expresses its conviction that the execution of the provisions set out in the present declaration and in the agreement on the cessation of hostilities creates the necessary basis for the achievement in the near future of a political settlement in Viet-Nam.

7. The Conference declares that, so far as Viet-Nam is concerned, the settlement of political problems, affected on the basis of respect for the principles of independence, unity and territorial integrity, shall permit the Viet-Namese people to enjoy the fundamental freedoms, guaranteed by democratic institutions established as a result of free general elections by secret ballot. In order to ensure that sufficient progress in the restoration of peace has been made, and that all the necessary conditions obtain for free expression of the national will, general elections shall be held in July 1956, under the supervision of an international commission composed of representatives of the Member States of the International Supervisory Commission, referred to in the agreement on the cessation of hostilities. Consultations will be held on this subject between the competent representative authorities of the two zones from 20 July 1955 onwards. . . .

12. In their relations with Cambodia, Laos and Viet-Nam, each member of the Geneva Conference undertakes to respect the sovereignty, the independence, the unity and the territorial integrity of the above-mentioned states, and to refrain from any interference in their internal affairs.

Source: U.S. House Committee on Armed Services, *United States-Vietnam Relations, 1945-1967: A Study Prepared by the Department of Defense*, 12 vols.; Vol. 9, *The Eisenhower Administration, 1953–1960* (Washington, D.C.: Government Printing Office, 1971), pp. 671–675.

Document 6
STATEMENT OF THE UNDERSECRETARY OF STATE
AT THE CONCLUDING PLENARY SESSION OF THE
GENEVA CONFERENCE
Walter Bedell Smith

The Government of the United States being resolved to devote its efforts to the strengthening of peace in accordance with the principles and purposes of the United Nations takes note of the agreements concluded at Geneva on July 20 and 21, 1954 . . . [and] declares with regard to the aforesaid agreements and paragraphs that (i) it will refrain from the threat or the use of force to disturb them, in accordance with Article 2(4) of the Charter of the United Nations dealing with the obligation of members to refrain in their international relations from the threat or use of force; and (ii) it would view any renewal of the aggression in violation of the aforesaid agreements with grave concern and as seriously threatening international peace and security.

Source: U.S. House Committee on Armed Services, *United States-Vietnam Relations, 1945–1967: A Study Prepared by the Department of Defense*, 12 vols., Vol. 9, *The Eisenhower Administration, 1953–1960* (Washington, D.C.: Government Printing Office, 1971), p. 675.

Note

1. Paul M. Taillon, "Geneva Conference, 1954," in *Encyclopedia of the Vietnam War,* ed. Stanley I. Kutler (New York: Charles Scribner's Sons, 1996), p. 206.

PRESIDENT EISENHOWER'S SUPPORT OF NGO DINH DIEM

Historian David L. Anderson argues that the decisions made about Vietnam by the Eisenhower administration were "pivotal" in the history of the Vietnam War.[1] Probably none was more important than the resolution to support the efforts of Ngo Dinh Diem to achieve a stable, noncommunist government. This letter from Eisenhower to Diem represents a first tentative step in that direction.

After the signing of the Geneva Accords, Saigon was a cauldron of political intrigue. Although officially named Prime Minister of the State of Vietnam in June of 1954, Diem was hardly without opposition. Various groups within southern Vietnam, including religious sects like the Cao Dai and Hoa Hao and a Saigon criminal gang called the Binh Xuyen plotted against Diem, as did rival politicians like General Nguyen Van Hinh. France, which retained troops and considerable influence in the South, preferred a prime minister who was not so anti-French as Diem. Even within the Eisenhower administration, Secretary of Defense Charles E. Wilson and the Joint Chiefs of Staff opposed American support for Diem. Wilson went so far as to assert that the United States should " 'get completely out of the area' . . . because he saw no chance 'of saving any part of Southeast Asia.' "[2]

Eisenhower was having none of that, however. After considerable debate within his National Security Council, he decided that Vietnam south of the 17th parallel had to be saved from communism and that Diem was probably the strongest viable leader in the south. On October 22, he ordered "a crash program to sustain the Diem government and establish security in Free Vietnam."[3] The next day, the president sent his letter of support. Although hardly a ringing and total endorsement of Diem, Eisenhower's offer of aid to help Diem prevent the imposition of "a foreign ideology on your free people" marked an important step on the road to American commitment.

Document 7
LETTER FROM DWIGHT EISENHOWER TO NGO DINH DIEM, 23 OCTOBER 1954

Dear Mr. President: I have been following with great interest the course of developments in Viet-Nam, particularly since the conclusion of the conference at Geneva. The implications of the agreement concerning Viet-

Nam have caused grave concern regarding the future of a country temporarily divided by an artificial military grouping, weakened by a long and exhausting war and faced with enemies without and by their subversive collaborators within.

Your recent requests for aid to assist in the formidable project of the movement of several hundred thousand loyal Vietnamese citizens away from areas which are passing under a *de facto* rule and political ideology which they abhor, are being fulfilled. I am glad that the United States is able to assist in this humanitarian effort.

We have been exploring ways and means to permit our aid to Viet-Nam to be more effective and to make a greater contribution to the welfare and stability of the government of Viet-Nam. I am, accordingly, instructing the American Ambassador to Viet-Nam to examine with you in your capacity as Chief of Government, how an intelligent program of American aid given directly to your Government can serve to assist Viet-Nam in its present hour of trial, provided that your Government is prepared to give assurances as to the standards of performance it would be able to maintain in the event such aid were supplied.

The purpose of this offer is to assist the Government of Viet-Nam in developing and maintaining a strong, viable state, capable of resisting attempted subversion or aggression through military means. The Government of the United States expects that this aid will be met by performance on the part of the Government of Viet-Nam in undertaking needed reforms. It hopes that such aid, combined with your own continuing efforts, will contribute effectively toward an independent Viet-Nam endowed with a strong government. Such a government would, I hope, be so responsive to the nationalist aspirations of its people, so enlightened in purpose and effective in performance, that it will be respected both at home and abroad and discourage any who might wish to impose a foreign ideology on your free people.

Source: State Department Bulletin, November 15, 1954, pp. 735–36.

Notes

1. David L. Anderson, *Trapped by Success: The Eisenhower Administration and Vietnam, 1953–1961* (New York: Columbia University Press, 1991), p. 65.

2. Ibid., p. 83.

3. Ibid., p. 85.

THE SOUTHEAST ASIA TREATY ORGANIZATION

On September 8, 1954, the United States, Great Britain, France, Australia, New Zealand, the Philippines, Thailand, and Pakistan signed a treaty establishing the Southeast Asia Treaty Organization (SEATO). In es-

sence, this was a mutual security pact in which each signatory agreed
that an armed attack on any of these nations would be a threat to their
common peace and safety. Such an attack could then lead to military
action by any or all of the signatories to assist the nation under attack.
Such a military response would come only "in accordance with the
constitutional process" of each nation. Although the Geneva Accords
prevented the former Indochinese states from joining military alliances,
Laos, Cambodia, and South Vietnam were included as protected parties in a special protocol. Finally, the United States added a special understanding indicating that it would become involved militarily only if
the aggression was by communist forces.

The treaty was designed essentially as a stop-gap measure—in the
words of John Foster Dulles, a "no trespassing sign" to Russia and China
in regard to Southeast Asia. Dulles also called SEATO a " 'moral offensive' with no standing military commitment such as the United States had
in Europe."[1] In other words, the Eisenhower administration saw no auto-
matic American armed intervention in the event of a communist attack.

Whatever Eisenhower's intention, the treaty ultimately became a
major component of America's justification for military intervention in
Vietnam. When the government of Vietnam felt sufficiently besieged by
communist forces, it requested American assistance under SEATO. The
result, ultimately, was massive intervention.

Document 8
SOUTHEAST ASIA COLLECTIVE DEFENSE TREATY
ARTICLE IV

1. Each party recognizes that aggression by means or armed attack in the
treaty area against any of the parties or against any state or territory which
the parties by unanimous agreement may hereafter designate, would endanger its own peace and safety, and agrees that it will in that event act to meet
the common danger in accordance with its constitutional processes. Measures taken under this paragraph shall be immediately reported to the Security Council of the United Nations.

2. If, in the opinion of any of the parties, the inviolability of the integrity of
the territory or the sovereignty or political independence of any party in the
treaty area or of any state or territory to which the provisions of paragraph 1 of
this article from time to time apply is threatened in any way other than by
armed attack or is affected or threatened by any fact or situation which might
endanger the peace of the area, the Parties shall consult immediately in order
to agree on the measures which should be taken for the common defense.

3. It is understood that no action on the territory of any state designated
by unanimous agreement under paragraph 1 of this article or on any territory

so designated shall be taken except at the invitation or with the consent of the government concerned.

UNDERSTANDING OF THE UNITED STATES OF AMERICA

The United States of America in executing the present Treaty does so with the understanding that its recognition of the effect of aggression and armed attack and its agreement with reference thereto in Article IV, paragraph 1 apply only to communist aggression but affirms that in the event of other aggression or armed attack it will consult under the provisions of Article II, paragraph 2.

Protocol to the Southeast Asia Collective Defense Treaty

Signed at Manila, September 8, 1954; entered into force as to the United States, February 19, 1955

DESIGNATION OF STATES AND TERRITORY AS TO WHICH PROVISIONS OF ARTICLE IV AND ARTICLE III ARE TO BE APPLICABLE

The parties to the Southeast Asia Collective Defense Treaty unanimously designate for the purposes of Article IV of the Treaty the states of Cambodia and Laos and the free territory under the jurisdiction of the state of Vietnam.

The parties further agree that the above mentioned states and territory shall be eligible in respect of the economic measures contemplated by Article III.

This protocol shall enter into force simultaneously with the coming into force of the Treaty.

Source: Richard A. Falk, ed., *The Vietnam War and International Law*, Vol. 1 (Princeton, N.J.: Princeton University Press, 1968), pp. 562, 564.

Note

1. David L. Anderson, *Trapped by Success: The Eisenhower Administration and Vietnam, 1953–1961* (New York: Columbia University Press, 1991), pp. 71, 72.

PRESIDENT KENNEDY'S SUPPORT OF NGO DINH DIEM

The crisis in South Vietnam intensified in the fall of 1961. Infiltration of men and materiel from the communist North was increasing, while National Liberation Front (NLF) forces launched a new offensive in the South. In reaction to these problems, on October 15, President John F. Kennedy sent advisors Walt Rostow and Maxwell Taylor to South Vietnam to assess the situation. The resulting Rostow-Taylor Report emphasized deep morale problems in South Vietnam and called for massive increases in American assistance to the government of President Ngo Dinh Diem. The most controversial proposal was Taylor's suggestion that eight thousand American troops be sent under the guise of being flood control workers. Among the soldiers would be some infantrymen—America's first "combat" troops.

Countering this proposal were suggestions by Chester Bowles, Undersecretary of State, and Averell Harriman, the chief American negotiator on Laos. Arguing that the United States was "headed full-blast up a dead-end street," Bowles joined Harriman in urging that a stronger commitment to Diem be deferred. If the Geneva Conference on Laos went well enough, it could be expanded to include Vietnam.[1]

Kennedy took a middle course, agreeing to send Diem additional assistance while foregoing the introduction of combat troops. He rejected any negotiations that might suggest that America was unwilling to live up to its commitments. Kennedy even refused to tie increased aid to demands that Diem reform his government and allow a larger American role in decision making. For Kennedy, the issue in late 1961 was not so much whether Diem was a just ruler but whether the United States could accept continued communist expansion into South Vietnam. Thus, Kennedy's December 14, 1961, letter to Diem focused almost entirely on stopping communism in Vietnam.

Document 9
LETTER FROM PRESIDENT KENNEDY
TO PRESIDENT DIEM
President John F. Kennedy

Dear Mr. President:

I have received your recent letter in which you described so cogently the dangerous condition caused by North Vietnam's efforts to take over your country. The situation in your embattled country is well known to me and to the American people. We have been deeply disturbed by the assault on your country. Our indignation has mounted as the deliberate savagery of the Communist program of assassination, kidnapping, and wanton violence became clear.

Your letter underlines what our own information has convincingly shown—that the campaign of force and terror now being waged against your people and your Government is supported and directed from the outside by the authorities at Hanoi. They have thus violated the provisions of the Geneva Accords designed to ensure peace in Vietnam and to which they bound themselves in 1954.

At that time, the United States, although not a party to the Accords, declared that it "would view any renewal of the aggression in violation of the

Agreements with grave concern and as seriously threatening international peace and security." We continue to maintain that view.

In accordance with that declaration, and in response to your request, we are prepared to help the Republic of Vietnam to protect its people and to preserve its independence. We shall promptly increase our assistance to your defense effort as well as help relieve the destruction of the floods which you describe. I have already given the orders to get these programs underway.

The United States, like the Republic of Vietnam, remains devoted to the cause of peace and our primary purpose is to help your people maintain their independence. If the Communist authorities in North Vietnam will stop their campaign to destroy the Republic of Vietnam, the measures we are taking to assist your defense efforts will no longer be necessary. We shall seek to persuade the Communists to give up their attempts of force and subversion. In any case, we are confident that the Vietnamese people will preserve their independence and gain the peace and prosperity for which they have sought so hard and so long.

Source: Department of State Bulletin, January 1, 1962, p. 14.

Note

1. George Herring, *America's Longest War*, 3rd ed. (New York: McGraw-Hill, 1996), p. 91. At the time, the United States was engaged in complicated negotiations to end a civil war in Laos between communist, anticommunist, and neutralist forces.

THE GULF OF TONKIN RESOLUTION, AUGUST 1964

The Gulf of Tonkin Resolution (1964), as the following document was popularly known, provided the legal basis for President Lyndon Johnson's escalation of the Vietnam War. The administration had been planning to introduce such a resolution for several months, and two allegedly unprovoked North Vietnamese gunboat attacks on American destroyers in the Gulf of Tonkin in early August 1964 seemed to provide the perfect opportunity. For Johnson the Resolution would eliminate the problems of congressional sniping of the kind President Harry Truman had faced when he fought the Korean War without similar approval. Moreover, it would provide him with considerable flexibility in prosecuting the war. Finally, at least in his public statements about the need for such congressional action, Johnson employed the usual rhetoric about America's "basic policy of assisting free nations of the area to defend their freedom."[1]

Most members of Congress were convinced that North Vietnam had illegally attacked American ships. Most also were convinced that the president would not have to call for the massive troop commitments that ultimately occurred. In fact, in his message to Congress accompanying the Resolution, the president firmly maintained that "the United States intends no rashness and seeks no wider war."[2] The Resolution was repealed in 1971, but by then President Richard Nixon argued that he no longer needed this authority to prosecute the war.

Document 10
RESOLUTION TO PROMOTE THE MAINTENANCE OF INTERNATIONAL PEACE AND SECURITY IN SOUTHEAST ASIA

Whereas naval units of the Communist regime in Vietnam, in violation of the principles of the Charter of the United Nations and of international law, have deliberately and repeatedly attacked United States naval vessels lawfully present in international waters, and have thereby created a serious threat to international peace; and

Whereas these attacks are part of a deliberate and systematic campaign of aggression that the Communist regime in North Vietnam has been waging against its neighbors and the nations joined with them in the collective defense of their freedom; and

Whereas the United States is assisting the peoples of southeast Asia to protect their freedom and has no territorial, military or political ambitions in that area, but desires only that these peoples should be left in peace to work out their own destinies in their own way: Now, therefore be it

Resolved by the Senate and the House of Representatives of the United States of America in Congress assembled.

That the Congress approves and supports the determination of the President as Commander in Chief, to take all necessary measures to repel any armed attack against the forces of the United States and to prevent further aggression.

SEC.2. The United States regards as vital to its national interest and to world peace the maintenance of international peace and security in southeast Asia. Consonant with the Constitution of the United States and the Charter of the United Nations and in accordance with its obligations under the Southeast Asia Collective Defense Treaty, the United States is therefore, prepared, as the President determines, to take all necessary steps, including the use of armed force, to assist any member or protocol state of the Southeast Asia Collective Defense Treaty requesting assistance in defense of its freedom.

SEC.3. This resolution shall expire when the President shall determine that the peace and security of the area is reasonably assured by international conditions created by action of the United States or otherwise, except that it may be terminated earlier by concurrent resolution of the Congress.

Source: U.S. Congress, Senate, "To Promote the Maintenance of Peace and Security in Southeast Asia," 88th Cong., 2nd sess., *Congressional Record*, Vol. 110, part 14 (August 4–August 12, 1964), p. 18132.

Notes

1. "Message from the President," Congressional Record, Vol. 110, part 14 (August 4–August 12, 1964), p. 18132.

2. Ibid.

THE JOHNS HOPKINS UNIVERSITY SPEECH

The following document consists of excerpts from a speech President Lyndon Johnson gave at Johns Hopkins University on April 7, 1965. In it, he indicates the basic reasons the United States was involved in the conflict in Vietnam. The tone of the speech is highly moralistic, with American motives stated in the most altruistic of terms. The first reason Johnson cites to justify American involvement is the American desire to help build "a world where every country can shape its own destiny." The president also argues that American self-interest in the Cold War demanded military assistance; otherwise, the loss of Vietnam to communism would create doubts about American credibility and lead to further communist aggression. Johnson also offers "unconditional discussions" with the North, promising a huge Southeast Asian New Deal as incentive. Many observers have seen this as an example of Johnson's naiveté in dealing with the North Vietnamese leadership. Presidential advisor Bill Moyers recalls that before the speech, Johnson told him "Old Ho, he can't turn that down." To Moyers, Johnson's offer of economic aid smacked of classic American political back-scratching: "Had Ho been [AFL-CIO] president George Meany," Moyers concluded, "he would have agreed."[1] Ho did not accept the offer; instead, he demanded that "the internal affairs of South Vietnam must be settled by the South Vietnamese people themselves in *accordance with the program of the South Vietnam National Front for Liberation* [NLF/Vietcong], without any foreign interference" (italics mine).[2] From the American point of view, acceptance of this condition would lead to a communist takeover of the south, and so it was rejected. The Johns Hopkins speech remains an excellent summary of the public rationale for the war, one that never substantially changed.

Document 11
SPEECH, JOHNS HOPKINS UNIVERSITY, 7 APRIL 1965
President Lyndon B. Johnson

Viet-Nam is far away from this quiet campus. We have no territory there, nor do we seek any. The war is dirty and brutal and difficult. . . .

Why must we take this painful road? . . .

We fight because we must fight if we are to live in a world where every country can shape its own destiny. And only in such a world will our own freedom be finally secure. . . .

The first reality is that North Viet-Nam has attacked the independent nation of South Viet-Nam. Its object is total conquest.

Of course, some of the people of South Viet-Nam are participating in attack on their own government. But trained men and supplies, orders and arms, flow in a constant stream from north to south. . . .

Over this war—and all Asia—is another reality: the deepening shadow of Communist China. The rulers in Hanoi are urged on by Peking. . . .

Why are these realities our concern? Why are we in South Viet-Nam?

We are there because we have a promise to keep. Since 1954 every American president has offered support to the people of South Viet-Nam. We have helped to build, and we have helped to defend. Thus, over many years, we have made a national pledge to help South Viet-Nam defend its independence.

And I intend to keep that promise. . . .

We are also there to strengthen world order. Around the globe, from Berlin to Thailand, are people whose well-being rests, in part, on the belief that they can count on us if they are attacked. To leave Viet-Nam to its fate would shake the confidence of all these people in the value of an American commitment and in the value of America's word. The result would be increased unrest and instability, and even wider war.

We are also there because there are great stakes in the balance. Let no one think for a moment that retreat from Viet-Nam would bring an end to the conflict. The battle would be renewed in one country and then another. The central lesson of our time is that the appetite of aggression is never satisfied. To withdraw from one battlefield means only to prepare for the next. We must say in southeast Asia—as we did in Europe—in the words of the Bible: "Hitherto shalt thou come, but no further." . . .

Our objective is the independence of South Viet-Nam, and its freedom from attack. We want nothing for ourselves—only that the people of South Viet-Nam be allowed to guide their own country in their own way.

We will do everything necessary to reach that objective. And we will do only what is absolutely necessary.

In recent months attacks on South Viet-Nam were stepped up. Thus, it became necessary for us to increase our response and to make attacks by air. This is not a change of purpose. It is a change in what we believe that purpose requires. . . .

... [P]eace demands an independent South Viet-Nam—securely guaranteed and able to shape its own relationships to all others—free from outside interference—tied to no alliance—a military base for no other country.

These are the essentials of any final settlement.

We will never be second in the search for such a peaceful settlement in Viet-Nam.

There may be many ways to this kind of peace: in discussion or negotiation with the governments concerned; in large groups or in small ones; in the reaffirmation of old agreements or their strengthening with new ones.

We have stated this position over and over again, fifty times and more, to friend and foe alike. And we remain ready, with this purpose, for unconditional discussions.

These countries of southeast Asia are homes for millions of impoverished people. Each day these people rise at dawn and struggle through until the night to wrestle existence from the soil. They are often wracked by disease, plagued by hunger, and death comes at the early age of 40. ...

For our part I will ask the Congress to join in a billion dollar American investment in this effort as soon as it is underway. ...

The task is nothing less than to enrich the hopes and the existence of more than a hundred million people. And there is much to be done.

The vast Mekong River can provide food and water and power on a scale to dwarf even our own TVA. ...

Source: Public Papers of the Presidents of the United States: Lyndon B. Johnson, 1965 (Washington, D.C.: Government Printing Office, 1966), pp. 394–97.

Notes

1. Robert D. Schulzinger, *A Time for War: The United States and Vietnam, 1941–1975* (New York: Oxford University Press, 1997), p. 173.

2. William Conrad Gibbons, *The U.S. Government and the Vietnam War: Executive and Legislative Rolls and Relationships, Part III: January—July 1965* (Princeton, N.J.: Princeton University Press, 1989), p. 218.

"CREDIBILITY" AS THE CENTRAL RATIONALE FOR VIETNAM POLICY

Lyndon Johnson's speech at the Johns Hopkins University on April 7, 1965, offered a public rationale for American involvement in Vietnam. A top-secret memorandum, dated two weeks earlier, from Assistant Secretary of Defense John T. McNaughton, suggests a different hierarchy of motives. McNaughton, who came to Defense in 1964 from Harvard Law School, was one of Secretary of Defense Robert McNamara's "Whiz Kids," a civilian analyst with a sharp eye for statistics. At the time he wrote the following document, he was Assistant Secretary of Defense.

In March 1965, McNaughton was part of a team trying to develop both rationales and strategies for the war. In this memo, McNaughton clearly thinks that the altruistic motive of helping "the people of SVN [South Vietnam] enjoy a better, freer way of life" is only a miniscule part of American aims in Vietnam. The president's Johns Hopkins speech indicated just the opposite. For McNaughton, credibility— protecting America's "reputation as a guarantor"—was far more important than freedom for South Vietnam.

This memorandum also showed McNaughton's perception of the deteriorating military and political situation in South Vietnam. His insights became part of the official justification for escalating the war in 1965.

McNaughton, like his boss, grew increasingly pessimistic about America's role in Vietnam. By the summer of 1967 he was warning McNamara that the war was becoming such a problem that it "could cause the worst split in our people in more than a century."[1] McNaughton and his family died in a plane crash shortly after this prophetic admonition.

Document 12
MCNAUGHTON DRAFT FOR McNAMARA ON "PROPOSED COURSE OF ACTION"
John T. McNaughton

1. U.S. Aims:

   70%—To avoid a humiliating U.S. defeat (to our reputation as a guarantor).

   20%—To keep SVN (and the adjacent) territory from Chinese hands.

   10%—To permit the people of SVN to enjoy a better, freer way of life.

   ALSO—To emerge from crisis without unacceptable taint from methods used.

   NOT—to "help a friend," although it would be hard to stay in if asked out.

2. The Situation:

The situation in general is bad and deteriorating. The VC have the initiative. Defeatism is gaining among the rural population, somewhat in the cities, and even among the soldiers—especially those with relatives in rural areas. The Hop Tac area around Saigon is making little progress; the Delta stays bad; the country has been severed in the north. GVN control is shrinking to the enclaves, some burdened with refugees.

Source: John T. McNaughton, "McNaughton Draft for McNamara on 'Proposed Course of Action,' " in *The Pentagon Papers*, ed. Neil Sheehan, et al. (New York: Bantam Books, 1971), pp. 432–33.

Note

1. John S. Leiby, "McNaughton, John Theodore," in *Dictionary of the Vietnam War*, ed. James Olson (New York: Peter Bedrick Books, 1990), p. 273.

GEORGE BALL'S DISSENT

George Ball, Undersecretary of State in President Lyndon Johnson's administration, was consistently skeptical of American policy in Vietnam. In the summer of 1965, the president and his advisors were going through yet another agonizing reappraisal of America's role in Southeast Asia. The first results of Operation Rolling Thunder and limited and largely defensive American ground force activity were not promising. According to military leaders, the enemy was still winning the conflict, and massive escalation would be necessary to stop the communist advance in South Vietnam.

As Ball's July 1, 1965, memorandum to President Johnson argues, any escalation would be folly. Additional American ground forces would turn the conflict into a white people's war against "yellow" people in Asian jungles. And once Americans began dying in large numbers, it would be increasingly difficult to withdraw American forces. Finally, Ball was simply not convinced that the United States could win no matter how many troops we sent.

President Johnson rejected Ball's plea not to escalate, largely because of his firm commitment to a noncommunist South Vietnam and his fear of a right-wing backlash if yet another nation "fell" to communism. But neither did he give the military the kind of full-scale escalation it wanted. Rather, he authorized an additional 150,000 troops and hoped that this slow "squeeze" would convince Hanoi to quit the South. Although not accepted, Ball's analysis of what further escalation would bring proved remarkably prophetic.

Document 13
MEMORANDUM TO LYNDON JOHNSON, 1 JULY 1965
George Ball

The South Vietnamese are losing the war to the Viet Cong. No one can assure you that we can beat the Viet Cong or even force them to the conference table on our terms, no matter how many hundred thousand *white foreign* (U.S.) troops we deploy.

No one has demonstrated that a white ground force of whatever size can win a guerrilla war—which is at the same time a civil war between Asians—in jungle terrain in the midst of a population that refuses cooperation in the white forces (and the South Vietnamese) and thus provides a great intelligence advantage to the other side. Three recent incidents vividly illustrate this point. . . .

The decision you face now, therefore, is crucial. Once large numbers of U.S. troops are committed to direct combat, they will begin to take heavy casualties in a war they are ill-equipped to fight in a non-cooperative if not downright hostile countryside.

Once we suffer large casualties, we will have started a well-nigh irreversible process. Our involvement will be so great that we cannot—without national humiliation—stop short of achieving our complete objectives. *Of the two possibilities I think humiliation would be more likely than the achievement of our objectives—even after we have paid terrible costs.* . . .

On balance, I believe we would more seriously undermine the effectiveness of our world leadership by continuing the war and deepening our involvement than by pursuing a carefully plotted course toward a compromise solution. In spite of the number of powers that have—in response to our pleading—given verbal support from feeling of loyalty and dependence, we cannot ignore the fact the war is vastly unpopular and that our role in it is perceptively eroding the respect and confidence with which other nations regard us. We have not persuaded either our friends or allies that our further involvement is essential to the defense of freedom in the cold war. Moreover, the more men we deploy in the jungles of South Vietnam, the more we contribute to a growing world anxiety and mistrust.

Source: George W. Ball, "A Compromise Solution in South Vietnam," memorandum to Lyndon Johnson, 1 July 1965, in *The Pentagon Papers,* ed. Neil Sheehan et al. (New York: Bantam Books, 1971), pp. 449–54.

PRESIDENT JOHNSON'S WITHDRAWAL SPEECH

The 1968 Tet Offensive by communist forces and General William Westmoreland's request for 206,000 additional American combat troops caused a major reappraisal of American strategy in Vietnam. In March 1968, President Johnson, waffling between conciliation and escalation, ultimately reassembled "the Wise Men," a group of current and former presidential advisors whom he had relied on for counsel in the summer of 1965. Led by former Secretary of State Dean Acheson, most of these men urged the president toward the path of peace, essentially reversing their more hawkish stand of three years earlier. Acheson condemned America's attempts to force a victory, arguing that "the old slogan that success is just around the corner won't work." McGeorge Bundy also changed his tune, urging a negotiated settlement of the war.[1]

Johnson was ultimately convinced by this advice. In his March 31, 1968, address to the nation, he began by talking about "peace in Vietnam," rather than the Vietnam War. He offered a partial bombing halt without demanding any concessions from the North, only "assum[ing]" that the DRV would not "take advantage of American restraint."

The final announcement in the speech was no doubt its most explosive component. Johnson's decision not to run for president came as a complete shock to all but a few of his intimate friends and advisors. Although we may never know the real reasons for his decision, Johnson says clearly that health concerns were uppermost in his mind: "I frankly did not believe in 1968 that I could survive another four years of the long hours and unremitting tensions that I had just gone through."[2]

Ultimately, the North Vietnamese accepted Johnson's call for negotiations. The peace talks that grew out of this speech were contentious, sporadic, and successful only after almost four additional years of fighting. But this address did mark the beginning of that process.

Document 14
THE PRESIDENT'S ADDRESS TO THE NATION ANNOUNCING STEPS TO LIMIT THE WAR IN VIETNAM
President Lyndon B. Johnson

Good evening, my fellow Americans:

Tonight I want to speak to you of peace in Vietnam and Southeast Asia.

No other question so preoccupies our people. No other dream so absorbs the 250 million human beings who live in that part of the world. No other goal motivates Amerian policy in Southeast Asia. . . .

There is no need to delay the talks that could bring an end to this long and bloody war.

Tonight, I renew the offer I made last August—to stop the bombardment of North Vietnam. We ask that talks begin promptly, that they be serious talks on the substance of peace. We assume that during those talks Hanoi will not take advantage of our restraint.

We are prepared to move immediately toward peace through negotiations.

So, tonight, in the hope that this action will lead to early talks, I am taking the first step to deescalate the conflict. We are reducing—substantially reducing—the present level of hostilities.

And we are doing so unilaterally, and at once.

Tonight, I have ordered our aircraft and our naval vessels to make no attacks on North Vietnam, except in the area north of the demilitarized zone where the continuing enemy buildup directly threatens allied forward positions and where the movement of their troops and supplies are clearly related to that threat.

The area in which we are stopping our attacks includes almost 90 percent of North Vietnam's population, and most of its territory. Thus there will be no attacks around the principal populated areas, or in the food-producing areas of North Vietnam. . . .

I believe that a peaceful Asia is far nearer to reality because of what America has done in Vietnam. I believe that the men who endure the dangers of battle—fighting there for us tonight—are helping the entire world avoid far greater conflicts, far wider wars, far more destruction, than this one.

The peace that will bring them home someday will come. Tonight I have offered the first in what I hope will be a series of mutual moves toward peace.

I pray that it will not be rejected by the leaders of North Vietnam. I pray that they will accept it as a means by which the sacrifices of their own people may be ended. And I ask your help and your support, my fellow citizens, for this effort to reach across the battlefield toward an early peace. . . .

Through all time to come, I think America will be a stronger nation, a more just society, and a land of greater opportunity and fulfillment because of what we have all done together in these years of unparalleled achievement.

Our reward will come in the life of freedom, peace, and hope that our children will enjoy through ages ahead.

What we won when all of our people united must not now be lost in suspicion, distrust, selfishness, and politics among any of our people.

Believing this as I do, I have concluded that I should not permit the Presidency to become involved in the partisan divisions that are developing in this political year.

With America's sons in the fields far away, with America's future under challenge right here at home, with our hopes and the world's hopes for peace in the balance every day, I do not believe that I should devote an hour or a day of my time to any personal partisan causes or to any duties other than the awesome duties of this office—the Presidency of your country.

Source: "The President's Address to the Nation Announcing Steps to Limit the War in Vietnam," in *Public Papers of the Presidents*, Vol. 1 (Washington, D.C.: Government Printing Office, 1970), pp. 469–76.

Notes

1. Frank Vandiver, *Shadows of Vietnam: Lyndon Johnson's Wars* (College Station, Tex.: Texas A&M University Press, 1997), p. 326.

2. Lyndon Baines Johnson, *The Vantage Point: Perspectives of the Presidency, 1963–1969* (New York: Holt, Rinehart and Winston, 1971), pp. 425–26.

PRESIDENT NIXON'S PLEA FOR SUPPORT OF VIETNAMIZATION

During the 1968 presidential campaign, Richard Nixon had promised the American people that he had devised a "secret" plan to end the Vietnam War, the details of which he would divulge after the election. In fact, as president, Nixon found himself on the horns of a dilemma very similar to that of Lyndon Johnson. Given growing American war-weariness, he could not increase American troop levels. But because he and his National Security Advisor Henry Kissinger believed that American credibility was at stake in Vietnam, that, in the words of historian Robert Schulzinger, "a forced departure from Vietnam would embolden American rivals elsewhere in the world," withdrawal was not a viable option.[1] Therefore, he sought to reduce U.S. exposure in the war by adopting a plan originally proposed by Robert McNamara—turning more of the fighting over to the South Vietnamese. Although "Vietnamization," as the strategy was dubbed, meant withdrawal of American combat troops, it also involved increased use of American air power, especially in neutral Cambodia.

In this address to the nation, President Nixon publicly explains the new strategy (the implementation of which had actually begun several months earlier), seeking to rally the support of "the great silent majority" of Americans for Vietnamization. He also not so subtly attacks the antiwar movement, noting that he would not allow policy to "be dictated by [a] minority . . . mounting demonstrations in the street." In the short run, the speech was quite effective; a Gallup Poll taken shortly after the address showed a 68 percent approval rating for the president.[2] In the long-run, of course, the policy failed, as South Vietnam was overwhelmed by communist forces in 1975.

Document 15
ADDRESS TO THE NATION ON THE WAR IN VIETNAM, NOVEMBER 3, 1969
President Richard M. Nixon

Good evening, my fellow Americans:

Tonight I want to talk to you on a subject of deep concern to all Americans and to many people in all parts of the world—the war in Vietnam. . . .

My fellow Americans, I am sure you can recognize . . . that we really only have two choices open to us if we want to end this war.

—I can order an immediate, precipitate withdrawal of all Americans from Vietnam without regard to the effects of that action.

—Or we can persist in our search for a just peace through a negotiated settlement if possible, or through continued implementation of our plan for

Vietnamization if necessary—a plan in which we will withdraw all our forces from Vietnam on a schedule in accordance with our own program, as the South Vietnamese become strong enough to defend their own freedom.

I have chosen this second course.

It is not the easy way.

It is the right way.

It is a plan which will end the war and serve the cause of peace—not just in Vietnam but in the Pacific and in the world. . . .

I recognize that some of my fellow citizens disagree with the plan for peace I have chosen. Honest and patriotic Americans have reached different conclusions as to how peace should be achieved.

In San Francisco a few weeks ago, I saw demonstrators carrying signs reading: "Lose in Vietnam, bring the boys home."

Well, one of the strengths of our free society is that any American has a right to reach that conclusion and to advocate that point of view. But as President of the United States, I would be untrue to my oath of office if I allowed the policy of this Nation to be dictated by the minority who hold that point of view and who try to impose it on the Nation by mounting demonstrations in the street. . . .

Let historians not record that when America was the most powerful nation in the world we passed on the other side of the road and allowed the hopes for peace and freedom of millions of people to be suffocated by the forces of totalitarianism.

And so tonight—to you, the great silent majority of my fellow Americans—I ask for your support.

I pledged in my campaign for the Presidency to end the war in a way that we could win the peace. I have initiated a plan of action which will enable me to keep the pledge.

The more support I can have from the American people, the sooner the pledge can be redeemed; for the more divided we are at home, the less likely the enemy is to negotiate at Paris.

Let us be united for peace. Let us also be united against defeat. Because let us understand: North Vietnam cannot defeat or humiliate the United States. Only Americans can do that.

Source: Richard M. Nixon, "Address to the Nation on the War in Vietnam, November 3, 1969," in *Public Papers of the Presidents of the United States: Richard Nixon, 1969* (Washington, D.C.: Government Printing Office, 1971), pp. 901–9.

Notes

1. Robert D. Schulzinger, *A Time for War: The United States and Vietnam, 1941–1975* (New York: Oxford University Press, 1997), p. 276.

2. Ibid., p. 282.

THE COMBAT EXPERIENCE

Ralph Strang, a native of South Bend, Indiana, joined the Marine Corps in the summer of 1967 the second time he tried. Earlier, he had failed the physical examination because of severe acne. He enlisted because he felt "this tremendous obligation to the United States." He joined the Marines because "that's what my dad was."[1]

Strang went to Vietnam in early 1968, during the Tet Offensive, and served in Alpha Company, First Battalion, Seventh Marine Regiment, First Marine Division. He spent most of his tour just south of Danang. After putting in his thirteen months, he returned to his South Bend home in March 1969.

The passage presented here is a segment of an interview his daughter Rochelle conducted with him in early 1997 as part of her Honors Thesis at Ball State University. Strang describes his first major firefights in-country, as he focuses on the confusion, fear, and pain they engendered. Significantly, by the end of his second one, he decided that his major purpose in Vietnam was to "save your friends, you save yourself, and it didn't matter about anything else—the United States, Mom, apple pie." This is an accurate reflection of the disillusionment felt by many American combat troops in the war.

Document 16
INTERVIEW WITH ROCHELLE STRANG
Ralph Strang

The first firefight I was ever in, the hill got hit one night, I mean I had actually gone to my lieutenant and I said, "Hey, I joined the Marine Corps to come over here and fight, and the gunny's got me picking up cigarette butts during the day." And I said, "You know, I mean what can I do to get out of picking up cigarette butts?" And he said, "Aw, just, soon enough, soon enough." And just a couple days after that we were on the hill getting ready to go out on a night patrol, and we got mortared. There is no speed like getting into a trench when somebody's dropping mortar rounds on you. Then one of the squads that was down off of the hill a ways got in a firefight with somebody, I don't know who with or how many or anything like that. So there were incoming rounds from that, coming over the hill. And we got down in the trench, and it was real exciting. I happened to run into the lieutenant. He was checking the lines and I said, "Man, you got any cigarette butts that need picked up?" Because it doesn't take much of that combat stuff, and you realize that it is not a healthy situation. So that was the first actual firefight that I was in.

The first patrol I was ever on [April 8] that anything bad happened to [us]; we went out on the river patrol. It was a deal where the navy had some big flat bottom boats they ran up and down the rivers over there. It was faster to get to some places by river than if you had to go over land to check out different places where the enemy was supposed to be. There was like, I think we had 12–13 guys that day, not counting the navy guys who were running the boat. Two of us were, two boatloads were on one side of the river, and the boat with the corpsman in it was on the other side. We started out, and it was a nice ride. We had a breeze because the boat was moving. It wasn't all that bad. One of the guys in the company a few months before I got there had been killed on the river. He got shot. But, yeah, the river patrol was this cool thing that everybody wanted to do, and I, of course, wanted to do it. I had volunteered a couple times previous, and they said, "No, you haven't been here long enough to be able to go out there." Because it was more dangerous, if that's possible, than what we did everyday anyway. So we were cruising along; and they always said that on the river patrol when you stopped somewhere to check out a village or a house or a cave or whatever it might be. That's where all the bad stuff is gonna happen anyway. So when we stopped and got out of the boat, we were walking very gingerly, looking around. We were in elephant grass over our heads. You couldn't see anything anyway, but we were trying to check out this little village like thing with half dozen hooches maybe. So I was stepping pretty light, and I had just picked up my right foot, looked around to see where I was going to put my right foot to take another step, and as soon as I did that I heard a horrendous explosion. I looked up in the air, and there was this big cloud of black smoke. And I figured, "Oh yeah, I'm dead." But then I realized that if I would have been dead, I wouldn't have been able to look up and see this big cloud of black smoke and all that. So I realized it was somebody else, or I figured it was. The point man came running out of the treeline ahead of us hollering for the corpsman. I said, "Who was hit?" And he said, "The whole first fire team." Well, I knew he was little excited because he was a part of the first fire team, and there was nothing wrong with him. Before I even knew it, before he ever got over the river to holler at the other boat, the corpsman and the other guys were across. They obviously knew what was going on. What had happened, there had been hand-detonated mine on this trail, and when the radioman, the lieutenant, and two other guys got pretty close to it, they touched it off. The lieutenant was killed right away. His radioman died about an hour later because the doc had set him up pretty good with IV's and all this other stuff. He woke up and started fighting the corpsman and pulling out all the stuff that he had done to him, and he died. A friend of mine got hit in the head but just a little bit. The guy that was, I guess he was standing on it, I mean it looked like he was standing on it when we finally found him, was dead too. And then you really started thinking seriously about what the hell you were doing over there when your first friends start dying. . . .

[T]hat was the first real firefight I was in, and after that when I realized that not only could people die that you just heard stories about, you know, how great they were and all that, but people could who you actually knew and cared about. Then it started to become a whole different deal. Then it was just surviving. Save your friends, you save yourself, and it didn't matter about anything else—the United States, Mom, apple pie, the girl you left behind—all that stuff was just for movies and books and all that. And the rest of it was just living from one second to the next and hoping that the seconds added up to minutes and hours and days and months so you could go home.

Source: Ralph Strang, interview by Rochelle Strang, in Rochelle Strang, "A Comparison of American and Vietnamese Soldiers in the Vietnam Conflict" (Honors Thesis, Ball State University, May 1997), pp. 13–17.

Note

1. Ralph Strang, interview by Rochelle Strang, in Rochelle Strang, "A Comparison of American and Vietnamese Soldiers in the Vietnam Conflict" (Honors Thesis, Ball State University, May 1997), appendix, p. 1.

FIGHTING THE WAR AS SEEN BY A POET-VETERAN

These poems by one of the most important American Vietnam veteran-poets, Bill Ehrhart, look at combat from two different perspectives. Ehrhart spent 1967–1968 in Vietnam as an Assistant Intelligence Chief in the 1st Battalion of the 1st Marine Division. Like most Marines, regardless of Military Occupational Speciality (MOS), Ehrhart saw considerable combat. Many of his poems are based on this experience.

"Night Patrol" uses concrete images—fish smells, stale urine, crunching gravel—to create the sensations involved in setting up an ambush at night. The key image in the second stanza—"A mangy dog/pits the stomach"—suggests the chilling fear accompanying combat situations. "Farmer Nguyen" tries to see the war from the point of view of the innocent Vietnamese villager. Nguyen is caught between the two sides of the war, as both Americans and Vietcong exploit him. Like many Vietnamese peasants, he probably cared more about the war ending than its political outcome.

Since the end of his tour of duty, Ehrhart has become a major spokesman for veterans who write about the war. He has written three volumes of memoirs and several collections of poetry. He also edited *Carrying the Darkness* (1985), probably the most important collection of works by poets of the Vietnam generation.

Document 17
NIGHT PATROL
and
FARMER NGUYEN
W. D. Ehrhart

NIGHT PATROL

Another night coats the nose and ears:
smells of fish and paddy water,
smoke from cooking fires and stale urine
drift uneasily, cloaked in silence;
the marketplace deserted, shuttered
houses, empty paths, all cloaked in silence;
shadows bristle.

Our gravel-crunching boots tear great
holes in the darkness, make us wince
with every step. A mangy dog
pits the stomach: rifles level;
nervous fingers hit the safety catch.

FARMER NGUYEN

When we swept through farmer Nguyen's hamlet,
some people said that farmer Nguyen
had given rice to the Vietcong.
        You picked the wrong side, farmer Nguyen.
        We took you in, and beat you,
        and put you in a barbed wire cage.

When the Vietcong returned to farmer Nguyen's hamlet,
some people said that farmer Nguyen
had given information to the Round Eyes.
        Wrong again, farmer Nguyen.
        They took more rice, and beat you,
        and made you carry supplies.

Source: W. D. Ehrhart, ed., *Carrying the Darkness: American-Indochina—The Poetry of the Vietnam War* (New York: Avon Books, 1985), pp. 93, 92.

THE AIR WAR

The American air war in Vietnam was an enormously complex phenomenon. It was fought simultaneously by six different air forces—the

U.S. tactical Air Force, Navy, Marines, Army, Strategic Air Force, and the South Vietnamese Air Force. Moreover, it was divided into distinct although sometimes overlapping missions: tactical air support of ground forces, air attacks against North Vietnam (Rolling Thunder), interdiction attacks against the Ho Chi Minh Trail, and air attacks in Laos and Cambodia. Within these missions, there were myriad types of aircraft, ranging from B-52 bombers to small LOH observation helicopters, as well as a variety of military personnel prosecuting the air mission.

These complexities probably meant little to individual pilots assigned to carry out the basic purpose of the air war: to kill the enemy from above. In the following document, Robert Kirk, a native of Oklahoma City, remembers what it was like to fly combat missions. Kirk enlisted in the Air Force in 1969 when his request for a draft deferment was denied, and he became an F-4 fighter pilot in the 480th Tactical Fighter Squadron in Danang between 1969 and 1970. His experiences as a pilot combined a sense of pride, courage, fear, and frustration when he saw the utter futility—indeed, craziness—of some of what he was asked to do. His main goal as a pilot became to "make it back home."

Document 18
MEMOIR
Robert Kirk

I felt like a gladiator. They put us in module barracks. We had air conditioning, steaks on ice. Officers' club, movies, ice cream. But every day, essentially, we all knew we were going to have to do things that might get us killed. Nobody got shot at more than the fighter pilot. The difference is: if you don't get hit, it doesn't exist, it's not happening; but if you do get hit, you're probably dead or in prison. There was a lot of fear, and it was strongest just before you went in. But once your run started, you were too busy; there were just so many things to do you didn't have time for fear.

Soon for me the war came down to three important truths. First, make it back home. Second, put it all out on the line only if friendly troops needed help or your friends were in trouble. Third, there were a lot of things in Vietnam not worth doing. . . .

We were running down the valley again at 500 knots, and we take a hit in the stabulator. The F-4 has a stabulator, a slab in the back that controls the pitch of the aircraft. An antiaircraft shell had exploded right beneath us. The aircraft pitched straight up! We pulled 8 1/2 G's with the first pitch. If we had pitched down, we would have been dead. The force of the explosion caused us to pitch over and back, a slapping up-and-down motion in the air. We were out of control. We both grabbed the stick and froze it. That's the procedure.

Here we were running this valley, pitching up and down. I could see the ground when we pitched down, and I could see the ridge when we pitched up. I saw that we were heading right for the wall at the end of the valley. The pitching motion dampened, and we both pulled back on the stick as hard as we could. We came to the ridge, and there was ground all around us. There was an instant's pause—I remembered wondering what it would be like to smash into a wall at 500 knots—and then the ridge just shot away from us and we were in the light of the sky. . . .

Absurd. I received a Distinguished Flying Cross. Someone put me in for it. I wasn't even sure then what mission it was for! The absurdity of it all hit me hardest one in-country mission. We made our runs with 500–pound high-drag bombs, very accurate. The forward air controller called our runs. We were hitting a suspected troop concentration in a bunker complex. We had made several runs when the FAC told us an old man had walked out of one of the bunkers and was sitting on a log. He had staggered out of a bunker into full view, just sitting there (my guess dying), with all this destruction around him. I don't know what was going through his mind, but I felt sorrow for him.

The FAC came back on the radio and was going crazy. He was shouting, "Kill him, kill him!" Our wingman made a run at the old man with a 20–mm cannon. He opened up and somehow missed him. What must the old man be thinking? He's just trying to die, and here are these crazies risking a two-million-dollar aircraft and two pilots to kill an old man. It was ludicrous. The FAC screamed again, "You missed! Kill him, kill him!" It was madness. I came on the radio and said, "Let's go home."

Source: Stanley W. Beesley, ed., *Vietnam: The Heartland Remembers* (Norman, Okla.: University of Oklahoma Press, 1987), pp. 75–76, 97–99.

AN AFRICAN AMERICAN IN VIETNAM

African Americans comprised slightly more than 9 percent of active duty military personnel sent to Vietnam. In the early stages of the war, prior to 1968, the majority of African Americans viewed the military and the war itself favorably. As historian James E. Westheider points out, "Military service was viewed [by African Americans] . . . as an opportunity, a chance for both social and economic advancement."[1] By 1968, however, black opposition to the war had increased, led by Martin Luther King, Jr., while racial problems began to surface in the armed services. Indeed, racial tension resulted in a number of violent incidents in the military both in and outside Vietnam. Many African Americans perceived subtle and not-so-subtle examples of white racism, ranging from fewer promotions of blacks in the services to Ku Klux Klan outfits being worn by white service personnel at Cam Ranh Bay after the assassination of Martin Luther King, Jr.

The experience of black Marine Rudolph Bridges in Vietnam in 1967–1968 illustrates these conflicting images of mobility and racism. Bridges, a native of Muskogee, Oklahoma, notes the disparity between the pride he felt at having served in Vietnam and the reception he received while trying to be served in an American restaurant. Moreover, blacks experienced a variety of attitudes from whites in Vietnam, from closeness, especially in combat situations, to downright hostility. Ironically, Bridges felt he got along better with Vietnamese than with whites.

Document 19
MEMOIR
Rudolph Bridges

I knew I would go to Vietnam. I had mixed emotions about it. I was a little gung ho and I was scared, too. I wanted to prove myself, I wanted to test my manhood, but I was very worried about my mother and father. I knew it would be hard on them.

I was very rebellious. Didn't want to take orders from a white man. There was so much prejudice and discrimination in the military that resentment just kept building up on the part of the brothers. We did all we could to hassle the Man, y'know. We would crush our caps and grow beards and not blouse our boots. We did it to irritate.

A lot of what I saw in Nam bothered me. I even began to think atheist from the things I saw happening. Fortunately, later I came to my senses because I do believe in God the Almighty. Most black guys, I think, didn't know what we were fighting for. Some thought there was a war going on back home in the streets. It was tough enough back there, so why did we have to come over here and fight? For the black man, Vietnam became more of a survival thing.

I heard of blacks and whites being real close to each other in the bush. But I know a black kid, a grunt, whose unit was hit bad. A white guy got hit, was hurt bad. And this young brother he risked his life going back in to get him. He carried this white dude out who was hurt bad, and the gooks firing at them, and this guy kept saying, "Put me down, nigger."

We were so close to the DMZ we could watch the little suckers load up on us every day. From January to March, we lived in a hole like rats. We took incoming every day. The rounds hit close. It was funny about whites and blacks then, too. White guys had this John Wayne thing, y'know, like they wanted in the action. They would jump up out of the trenches and on top of the bunkers. Crazy! And get killed, too. No way a brother was going to do something like that. We fought, but we knew how to survive, too. In fact, I think more blacks fought in the field than whites, percentagewise.

Black men got along better with the Vietnamese, I think, because there was an empathy between us. They knew something about what we'd been through. Especially the kids. They looked up to us. Liked our jive talk, and they caught on to the con game a lot of black guys know. I used to stay with the villagers. I'd go off limits into the villages, where we weren't supposed to go. What was they gonna do to me? I was already in Nam. I'd take my weapon with me, but still it was a little crazy, looking back at it. I'd jump off the truck, roll off the road, and hide in the weeds for a little while. I'd sneak into the village and stay for two or three days at a time. I liked the Vietnamese, but I never completely trusted them. . . .

When first back, I flew into Dallas. I had on my uniform with my medals, feeling pretty good about myself. Proud, too. I'd done something. I had served thirteen months in Vietnam for my country. I don't know, maybe I was looking for special treatment. I go to this restaurant, and I sit down. I sat and sat and sat. A long time. Finally a waitress came over, and the look in her eyes was, "What are you doing in here?" It really hurt me. Tears came into my eyes. I had been looking for something that wasn't there.

Source: Stanley W. Beesley, ed., *Vietnam: The Heartland Remembers* (Norman, Okla.: University of Oklahoma Press, 1987), pp. 15–16.

Note

1. James E. Westheider, *African Americans and the Vietnam War: Fighting on Two Fronts* (New York: New York University Press, 1997), p. 2.

AMERICAN WOMEN IN THE WAR

During the years from 1962 to 1973, between thirty-three thousand and fifty-five thousand American women served in the Vietnam War theater. Approximately eleven thousand served in the military, and the rest were in civilian positions. Roughly 80 percent of the women in the military were nurses; civilian women held a variety of positions, from Red Cross workers to stewardesses to librarians. Much like their male counterparts, women who served in Vietnam underwent a bewildering variety of experiences and held very different views of the war. As nurse/historian Elizabeth Norman rightly argues, "[T]here was no standard experience or common reaction to the war."[1]

Lily Lee Adams was an army nurse in Vietnam from October 1969 to October 1970, serving at the 12th Evacuation Hospital at Cu Chi. While at nursing school in 1967, she was impressed by the pitch of an Army recruiter. Recalling the inaugural address of John F. Kennedy, she decided to "do" something for her country by joining the Army as a nurse. She was ordered to Vietnam in 1969.

Adams's time in-country represented the kind of immersion into horror that many women, especially nurses, experienced there. The selection presented here describes some of her experiences in various units within the hospital where she was stationed.

Eight nurses died in Vietnam. They and other women who served and died were honored when the Vietnam Women's Memorial was added to the National Vietnam War Memorial in Washington, D.C., in 1993.

Document 20
MEMOIR
Lily (Lee) Adams

I liked triage. We got all kinds of stuff—Lambretta accidents, babies from the orphanages, GIs coming in drunk—the light stuff as well as the heavy. But the mass-cals were heavy. Setting aside the guys that weren't going to make it to the OR—well, I had some very heavy experiences. I remember one guy who knew he was dying and kept thinking I was his wife. He was saying, "Mary, Mary—hold my hand!" So I held his hand. "Mary, Mary—I just want to let you know I love you!" At the time I did not know much about dealing with dying people except what I knew by instinct—I have since done some work with Elisabeth Kubler-Ross—but my instincts told me it would not be right to say, "Hey, you're dying in muddy fatigues and this is a war zone and I am not your wife." I mean, it was his last time on earth and I did not want to screw up his fantasy, even though I felt guilty that, in a way, I was lying to him. Well, my response was, "You're going to be OK," meaning either way—you're going to live or you're going to die, but you're going to be OK.

Another guy, I remember, lay there and told me he was dying for nothing. I was just about to talk about the domino theory and try to make him feel better, but something told me, "He doesn't want to listen to that ———." So I said, "Yeah, you're right." And he died peacefully. They all died peacefully. I always thought guys in a war zone would die like in an Edgar Allan Poe story. But they always died so peacefully that it gave me a sense of peace.

The ones that would come in that were OR material—they'd come in and say things like, "Oh, s——t." And then they'd go, "Oh, I'm sorry, ma'am, I didn't mean to curse in front of you." And I'd say, "You can curse any way you want." For some reason I always ended up getting stuck with the Southern boys—I think we got more Southern boys in Vietnam than we got Northerners. Because I was always running into the Southern accent and the "Yes, ma'am, no, ma'am" s——t. I'm used to it now, but in those days I always felt like an old lady when those guys said "ma'am" to me.

So after they cursed and apologized they always said, "You smell so good." I mean, I've got guys in shock, wide awake, telling me how good I smell. So I wrote home . . . and said, "Send me bottles and bottles of perfume." I wore Chantilly. And you know, I'm still wearing it—I'm wearing it because I'm hoping to run into my patients, hoping that even if they don't recognize my face they'll recognize my smell. For the longest time I didn't wear it, though, because it reminded me of Vietnam.

Of course, I have yet for a vet to come up to me and say, "Hey, you smell familiar." But wearing Chantilly now is just something I have to do. . . .

Yeah, I miss the devotion. I miss the respect I got as a nurse in Vietnam. One day, I remember, there was this infantry captain who came through my triage. He says to me, "Ma'am, I have all the respect in the world for you." I say, "What for?" He says, "Ma'am, I couldn't do what you are doing. I'd rather be out in the boonies ducking from Charlie than be in here doing your job." I heard that over and over in Vietnam. I didn't have to ask for respect over there—I got it.

Source: "Lily Lee Adams," in *In the Combat Zone* by Kathryn Marshall (New York: Penguin Books, 1988), pp. 206–29.

Note

1. Elizabeth M. Norman, *Women at War: The Story of Fifty Military Nurses Who Served in Vietnam* (Philadelphia: University of Pennsylvania Press, 1990), p. 2.

REAR ECHELON TROOPS IN THE WAR

Those who have learned about the Vietnam War from motion pictures probably see it as a confusion of explosions, gunfire, and young men dashing from helicopters, crouched low and ready to face a cagey, often unseen enemy. For many of us, war means combat. In fact, the majority of American military personnel who were stationed in Vietnam were not combat troops based on their Military Occupational Specialty (MOS). Indeed, between 60 and 80 percent of Americans who served in Vietnam were designated as "Service and Support," called by combat troops "the rear," or less charitably "Rear Echelon Mother F——s" (REMFs). The jobs held by those who served behind military lines ranged from cooks to supply officers to computer programmers to mechanics, and more.[1] Obviously necessary to the smooth functioning of modern armed forces, the forces provided the logistical backbone of America's military effort.

Generally, those in the rear faced a much less harrowing war than did combat forces, although occasionally enemy strikes did threaten cities and units behind combat areas, as in the case of the Tet Offensive. For most Service and Supply forces, however, the war was a predictable 9:00–5:00 affair, with frequent trips to the Post Exchange, movies, and clubs located near by. In some ways, this "other war" was in fact the "typical" Vietnam War for most Americans who served.

The following document is part of an interview with one such veteran, Scott Higgins. Higgins was a supply officer with the I I Field Force headquarters in Bien Hoa from 1967 to 1968. Higgins focuses on the less-than-dangerous tasks he undertook, as well as some of the shadier activities of some of his cohorts in the rear.

Document 21
MEMORIES OF THE WAR
Scott Higgins

My first job was to go down to Saigon and hire bar girls. . . . I went to the Saigon bars and talked to the girls and decided whether they had pleasing enough personalities and looked at the bands to hire for the officers' club in Bien Hoa. The first three weeks I was on the job I would get up at ten in the morning and take a jeep down to Saigon, go around these bars checking out the groups and the gals, hire few and then come back. In the evening I'd be in the Bien Hoa officers' club.

Saigon was an incredible city, an incredibly active, bustling town. There were probably fifty thousand prostitutes by the time I left. Some unbelievable French restaurants were still there. Supposedly you could walk into this elegant French restaurant with a .45–caliber pistol on. There were still some vestiges of French occupation there.

At Bien Hoa there really wasn't very much to do. The club officer was a captain, I was a lieutenant. We had this old villa on the most expensive street in Bien Hoa. At that time Bien Hoa was considered a safe town. There wasn't any curfew. It was one of the larger towns, with about a half million people—hell, it could have been a million. It was a big town. . . .

Sometimes there was no question about it that people in headquarters got privileges that people in the field didn't. One guy literally stubbed his toe and got a Purple Heart. He was jumping from his trailer on the night of Tet. (High-ranking officers and some of the generals had their own trailers.) So he jumped out of his trailer and stubbed his toe and got himself a Purple Heart. Isn't that incredible? I mean, he didn't even write it up as stubbing his toe. "During the course of enemy action, he was injured. Injury sustained to his foot, abrasions on his leg" and so forth. It was bull———. What he did was stub his toe. When the story went around, everybody. . . . But who's going to question that, you know? I mean, if it doesn't stop at the top and there was a lot of that. A lot of Air Medals went out that way, the kind you get for hazardous duty, for acts of valor in the air. A lot of officers would go out and just fly around and put themselves in for Air Medals or a Service Cross. . . .

My initial experiences the first couple of months over there were sort of unrealities, living in this compound, in a room with a high ceiling fan, and in a villa. Each officer had his own room or we doubled up at that time. It depended, but there was no lack of space.

Source: Al Santoli, ed., *Everything We Had: An Oral History of the Vietnam War by Thirty-three American Soldiers Who Fought in It* (New York: Random House, 1981), pp. 87–99.

Note

1. Charles R. Anderson, *Vietnam: The Other War* (Novato, Calif.: Presidio, 1982), p. 2.

AN NCO IN ARMY INTELLIGENCE REMEMBERS THE WAR

Although many veterans of the war are ambivalent about the experience, others clearly retain a sense of deep commitment to what they see as the honorable purposes of the war. Walter McIntosh is such a person. Born in Pomona, California, in 1937, he joined the Army in 1954, a seventeen-year-old boy who had worked since he was twelve. He served in various capacities in Vietnam for much of the war, arriving in 1961 as an army intelligence specialist and ending his multiple tours as a CIA operative in Tay Ninh in 1975. McIntosh now lives in Hawaii where he works as an insurance investigator.

Walter McIntosh saw the war from several perspectives, but given his training in the Vietnamese language, he spent most of his time in Vietnam working with elements of the South Vietnamese Army. He developed a great deal of compassion and sympathy for his South Vietnamese counterparts, unlike many Americans who tended to denigrate the efforts of ARVN units. As he notes in his memoir, he still feels "a very real commitment to the Vietnamese people who were promised . . . a chance to earn a life that included freedom from the enslavement of Communism." American motives, he would argue, were noble ones indeed.

Document 22
MEMORIES OF THE WAR
Walter McIntosh

In 1959 [at the army language school in Monterey, California] . . . I was told to report to . . . a class . . . in Vietnamese. Had they said Annamese or even Tonkinese, I might have known what they were talking about, but Vietnam had not yet entered our vocabulary. Along with three other army enlisted men and three Marine enlisted men and one army officer I studied the Vietnamese language for the next 48 weeks. This was the 16th class of Vietnamese language students since the inception of the school during WWII. Brigadier General Collins, the son of Lawton Collins, was the C.O. of the school. During this period of time, a lot was going on. The stagnation of Ike's period was coming to an end. JFK got elected. The Peace Corps was established. The *Ugly American* was read by all. The Special Forces was JFK's pet. There was a great sense that we, all of us, could be the positive agents of change. "Ask not what your country can do for you, as what you can do for your country!"

In May 1961 I graduated and got assigned to Columbia University for four weeks to go through Nguyen Van Hoa's PhD material and his reference material he used in writing his Vietnamese-English dictionary. I spent all the month living on the fifth level down in the stacks of the library and taking in Manhattan, meeting all the Vietnamese people that I could, particularly using the offices of "the Friends of Vietnam," a lobbying office for the Diem government. I was then assigned to a military intelligence platoon in Fort Hood, Texas. After only a few weeks at Fort Hood I got orders to Vietnam. Assigned to the Army Security Agency, I spent about three weeks in the Philippines where I studied the technical problems that we were facing. I was also told that since my presence in Vietnam was over the allotment of military personnel allowed by the 1954 and 1962 Geneva Agreements, I would be given $300.00 to purchase mufti for my travel and duty wear.

I arrived in Saigon in late September 1961. I was assigned to the 3rd RRU, an Army Security Agency unit that had been assembled a couple of months earlier by taking personnel from the existing units. I found the unit had one Vietnamese linguist. He had mostly been employing himself by assisting some of the code breakers in breaking low-level field codes used by VC main force and local units. I kept myself busy mainly by assisting our commanding officer and executive officer with interpreting and negotiating deals on property and getting construction projects to get the unit in an operational mode. I was asked to run a radio survey of the country. This was an exciting time. I was assigned to head up a seven-man ARVN unit of radio intercept operators. We outfitted an Army 3/4 truck/van with radios and antennas. We would drive over to Tan Son Nhut Airport and up onto a flying bumble bee C-123 aircraft, tell the pilot to take us somewhere, drive off and then drive to the nearest hill top and set up our antennas. We kept track of all the radio signals that we heard at each site. It was a very fun time. Then we determined that in emergency situations the VC did use short range voice communications. So we went off and joined ARVN units wherein it appeared there was going to be active firefights in order to determine if an intercept unit would be tactically helpful to the ARVN commander.

In late 1962 I brought my wife and young baby boy to Saigon. My unit CO was not too happy about this, but during that time it was allowed as I was an NCO with several years seniority. During this period I spent all of my time with ARVN, mostly NCO's. I heard their stories or at least what they wanted to tell me. The senior ARVN NCO in my unit, in a very dramatic action/moment, saved my life during one of these missions. It was a major turning point regarding my commitment to the cause of at least this man's dream of living in a free sociey and his dream that his children not grow up with the suffering that he had endured during the last fifteen years.

In 1963 my tour was up. I had been offered a warrant officer's slot if I reenlisted, but at the same time I had been offered a job with the Central Intelligence Agency if I cut my ties to the military. I had met and worked with several people that seemed to be CIA (all but one I had so identified were in fact Agency), and I was enamored with the fact that it seemed that they actually had the ability to issue reports about what was happening that might actually make a difference to our efforts there. I went back to CONUS (mainland USA) and got a job translating Vietnamese language newspapers into English which paid $9.00 per thousand words. I had a damn hard time raising a family on this income so I got a second job as security officer at a Nike missile base in San Francisco area. Now I was making too much money and was missing the excitement of the mission in Vietnam. In order to push the Agency a bit on my employment with them, I took a job in the Washington D.C. area transcribing Vietnamese language tapes into English. After almost a year of this, the Agency job finally came through. After training I was immediately sent back to Saigon.

I worked as a technician and for the most part spent my time teaching forensic sciences to South Vietnamese civilian and military intelligence units, particularly the Special Branch of the police. The training was in Identikit, explosives detection, metal and trace metal detection. I also studied North Vietnam's security and population control measures by setting up programs and personally debriefing NVA infiltratees who had been captured in South Vietnam. After three years of this, I was promoted to so called Special Case Officer status and sent to Dalat as advisor to both the Special Branch Chief and National Police Chief. I assisted the South Vietnamese police in every way I could. Of particular interest at that time was a very active sapper unit in Dalat that was blowing up a government building at least once a week. After 120 days we managed to penetrate the sapper organization and after some cat and mouse games, the stuff that intelligence is all about, we rolled up the sapper unit that had over 115 members, with only six or seven actually illegal VC and the rest legal support elements within Dalat City. Unilaterally I was also involved in running cross border intelligence gathering operations into north east Cambodia and some internal political intelligence operations as well.

By the Easter Offensive of 1972, my wife, now in New York, wanted a divorce. I took off for nine months and went sailing in Europe and got the divorce at the same time. I reported back to work in Washington on 1 January 1973. I started working on anti-terrorist operations as a technician, but when an officer in Tay Ninh committed suicide I was shipped out post haste to hold the fort. Unfortunately, by the time I got there they had filled the post with someone senior to me who had just been assigned to Saigon. This was John Stockwell. So my last two years in Vietnam I worked directly for a man who, in my view, became a traitor to his country.

I was in Vietnam for a very long time, got shot once, was injured a bit more seriously by an errant water buffalo, but I survived. And in spite of the fact that my experience has made me a serious cynic, I still feel a very real commitment to the Vietnamese people who were promised at least a chance to earn a life that included freedom from the enslavement of communism and a hope for a future for their children.

Source: Walter McIntosh to Anthony Edmonds, electronic mail messages, January 25, 28, 31, 1998, in author's possession.

A NORTH VIETNAMESE SOLDIER WRITES ABOUT THE WAR

This poem is one of thousands of enemy documents from the war as gathered by "The Combined Documents Exploitation Center Collection of Captured Documents." This joint effort by American and South Vietnamese intelligence services between 1966 and 1972 resulted in "nineteen miles" of 35mm microfilm providing "significant documentation of the revolutionary side of the American war in Vietnam."[1]

Among these documents were a large number of diaries kept by North Vietnamese and PLAF troops, many of them dotted with poetry. This was not surprising, given the long historical tradition of poetry writing in Vietnam. Indeed, according to translator Thanh T. Nguyen, "All Vietnamese wrote poetry . . . especially when they were separated from their loved ones."[2] This particular poem, whose author we know nothing about beyond his name, Ong Giang, expresses a disillusionment with war that soldiers have shared for centuries. Giang's particular *bêtes noires* are "corrupt people," presumably political and military officers who spy on their troops even as they go to the bathroom. The soldier longs for the war to be over so that he can move beyond his "wandering life"—if he lives, because "Life in war is so short."

Texts like this one help humanize the enemy, challenging the stereotypes of PAVN and PLAF soldiers as mindless automatons ideologically
programmed by their political cadres. As Vietnam veteran-poet Bruce
Weigl concludes, "The Vietnamese [enemy] . . . suffered the same long-
ing . . . the same exhaustion . . . the same daily frustrations" as did many
American soldiers.[3]

Document 23
MY THOUGHTS
Ong Giang

I want to write, in my little book,
Many pages of what I long for, what I feel.
A wandering life is no life at all.
I'm sick and I'm tired of this damned life.

Corrupt people look down on us here.
They teach us meaningless lessons
On how to s——t, how to sleep.
They spy on who eats what and when.

They talk nonsense and wonder
Why those who eat so little s——t so big.
If I had more teeth, I would eat a village of frogs.
I would eat a meal of rotten food
And see if they'd still want to watch.

"You're so rich, do something to me now," I'd say.
Until the victory, I'll try to believe in you.
Until my family can feast on fish, rice, and duck,
I will strike with my cane he who spies on me.
I have a life in this world.
Why stay quiet only to suffer loss?
Life in war is so short.

Source: Ong Giang, "My Thoughts," in *Poems from Captured Documents*, selected and
translated by Thanh T. Nguyen and Bruce Weigl (Amherst, Mass.: University of Massachusetts Press, 1994), p. 5.

Notes

1. Bruce Weigl, "Introduction," *Poems from Captured Documents*, selected
and translated by Thanh T. Nguyen and Bruce Weigl (Amherst, Mass.: University
of Massachusetts Press, 1994), p. viii.

2. Ibid., p. xi.

3. Ibid., p. viii.

VIETNAM VETERANS AGAINST THE WAR
SENATE TESTIMONY

John Kerry, a Navy veteran of the Vietnam War and spokesman for the Vietnam Veterans Against the War (VVAW), gave this testimony in April 1971 as part of a VVAW protest in Washington. The organization grew out of a 1967 demonstration in New York City and by 1971 counted several thousand members. In January 1971, at a "Winter Soldier" tribunal organized by the VVAW, over one hundred veterans testified that they had committed war crimes during their tours of duty in Vietnam. Over a thousand members participated in the April demonstration, dubbed "Operation Dewey Canyon III." A few tried to turn themselves into the Pentagon for their crimes in Vietnam, and some seven hundred threw their medals and ribbons over barricades onto the steps of the Capitol.

Kerry's testimony on April 22, 1971, was a passionate, articulate attempt to show members of Congress and the wider public that many who had participated in the war found it deeply offensive. His measured words and calm, nonmilitant demeanor seemed to have a more positive impact on public opinion than more-confrontational demonstrations by antiwar advocates who had not served in Vietnam. Polls after a major, militant antiwar protest in early May—one that did not feature veterans—indicated that 71 percent of the public disapproved and only 17 percent approved.[1] Similar polls taken after Dewey Canyon III showed that 32 percent of the public approved of the demonstration, but only 42 percent disapproved. Kerry himself became something of a hero who transcended the sectarianism of the antiwar movement and was later elected to the Senate from Massachusetts.

Document 24
TESTIMONY BEFORE THE SENATE FOREIGN
RELATIONS COMMITTEE. 22 APRIL 1971
John Kerry

Thank you very much, Senator Fulbright, Senator Javits, Senator Symington, Senator Pell. I would like to say for the record, and also for the men behind me who are also wearing the uniform and their medals, that my sitting here is really symbolic. I am not here as John Kerry. I am here as one member of the group of 1,000 which is a small representation of a very much larger group of veterans. . . .

In 1970 at West Point Vice President [Spiro] Agnew said "some glamorize the criminal misfits of society while our best men die in Asian rice paddies to preserve the freedom which most of those misfits abuse," and this was used as a rallying point for our effort in Vietnam.

But for us, as boys in Asia whom the country was supposed to support, his statement is a terrible distortion from which we can only draw a very deep sense of revulsion, and hence the anger of some of the men who are here in Washington today. It is a distortion because we in no way consider ourselves the best men of this country; because those he calls misfits were standing up for us in a way that nobody else in this country dared to; because so many who have died would have returned to this country to join the misfits in their efforts to ask for an immediate withdrawal from South Vietnam; because so many of those best men have returned as quadriplegics and amputees—and they lie forgotten in Veterans Administration Hospitals in this country which fly the flag which so many have chosen as their own personal symbol—and we cannot consider ourselves America's best men when we are ashamed of and hated for what we were called on to do in Southeast Asia.

In our opinion, and from our experience, there is nothing in South Vietnam which could happen that realistically threatens the United States of America. And to attempt to justify the loss of one American life in Vietnam, Cambodia or Laos by linking such loss to the preservation of freedom, which those misfits supposedly abuse, is to us the height of criminal hypocrisy, and it is that kind of hypocrisy which we feel has torn this country apart. . . .

We are also here to ask, and we are here to ask vehemently, where are the leaders of our country? Where is the leadership? We are here to ask where are McNamara, Rostow, Bundy, Gilpatric and so many others? Where are they now that we, the men whom they sent off to war, have returned? These are commanders who have deserted their troops, and there is no more serious crime in the laws of war. The Army says they never leave their wounded. The Marines say they never leave their dead. These men have left all the casualties and retreated behind a pious shield of public rectitude. They have left the real stuff of their reputations bleaching behind them in the sun in this country.

Finally, this administration has done us the ultimate dishonor. They have attempted to disown us and the sacrifices we made for this country. In their blindness and fear they have tried to deny that we are veterans or that we served in Nam. We do not need their testimony. Our own scars and stumps of limbs are witness enough for others and for ourselves.

We wish that a merciful God could wipe away our own memories of that service as easily as this administration has wiped away their memories of us. But all that they have done and all that they can do by this denial is to make more clear than ever our own determination to undertake one last mission—to search out and destroy the last vestige of this barbaric war, to pacify our own hearts, to conquer the hate and the fear that have driven this country these last ten years and more, so when 30 years from now our brothers go down the street without a leg, without an arm, or a face, and small boys ask why, we will be able to say "Vietnam" and not mean a desert, not a filthy obscene memory, but mean instead the place where America finally turned and where soldiers like us helped in the turning.

Thank you.

Source: John Kerry, "Testimony before the Senate Foreign Relations Committee," April 22, 1971, *Congressional Record*, Vol. 117:57.

Note

1. Tom Wells, *The War Within: America's Battle over Vietnam* (Berkeley, Calif.: University of California Press, 1994), p. 511.

THE FALL OF SOUTH VIETNAM

During the early months of 1975, the North Vietnamese overwhelmed the South Vietnamese army (ARVN) in a series of conventional military strikes, culminating in the fall of Saigon on April 30, 1975. South Vietnamese President Nguyen Van Thieu's responses to the Northern offensive were ineffectual; especially damaging was his decision to withdraw completely from the central highlands and establish a defensive perimeter around Saigon. In spite of some heroic stands by remnants of the ARVN, morale in the South rapidly collapsed as the Northern forces moved relentlessly forward. Seeing the handwriting on the wall, Thieu resigned the presidency nine days before the collapse of his country. Interestingly, in his resignation speech, he bitterly attacks the United States for deserting the South. By 1975 both congressional and public opinion in the United States overwhelmingly opposed any further assistance to South Vietnam beyond humanitarian aid. But it is doubtful that anything short of massive American military intervention could have saved the South.

North Vietnamese journalist Colonel Bui Tin saw the fall of Saigon from a very different perspective. Tin was one of the first ranking communist officers to enter Saigon in April 1975. As a journalist attached to *Nhan Danh*, the official communist party newspaper, he was especially observant. He particularly noted the "extraordinary" nature of the first days of independence in Saigon, a vivid contrast to the melancholy, accusatory mood of Thieu's resignation letter.

Document 25
RESIGNATION SPEECH
Nguyen Van Thieu

I have . . . told them (the Americans): you have asked us to do something that you failed to do with half a million powerful troops and skilled commanders and with nearly 300 billion dollars in expenditures over six long years. If I do not say that you were defeated by the communists in Vietnam, I must modestly say that you did not win either. But you found an honourable way out. And at present, when our army lacks weapons, ammunition, helicopters, aircraft and B-52's, you ask us to do an impossible thing like filling up the ocean with stones. This is like the case in which you give me only three dollars and urge me to go by plane, first class; to rent a room in the hotel for 30 dollars per day; to eat four or five slices of beefsteak and to drink seven or eight glasses of wine per day. This is an impossible, absurd thing.

Likewise, you have let our combatants die under the hail of shells. This is an inhumane act by an inhumane ally. Refusing to aid an ally and abandoning it is an inhumane act. This is the reason why, on the day a US congressional delegation came here, I told the congressmen that it was not the problem of 300 million dollars in aid, but it was the question of complying with the U.S. pledge to assist the Vietnamese people in the struggle to protect their independence and freedom and the ideal of freedom for which the Americans fought together with our people here and for which some 50,000 US citizens were sacrificed. . . .

Gentlemen, compatriots and brothers and sisters: All this has led to the current situation in our country. I accept the criticism of the world people and our ally as well as the correct criticism of our Vietnamese people. I admit that some, but not all, of our military leaders were cowardly and imbued with a defeatist spirit and lacked the bravery of combatants in recent battles. In some areas, our combatants fought valiantly and I don't think that our allied troops could have fought as valiantly as they did.

We must be just. Therefore, I have said that wrongdoers must be punished and those scoring military achievements must be properly awarded. We do not try to conceal the shortcomings of those wrongdoers. We are proud to say that, in some of the recent battles, we scored achievement that our US allied troops probably could not have scored if they had been there.

Source: Nguyen Van Thieu, "Resignation Speech, April 21, 1975," translated and edited by the Monitoring Service of the British Broadcasting Corporation.

Document 26
FOLLOWING HO CHI MINH
Bui Tin

Early on the morning of April 30, 1975, the day the war ended, I was in Cu Chi and it was simply by chance that I ended up at Independence Palace in Saigon. When I arrived there I saw a tank commander who had been wounded. I was told there had been fighting near the An Quang and Xa Loi pagodas which were the most militant in Saigon. Then Lt.-Col. Nguyen Van Han, the chief of security of the Fourth Army Corps with whom I had previously been closely associated, and Bui Van Tung, the political commissar of the 203rd Tank Regiment, informed me that Duong Van Minh—Big Minh as he was known—who had become president of South Vietnam two days earlier, was sitting inside the palace with all his cabinet, waiting. However there was nobody present of a rank high enough to go and talk to him. In the People's Army of Vietnam, only officers of the rank of colonel or above were considered to have sufficient authority and seniority to make decisions. Lt.-Col. Han said he had been ordered to wait for such an officer to arrive before entering the building. He then asked me to go in and talk to the president because I held the rank of colonel. I replied that I was only a journalist now, but Lt.-Col. Han persisted. Eventually I agreed. . . .

Those first days in Saigon after our unexpectedly easy victory were extraordinary. To celebrate this historic event the commanders of all the forces involved assembled at Independence Palace. They included the generals in charge of the four army corps and one special mixed corps which had participated in the campaign. Also present were the commanders of the Air Force, the Navy and those branches of the armed forces responsible for armoured, anti-aircraft and chemical warfare as well as propaganda and special operations. All these senior officers had been present twenty-one years earlier at Dien Bien Phu when, holding junior commands, they had been put to the test. Clearly the war against the French had been a sort of university, a stage on which to rehearse and learn about military theory and practise it as an officer. If it had not been for that war, the struggle against the Americans would not have turned out in the way it did.

Then on May 7, 1975, or thereabouts, General Vo Nguyen Giap arrived at Tan Son Nhut and was taken to Independence Palace which had just been transformed into an official guest house. There he was greeted by General Tran Van Tra, who had become the head of the Military Committee administering Saigon. I still recall that evening. An officer said that he had acquired a good-quality piano from a military base in the South which he would send to General Giap's home in Hanoi. I have never see Giap so angry. With his eyes blazing and uttering obscenities, he replied that it was impossible for him to accept such booty: what would everybody else who had participated in the campaign expect?

Source: Bui Tin, *Following Ho Chi Minh: Memoirs of a North Vietnamese Colonel* (Honolulu: University of Hawaii Press, 1997), pp. 84–85.

THE PARIS PEACE AGREEMENT

The Paris Accords, signed by North Vietnam, South Vietnam, the United States, and the southern-based Provisional Revolutionary Government (PRG), officially marked the end of the Vietnam War for the United States. The agreement's military component called for removal of all American troops from Vietnam within sixty days. The North Vietnamese would then release all American prisoners of war within the same time frame. Additionally, military forces, both communist and ARVN, would remain in place in the South. Politically, the government of South Vietnamese President Nguyen Van Thieu would remain in power in South Vietnam while the North and South would negotiate a peaceful reunification.

Both major combatants had made significant concessions, with America allowing communist troops to remain in the South and North Vietnam accepting the Thieu government. Both sides were no doubt war-weary, given the continued military stalemate. In addition President Nixon faced an increasingly hostile Congress that might well have cut off funds for the war had the negotiations failed.

In many ways, the chief "loser" in the Accords was South Vietnam. President Nguyen Van Thieu had bitterly opposed the retention of enemy troops in the South. He reluctantly went along when Nixon threatened to conclude the negotiations without Thieu's participation, while also promising an American military response should the North break the agreement. In fact, both sides violated the Accords, the North more flagrantly than the South, and by late 1974 NVA troops were poised to launch a final assault on South Vietnam. Richard Nixon had resigned from office, a victim of Watergate, and his successor, Gerald Ford, recognized that public and congressional opinion would never support America's reentry into the war. The fate of the South was sealed.

Document 27
THE PARIS ACCORDS, JANUARY 27, 1973

ARTICLE 1

The United States and all other countries respect the independence, sovereignty, unity, and territorial integrity of Viet-Nam as recognized by the 1954 Geneva Agreements on Viet-nam. . . .

ARTICLE 2

A cease-fire shall be observed throughout South Viet-Nam as of 2400 hours G.M.T., on January 27, 1973.

At the same hour, the United States will stop all its military activities against the territory of the Democratic Republic of Viet-Nam by ground, air and naval forces, wherever they may be based, and end the mining of the territorial waters, ports, harbors, and waterways of the Democratic Republic of Viet-Nam. The United States will remove, permanently destroy or deactivate all the mines in the territorial waters, ports, harbors, and waterways of North Viet-Nam as soon as this Agreement goes into effect.

The complete cessation of hostilities mentioned in this Article shall be durable and without limit of time. . . .

ARTICLE 4

The United States will not continue its military involvement or intervene in the internal affairs of South Viet-Nam.

ARTICLE 5

Within sixty days of the signing of this Agreement, there will be a total withdrawal from South Viet-Nam of troops, military advisers, and military personnel, including technical military personnel and military personnel associated with the pacification program, armaments, munitions, and war material of the United States and those of the other foreign countries to all paramilitary organizations and the police force will also be withdrawn within the same period of time.

ARTICLE 6

The dismantlement of all military bases in South Viet-Nam of the United States and of the other foreign countries mentioned in Article 3(a) shall be completed within sixty days of the signing of this Agreement.

ARTICLE 7

From the enforcement of the cease-fire to the formation of the government provided for in Article 9(b) and 14 of this Agreement, the two South Vietnamese parties shall not accept the introduction of troops, military advisers, and military personnel including technical military personnel, armaments, munitions, and war material into South Viet-Nam.

ARTICLE 8

(a) The return of captured military personnel and foreign civilians of the parties shall be carried out simultaneously with and completed not later than the same day as the troop withdrawal mentioned in Article 5. The parties shall exchange complete lists of the above-mentioned captured military personnel and foreign civilians on the day of the signing of this Agreement.

(b) The Parties shall help each other to get information about those military personnel and foreign civilians of the parties missing in action, to determine the location and take care of the graves of the dead so as to facilitate the exhumation and repatriation of the remains, and to take any such other measure as may be required to get information about those still considered missing in action. . . .

ARTICLE 11

Immediately after the cease-fire, the two South Vietnamese parties will:

—achieve national reconciliation and concord, end hatred and enmity, prohibit all acts of reprisal and discrimination against individuals or organizations that have collaborated with one side or the other;

—ensure the democratic liberties of the people: personal freedom, freedom of speech, freedom of the press, freedom of meeting, freedom of organization, freedom of political activities, freedom of belief, freedom of movement, freedom of residence, freedom of work, right to property ownership, and right to free enterprise. . . .

Source: *United States Treaties and Other International Agreements*, compiled and edited under the direction of the U.S. Secretary of State (1 U.S.C. 112A), vol. 24, part 1, 1973 (Washington, D.C.: Government Printing Office, 1974), pp. 1–225, passim.

VIETNAMESE IMMIGRATION TO THE UNITED STATES

One continuing legacy of the Vietnam War has been the migration of Vietnamese nationals to the United States and elsewhere as thousands have left their homeland. Between 1975 and 1985, almost half a million Vietnamese settled in the United States, and by 1990 the U.S. Census reported a Vietnamese population of 614,547.[1]

Most who came to the United States did so as political "refugees," escaping what they perceived as political repression, including the threat of imprisonment or death. Immigrants also came in several waves. The first wave, which began immediately after the fall of Saigon in late April 1975, generally contained well-educated, English-speaking Catholics with close connections to the American war effort. The second wave began in 1977 and consisted of additional ethnic Vietnamese and increasing numbers of ethnic minorities who were discriminated against or expelled by the communist government. Both of the waves were composed of migrants who clearly seemed to deserve asylum. Many of the later immigrants in the 1980s and early 1990s were economically and educationally disadvantaged, less clearly political refugees, and therefore not as easily admitted.

Nguyen Cong Hoan was among the second wave of immigrants. Although he served as a Representative to the National Assembly of the Socialist Republic of Vietnam, he concluded that communists "used [the Vietnamese] for a tragic end." He escaped from Vietnam in 1977. His expeience in America has been bittersweet. Like many Vietnamese-born immigrants, he hopes to return to a non-communist Vietnam some day.

Document 28
THE DREAM
Nguyen Cong Hoan

In April 1977, after the second assembly session in Hanoi, I left by boat from Nha Trang with thirty-three other people. Two other assemblymen were with me, among many different types of people in our boat, captained by a fisherman.

Our engine broke down on the high seas. We drifted for two days aimlessly. A Japanese ship rescued us and gave us passage to Tokyo.

Today, it's ironic to live in America, whose presence in my country I opposed for so many years. When I first arrived, I went to Washington and talked with congressmen. They had their own concerns and did not want to think about Vietnam. So I came to California to take care of my family, working in an electronics firm.

America has been good to us and offered many opportunities. But we Vietnamese have different customs. The young adapt more quickly than the old. To the Vietnamese, family cohesiveness is the most important thing in life. Vietnamese children are brought up with respect for their parents. But in the U.S., children have their own lives at seventeen or eighteen years old. They don't want to listen to their parents or stay at home.

Now, our children grow up without knowing their homeland, the customs, the scenery. They only hear the older people talk about it. Even though I now live well, I only think and dream to someday go back home.

I am very regretful that I did not understand the Communists before. The Communists always speak in lofty terms that appeal to the better part of people. Then they are used for a tragic end. I believed them, I was wrong. And now I can never be happy until I return to my country.

Source: Al Santoli, ed., *To Bear Any Burden: The Vietnam War and Its Aftermath in the Words of Asians and Southeast Asians* (New York: E. P. Dutton, 1985), pp. 332–33.

Note

1. Nazli Kibria, *Family Tightrope: The Changing Lives of Vietnamese Americans* (Princeton, N.J.: Princeton University Press, 1993), pp. 10–11. Kibria thinks

the Census figures are roughly one hundred thousand on the low side, probably because many ethnic Chinese who migrated from Vietnam designated themselves to census officials as "Chinese" rather than "Vietnamese" (p. 11n).

A POET-VETERAN'S LEGACY

The Vietnam War lives vividly in the minds of those who experienced it. From antiwar activists to combat troops to those who just happened to have lived during the Vietnam era, the war remains a part of the lives of millions of Americans. David Connolly fought in that war as a U.S. Army infantryman. He entered the service as a working-class youth from South Boston with high ideals and "the pumping vigor of early manhood."[1] By the end of his tour, his disillusionment with war in general and the American one in particular led him to join the Vietnam Veterans Against the War.

In "Why I Can't," Connolly vividly recalls a particularly horrific scene from his war. Two friends, "Ratshit" and "Weasel," die next to him in combat while Connolly watches helplessly. And, as he so poignantly describes it, "they've been taking turns/dying on me/again and again and again/ for all these long years." He will never "Forget Nam." David Connolly can stand as a symbol of the legacy of that war, which ranks among the most important crises in modern American history.

Document 29
WHY I CAN'T
David Connolly

Ratshit and the Weasel and I
are behind this dike, see,
and Victor Charlie,
he's giving us what for.
And Ratshit, he lifts his head,
just a little, but just enough
for the round
to go in one brown eye,
and I swear to Christ,
out the other.
And he starts thrashing,
and bleeding, and screaming,
and trying to get
the top of his head
to stay on,

but we have to keep shooting.

A B-40 tunnels into the dike
and blows the Weasel against me.
He doesn't get the chance
to decide whether or not
he should give up and die.
Now I'm crying
and I'm screaming, "Medic,"
but I have to keep shooting.
At this point, I always wake,
and big, black Jerome
and little, white William,
my brothers,
are not dying beside me,
even though
I can still smell their blood,
even though
I can still see them lying there.
You see, these two,
they've been taking turns
dying on me,
again and again and again
for all these long years,
and still people tell me,
"Forget Nam."

Source: Connolly, *Lost in America* (Woodbridge, Conn.: Burning Cities Press, 1994), pp. 68–69.

Note

1. "All the Stars Do Not Spangle," in *Lost in America*, David Connolly (Woodbridge, Conn.: Burning Cities Press, 1994), p. 9.

Glossary of Selected Terms

ARVN: Abbreviation for Army of the Republic of Vietnam; the regular forces of the South Vietnamese military; pronounced "arvin."

B-40: Rocket-propelled grenade launcher carried by Vietcong and North Vietnamese.

B-52: U.S. Air Force's major high altitude bomber during the war. Used primarily for saturation bombing attacks with 500-pound bombs. B-52 raids were called "Arc Lights" by GIs.

Betel nut: a mildly narcotic palm nut chewed by many Vietnamese; it stains teeth black after many years of use.

Bien Hoa City: Vietnamese city near Saigon and site of a major American air base.

Bush: GI slang for areas outside bases where attacks might take place. Also called "boonies."

Danang: Second largest city in South Vietnam and site of the landing of the first U.S. combat troops in 1965; also home of major American airbase.

Delta: Lowland, marshy geographical area of southern South Vietnam formed by the Mekong River and its tributaries.

DMZ: Abbreviation for Demilitarized Zone; a buffer zone between North and South Vietnam, fifteen miles on each side of the 17th parallel.

Dove: Term applied to those who vocally opposed the war.

DRV: Abbreviation for Democratic Republic of Vietnam; official name of what the Americans called North Vietnam.

F-4: A McDonnell/Douglas fighter-bomber, nicknamed "Phantom"; principal fighter-bomber used by the United States in the war.

FAC: Abbreviation for Forward Air Controller; usually airborne, FACs coordinated American air strikes in close support of ground troops.

Firefight: GI slang for combat against enemy forces, especially those involving small arms.

Gook: Common derogatory slang term applied by many American soldiers to Vietnamese, especially but not exclusively the enemy; other such terms included zip, slope, slant, and dink.

Grunt: GI slang for soldier fighting in the war; usually applied to infantrymen.

Gunny: Nickname for a Marine gunnery sergeant.

Hamlet: A small group of buildings, usually in rural areas of Vietnam; several hamlets made up a village.

Hawk: Term applied to those who vocally supported the war.

MACV: Abbreviation for Military Assistance Command, Vietnam; official name of American military mission and its headquarters in Vietnam from 1962 to 1973.

NLF: Abbreviation for National Liberation Front; political organization of the communist-dominated guerrilla forces in South Vietnam.

NVA: Abbreviation for North Vietnamese Army; used by Americans to refer to what the North Vietnamese officially called the People's Army of Vietnam (PAVN).

OSS: Abbreviation for Office of Strategic Services; World War II intelligence agency replaced by Central Intelligence Agency (CIA) in 1947.

PAVN: *See* NVA

PLAF: *See* Vietcong

Round-eye: GI slang for Westerner, especially a woman.

RVN: Abbreviation for Republic of Vietnam; official name of what Americans called South Vietnam.

Tan Son Nhut: Large airport near Saigon; served as headquarters for MACV.

Tet: The most important Vietnamese holiday, it celebrates the lunar new year. It is a multi-day celebration with a focus on family visits and homage to ancestors. In 1968, the communists launched a major military offensive during the Tet holiday.

Triage: Medical procedure for deciding the order in which casualties would be treated.

Vietcong (Viet Cong): Derogatory name given to the People's Liberation Armed Forces (PLAF), communist forces supported by North Vietnam who fought against Americans and the anticommunist South Vietnamese government; in GI slang, also called VC, Victor Charlie, Charles, Mr. Charles, and Chuck.

Vietminh: Contraction of Viet Nam Doc Lap Dong Minh Hoi (League for the Independence of Viet Nam). Founded by Ho Chi Minh as a patriotic front in 1941, it provided the leadership and troops in the struggle against Japanese and French rule in Vietnam.

Vietnamization: The term used by President Richard M. Nixon to describe his policy for conducting the war. It involved the withdrawal of American combat troops and relying upon South Vietnamese military forces to conduct the bulk of the fighting.

Annotated Bibliography

BOOKS: NONFICTION

Anderson, David L. *Trapped by Success: The Eisenhower Administration and Vietnam, 1953–1961*. New York: Columbia University Press, 1991. Scholarly account of Eisenhower policy toward Vietnam, which, argues Anderson, propped up Ngo Dinh Diem's regime and helped create a dependency on America by South Vietnam that would be part of what propelled the United States into the war.

Beesley, Stanley W., ed. *Vietnam: The Heartland Remembers*. Norman, Okla.: University of Oklahoma Press, 1987. An oral history of the war collected from Oklahomans who served. A variety of attitudes give a feeling for the role of "middle Americans" in the conflict.

Bergerud, Eric M. *Red Thunder, Tropic Lightning: The World of a Combat Division in Vietnam*. New York: Penguin Books, 1994. An examination of the war through the eyes of one combat division, the 25th Infantry, from 1966 to 1971. Relies heavily on personal recollections of those who served.

Bilton, Michael, and Kevin Sim. *Four Hours in My Lai*. New York: Viking, 1992. The most thorough account of the major American atrocity of the war and its aftermath. Argues that My Lai was an aberration, but an understandable one given American tactics.

Braestrup, Peter. *Big Story: How the American Press and Television Reported and Interpreted the Crisis of Tet 1968 in Vietnam and Washington*, abr. ed. Novato, Calif.: Presidio Press, 1994. A shorter version of the massively detailed two-volume study (of the same title) of the performance of the press during the Tet Offensive of 1968. Highly critical of media distortions that helped turn a military victory into a psychological defeat.

Broyles, William, Jr. *Brothers in Arms: A Journey from War to Peace.* New York: Avon, 1987. Memoir of a combat Marine who returned to Vietnam in 1984. Focuses on forgiveness and reconciliation.

Brune, Lester, and Richard D. Burns. *America and the Indochina Wars, 1945–1990: A Bibliographical Guide: Supplementing Wars in Vietnam, Cambodia, and Laos, 1945–1982.* Claremont, Calif.: Regina Books, 1992. Burns, Richard D., and Milton Leitenberg. *The Wars in Vietnam, Cambodia, and Laos, 1945–1982: A Bibliographic Guide.* Santa Barbara, Calif.: ABC-Clio, 1984. Companion-piece bibliographies that cover all aspects of American involvement in the war. Focus is on historical material, including books, articles, and dissertations. Unfortunately, not annotated.

Caputo, Philip. *A Rumor of War.* New York: Ballantine Books, 1987. One of the first and best memoirs by an American participant in combat. Shows the horror, disillusionment, and fascination of the war, as one Marine grows up very quickly.

DeBenedetti, Charles, with Charles Chatfield. *An American Ordeal: The Anti-War Movement of the Vietnam War Era.* Syracuse, N.Y.: Syracuse University Press, 1990. A balanced, detailed study of the antiwar movement. Argues that because the movement helped place the war in the public arena, it was at least partially successful.

Faas, Horst, and Tim Page, eds. *Requiem, by the Photographers Who Died in Vietnam and Indochina.* New York: Random House, 1997. A powerful collection of photographs by photojournalists—including communist ones—who died in the war or are missing. Includes brief firsthand accounts and essays by participants as well.

Franklin, H. Bruce, ed. *The Vietnam War in American Stories, Songs, and Poems.* New York: Bedford Books-St. Martin's Press, 1996. A variety of selections from creative literature about the war, most of them reflecting a critical attitude toward the war.

Garfinkle, Adam. *Telltale Hearts: The Origins and Impact of the Vietnam Antiwar Movement.* New York: St. Martin's Press, 1995. Critical analysis of the antiwar movement. Places some of the blame for the war's continuation on the more radical elements of the movement that garnered considerable media attention and alienated much of the American public.

Gettleman, Marvin E. et al., eds. *Vietnam and America: A Documented History.* Rev. and enl. 2nd ed. New York: Grove Press, 1995. Contains a selection of "major" documents by leading players from the late nineteenth century through 1975.

Gilbert, Marc Jason, ed. *The Vietnam War: Teaching Approaches and Resources.* Westport, Conn.: Greenwood Press, 1991. The best single-volume work on teaching the war, with fourteen essays by leading practitioners. Includes sample syllabi.

Halberstam, David. *The Best and the Brightest*, 20th Anniversary ed. New York: Random House, 1992. A classic account of the decisions that led the United States into the war. Largely critical of the role of the liberal Democratic establishment—the "best and the brightest"—for gradually escalating American involvement.

————. *Ho*. New York: McGraw-Hill, 1993. A brief sympathetic biography focusing on the period since 1954.

Hallin, Daniel. *The Uncensored War: The Media and Vietnam*. Berkeley, Calif.: University of California Press, 1986. Argues that for most of the war, the media was essentially supportive of the war effort and became only slightly less so after the Tet Offensive.

Herring, George. *America's Longest War: The United States and Vietnam 1950–75*. 3rd ed. New York: McGraw-Hill, 1996. The best brief, single-volume history of the war. Evenhanded, it focuses on political, strategic, and diplomatic aspects of the conflict.

————. *LBJ and Vietnam: A Different Kind of War*. Austin, Tex.: University of Texas Press, 1994. A study of President Johnson's decision-making style, noting how his tendency to overemphasize consensus and to micromanage helped exacerbate his difficulties.

————, ed. *The Pentagon Papers*, abr. ed. New York: McGraw-Hill, 1993. Includes key documents from this massive government study of the war, from Ho Chi Minh's 1946 appeal for help to General Wheeler's post–Tet Offensive report. The only edition of this key source in print as of late 1997. The best out-of-print version is *The Senator Gravel Edition*, 5 vols. Boston: Beacon Press, 1971.

Hess, Gary R. *Vietnam and the United States: Origins and Legacy of War*. Boston: Twayne Publishers, 1990. The best text available that focuses on the war from the Vietnamese perspective.

Isaacs, Arnold R. *Vietnam Shadows: The War, Its Ghosts, and Its Legacy*. Baltimore: Johns Hopkins University Press, 1997. A sensitive meditation on the legacies of the war for both Americans and Vietnamese. Argues that a sense of absurdity may be the war's most enduring result.

Jamieson, Neil L. *Understanding Vietnam*. Berkeley, Calif.: University of California Press, 1993. A detailed, nuanced study of the Vietnamese "mind." Focuses on Vietnamese writers and intellectuals in the nineteenth and twentieth centuries.

Karnow, Stanley. *Vietnam, A History*. New York: Viking Press, 1983. Companion piece to the PBS series, *Vietnam: A Television History*. Focuses on political and strategic aspects of the war, with substantial material on Vietnam before American involvement.

Kutler, Stanley I., ed. *Encyclopedia of the Vietnam War*. New York: Charles Scribner's Sons, 1996. The most thorough one-volume reference guide to the war. Contains 564 original signed articles, including several lengthy focused essays on major aspects of the war.

Lacouture, Jean. *Ho Chi Minh*. New York: Vintage Books, 1968. The most detailed biography available of Ho. Balanced, but tending toward sympathetic.

Mangold, Tom, and John Penycate. *The Tunnels of Cu Chi: The Untold Story of Vietnam*. New York: Berkeley, 1986. Gripping account of a major communist tunnel complex northwest of Saigon. Told from the points of view of the enemy who inhabited the tunnels and the American "tunnel rats" who tried to extricate them.

Marr, David. *Vietnam, 1945*. Berkeley, Calif.: University of California Press, 1995. A richly detailed analysis of this key year in Vietnamese history told from the differing perspectives of the major players. Sees Ho's capture of the independence movement as the result of both dedication and chance.

Marshall, Kathryn, ed. *In the Combat Zone: An Oral History of American Women in Vietnam*. New York: Penguin, 1988. An oral history based on interviews with twenty women who served in a variety of capacities in the war, from nurse to Red Cross volunteer. Reveals a wide spectrum of attitudes toward the war.

McMahon, Robert J., ed. *Major Problems in the History of the Vietnam War: Documents and Essays*. 2nd ed. Lexington, Mass.: D. C. Heath, 1995. A massive compilation of documents and historical essays, focusing on major figures with some attention paid to ordinary participants. Offers multiple points of view.

McNamara, Robert S., with Brian VanDeMark. *In Retrospect: The Tragedy and Lessons of Vietnam*. New York: Times Books, 1995. In this controversial memoir of his role in the war, the former Secretary of Defense admits that American military involvement in Vietnam was an error of judgment and capabilities.

Moise, Edwin E. *Tonkin Gulf and the Escalation of the Vietnam War*. Chapel Hill, N.C.: University of North Carolina Press, 1996. A meticulously detailed account of the Gulf of Tonkin incidents and the congressional resolution responding to them. Argues that the report of an alleged second attack by North Vietnamese boats was an honest error, not a lie developed to justify escalation.

Olson, James S., ed. *Dictionary of the Vietnam War*. Westport, Conn.: Greenwood Press, 1988. A compilation of nine hundred definitions of people, places, and events associated with the war. A considerably briefer treatment than the Kutler *Encyclopedia*.

Olson, James S., and Randy Roberts. *Where the Domino Fell: America and Vietnam, 1945–1995*, 2nd ed. New York: St. Martin's Press, 1996. Probably the most engagingly written of the general textbooks. Devotes roughly equal space to political, diplomatic, and military aspects of the war.

Palmer, Bruce, Jr. *The 25–Year War: America's Military Role in Vietnam*. New York: Da Capo Press, 1990. The best of the "revisionist" histories of the war. Focuses on military strategy and tactics. Places much of the blame for the ultimate failure of U.S. goals on political decisions made at the top.

Palmer, Laura, ed. *Shrapnel in the Heart: Letters and Remembrances from the Vietnam Veterans Memorial*. New York: Random House, 1987. Moving stories of twenty-nine families who lost members in the war. Based on objects left by survivors at the Vietnam Memorial in Washington, D.C.

Reinberg, Linda. *In the Field: The Language of the Vietnam War*. New York: Facts on File, 1991. A dictionary focusing on language and terms used by American participants in the war, especially slang. Almost five thousand entries.

Shay, Jonathan. *Achilles in Vietnam: Combat Trauma and the Undoing of Character*. New York: Atheneum, 1994. A psychiatrist's imaginative comparison of the Trojan and Vietnam Wars. Focuses on the nature and causes of Post–Traumatic Stress Syndrome (PTSD).

Sheehan, Neil. *A Bright Shining Lie: John Paul Vann and America in Vietnam*. New York: Random House, 1988. A sprawling combination of the history of the war, the personal trials of American military advisor John Paul Vann, and an analysis of his contributions and critique of the war effort. A monumental work.

Terry, Wallace, ed. *Bloods: An Oral History of the Vietnam War by Black Veterans*. New York: Ballantine Books, 1985. The edited recollections of twenty African Americans who fought in the war. Most focus on the racism encountered in the military as well as disillusionment with the war.

Thayer, Thomas C. *War without Fronts: The American Experience in Vietnam*. Boulder, Colo.: Westview Press, 1986. A major statistical look at the war, with charts and tables dealing with virtually all aspects of combat. An invaluable reference.

Van Devanter, Lynda, and Christopher Morgan. *Home before Morning*. New York: Warner Books, 1983. A graphic memoir by an army nurse. Focuses on the horrors of war and an idealistic young woman's disillusionment.

The Vietnam Experience, 23 vols. Boston: Boston Publishing Company; Addison-Wesley, 1981–1988. A massive examination of the war including both chronological and topical volumes. Especially stunning use of photographs, drawings, and paintings.

Wells, Tom. *The War Within: America's Battle over Vietnam*. Berkeley, Calif.: University of California Press, 1994. A richly detailed, largely sympathetic account of the antiwar movement. Argues that it was essentially successful in helping to end the war.

BOOKS: FICTION AND POETRY

Bao Ninh. *The Sorrow of War: A Novel of North Vietnam*. Translated by Phan Thanh Hao, edited by Frank Palmos. New York: Pantheon, 1995. Fictionalized account of a North Vietnamese soldier's years in the war. Suggests the universality of the combat experience.

Duong Thu Huong. *Novel without a Name*. Translated by Phan Huy Duong and Nina McPherson. New York: Morrow, 1995. A novel that focuses on the loss of innocence of North Vietnamese combat soldiers in the war.

Ehrhart, W. D. *The Distance We Travel*. Easthampton, Mass.: Adastra Press, 1993. Poems that directly and indirectly deal with the poet's experience in Vietnam. Shows profound sympathy for the victims of the war and the poet's opposition to it.

Ehrhart, W. D., ed. *Carrying the Darkness: The Poetry of the Vietnam War*. Lubbock, Tex.: Texas Tech University Press, 1989. The first major collection of Vietnam War-related poetry. Contains a variety of authorial voices, including a large concentration of veterans.

Heinemann, Larry. *Paco's Story*. New York: Pocket Books, 1986. A novel of the postwar experience of one veteran. Focuses on his "ghosts" as memories and nightmares pursue him.

O'Brien, Tim. *Going after Cacciato*. New York: Dell, 1992. Surrealistic novel focuses on a squad trying to capture an American soldier who escaped the war by walking to Paris. Suggests the absurdity of the war.

———. *The Things They Carried*. New York: Penguin, 1991. Interrelated short stories and memoiristic essays dealing with the war and its legacy for those who participated in it. Focuses on the importance of telling stories about the experience.

Van Devanter, Lynda, and Joan A. Furey, eds. *Visions of War, Dreams of Peace: Writings of Women in the Vietnam War*. New York: Warner Books, 1991. A collection of poems by forty women who served in Vietnam, including six Vietnamese. Focuses on the tragedy of war and the necessity for reconciliation.

FILMS, WEB SITES, AND CD-ROMS

The Anderson Platoon. Public Media/Films, Inc., 1967. A documentary film, made in cinema verité style, with a camera following one infantry platoon for six weeks in 1966.

Apocalypse Now. Paramount Home Video, 1979. This commercial film is a controversial Francis Ford Coppola epic that recasts Joseph Conrad's novel, *The Heart of Darkness*. More a series of metaphors than a literal version of the war.

As the Mirror Burns. Women Making Movies, 1993, 1990. Documentary film focusing on women who fought as Vietcong guerrillas. Also deals with their lives after the war.

Berkeley in the Sixties. California Newsreel, 1991. Documentary film based on film clips and interviews with activists. Considerable emphasis on the antiwar movement in northern California.

Born on the Fourth of July. MCA/Universal Home Video, 1989. Commercial film version of Ron Kovic's memoir. Traces Kovic's journey from an idealistic young Marine to a disabled veteran who became active in the antiwar movement.

The Deer Hunter. MCA/Universal Home Video, 1978. Complex story of three working-class friends who served in Vietnam. Focuses on different impacts of the war on veterans, from obsession to reconciliation.

84 Charlie Mopic. Columbia Tri-Star Home Video, 1989. An American Army patrol as seen from the point of view of a combat cameraman. Generally considered one of the most realistic commercial films dealing with combat.

Go Tell the Spartans. Image Entertainment, 1978. The only major commercial film focusing on the American advisory effort. Follows a Vietnamese military unit and its advisors as they try to pacify an area infested with Vietcong.

Indochine. Columbia Tristar Home Video, 1993. One of the few films dealing with French rule in Vietnam. Shows the complexity of the relationship between French colonists and Vietnamese subjects.

No Time for Tears: Vietnam, The Women Who Served. West End Films, 1993. A powerful documentary film examining seven women who served in the war in various military and civilian capacities. Interviews interspersed with film footage and still photographs.

Passage to Vietnam: Through the Eyes of Seventy Photographers. CD-ROM created by Rick Smolan and Jennifer Erwitt. Windows and Macintosh. Against All Odds/Interval Research, 1995. Companion to coffee-table book of the same title. Includes stunning video footage and still photographs of contemporary Vietnam, interviews with the photographers, and a sound track of Asian music.

Platoon. Live Home Video, 1986. Commercial film creating a morality play as good and evil American sergeants approach the war in diametrically opposite ways. Focuses on a new member of an infantry company.

The Scent of Green Papaya. Columbia Tristar Home Video, 1995. Vietnamese-produced study of a family living in Saigon in the 1950s. Presents a view of Vietnam outside the context of the war.

Sixties Project: http://www.jefferson.village.virginia.edu/sixties/. A web page with collections of works on all aspects of the 1960s. Includes articles and sample syllabi.

Viet Nam. CD-ROM, Windows and Macintosh. Medio, P.O. Box 2949, Richmond, WA 98052. Features the text of the second edition of Herring's *America's Longest War*, as well as interviews, photographs, and ABC television film footage.

Vietnam: A Television History. Public Media/Films, Inc., 1983. A thirteen-part PBS retrospective covering virtually all aspects of the war. Contains both interviews and film footage, presenting a generally balanced view.

Vietnam Veterans Home Page: http://www.vietvet.org/. Interactive web page featuring mainly veterans of the war and their families and friends. Includes art, photographs, stories, songs, and links to other Vietnam-related web sites.

The War in Vietnam: A Multimedia Chronicle. CD-ROM, Windows and Macintosh. Macmillan Digital, 1995. Uses articles from the *New York Times* and CBS film footage to create an interactive history of the war. Includes maps and photographs.

Index

About the Author

ANTHONY O. EDMONDS is Professor of History at Ball State University in Muncie, Indiana. He is author of two books, including *A Resource Guide for Teaching the Vietnam War* (1992), and numerous articles and chapters on the war in Vietnam.